Combined and Uneven Development: Towards a New Theory of World-Literature

Postcolonialism across the Disciplines 17

Postcolonialism across the Disciplines

Series Editors
Graham Huggan, University of Leeds
Andrew Thompson, University of Exeter

Postcolonialism across the Disciplines showcases alternative directions for postcolonial studies. It is in part an attempt to counteract the dominance in colonial and postcolonial studies of one particular discipline – English literary/ cultural studies – and to make the case for a combination of disciplinary knowledges as the basis for contemporary postcolonial critique. Edited by leading scholars, the series aims to be a seminal contribution to the field, spanning the traditional range of disciplines represented in postcolonial studies but also those less acknowledged. It will also embrace new critical paradigms and examine the relationship between the transnational/cultural, the global and the postcolonial.

Combined and Uneven Development

Towards a New Theory of World-Literature

WReC
(Warwick Research Collective)

Liverpool University Press

Warwick Research Collective:
    Sharae Deckard
    Nicholas Lawrence
    Neil Lazarus
    Graeme Macdonald
    Upamanyu Pablo Mukherjee
    Benita Parry
    Stephen Shapiro

First published 2015 by
Liverpool University Press
4 Cambridge Street
Liverpool L69 7ZU

Copyright © 2015 Sharae Deckard, Nicholas Lawrence, Neil Lazarus, Graeme Macdonald, Upamanyu Pablo Mukherjee, Benita Parry and Stephen Shapiro

The right of Sharae Deckard, Nicholas Lawrence, Neil Lazarus, Graeme Macdonald, Upamanyu Pablo Mukherjee, Benita Parry and Stephen Shapiro to be identified as the authors of this book has been asserted by them in accordance with the Copyright, Design and Patents Act 1988. All rights reserved. No part of this book may be reproduced, stored in a retrieval system, or transmitted, in any form or by any means, electronic, mechanical, photocopying, recording, or otherwise, without the prior written permission of the publisher.

British Library Cataloguing-in-Publication data
A British Library CIP record is available

ISBN 978-1-78138-189-2 cased
ISBN 978-1-78138-191-5 limp

Typeset in Amerigo by Carnegie Book Production, Lancaster
Printed and bound by BooksFactory.co.uk

The periphery is where the future reveals itself.
– J.G. Ballard

Contents

A Note on Collaborative Method   ix

1 World-Literature in the Context of Combined and Uneven Development   1

2 The Question of Peripheral Realism   49

3 'Irrealism' in Tayeb Salih's *Season of Migration to the North*   81

4 *Oboroten* Spectres: Lycanthropy, Neoliberalism and New Russia in Victor Pelevin   96

5 The European Literary Periphery   115

6 Ivan Vladislavic: Traversing the Uneven City   143

Works Cited   168

Index   188

A Note on Collaborative Method

This book is the product of intensive discussion and debate. Although our individual specialisms vary widely, from postcolonial studies to American studies to modern European and Scottish literary studies, we are motivated by a common conviction that the existing paradigms of literary analysis, in whatever field, are not equal to the challenge of theorising 'world literature' in the new millennium. With a linked history of co-teaching as our departure point, alongside the co-organising of reading groups, conferences and symposia, we approached the task of writing from a basis not simply of shared theoretical interests and determination but of already extensive conversation on the central problems, as we saw them, of our respective sub-fields and of the emerging field of world-literary studies.

That said, the process of collaboration should never be mistaken for the harmonious reconciliation of differences. Several of our disagreements and divergent emphases are sedimented in this work, and our applications of its proposals continue to evolve in different ways. At the same time, and especially in the face of an increasingly hostile environment for critical studies of this kind, we have benefited enormously from the mutual attention, support and unstinting engagement that comes with collective endeavour.

Individual members of the collective drafted sections of the book after its main arguments were established in draft form. These were then edited, revised and rewritten in a multi-phase process by several hands. The result could indeed be termed combined and unequal – but in ways that perhaps highlight, rather than negate, the values of solidarity on which the work is premised.

CHAPTER ONE

World-Literature in the Context of Combined and Uneven Development

The way we imagine comparative literature is a mirror of how we see the world. (Franco Moretti 2003: 81)

These are testing times for literary studies. The challenges confronting the discipline today are legion and multiform; they range from the field-specific to the institutional, from the university to the wider spheres of politics and the economy. In addition to internal debates about the coherence and sustainability of the established forms of disciplinary literary studies, we might reference in this connection the ongoing subordination of culture generally to the laws of the market,[1] the apparently declining significance, relatively speaking, of literature itself as a cultural form,[2] and the steady assault on the autonomy of the humanities – and indeed of the university itself in its historical guise as, for better and worse, an ivory tower, a 'world apart' – by government, business and media regimes, all bent in their various ways on incorporation, control and instrumentally defined regulation.[3]

---

1 See Huggan 2001; Brouillette 2007; Strongman 2002; English 2005; and Casanova 2004, all of whom have interesting things to say about the commodification and marketing of literary prestige.
2 See Fredric Jameson: 'My sense is that this is essentially a visual culture, wired for sound – but one where the linguistic element [...] is slack and flabby, and not to be made interesting without ingenuity, daring, and keen motivation' (1995: 299).
3 Jameson speaks thus, of the 'subsumption of whole fields and disciplines under the patronage of private business and, as it were, the assimilation to wage labor of the standard nonacademic type of researchers whose work is subsidized by monopolies who set the agenda and are likely to profit from the results' (2008: 571). See, among others, Furedi 2006; Maskell and Robinson 2001; Miyoshi 1998, 2000, 2005; Ohmann 2003; Readings 1996; Teeuwen and Hantke 2007; and

The suggestion that literary studies is in crisis has been made before, of course. As long ago as 1981, for instance, Raymond Williams argued that English literary studies had stumbled into incoherence – on the one hand, because the idea of 'literature' no longer provided a stable evidentiary basis of study; on the other, because the connotations of 'English' were so densely problematical.[4] Asking whether the 'English' in 'English literary studies' identified 'the language or the country', Williams wrote that '[i]f it is the language, there are also fifteen centuries of native writing in other languages: Latin, Welsh, Irish, Old English, Norman French. If it is not the language but the country, is that only "England" or is it now also Ireland, Wales, Scotland, North America, Old and New "Commonwealths"?' (1991a: 194).

In the 30 years since that Cambridge-centred 'crisis in English Studies',[5] arguments as to the instability – indeed, on Williams's reading, the strict *unviability* – of disciplinary literary studies overall have been sounded with increasing resonance. Scholars in the field have been proposing that the received modes of procedure are in need of radical overhaul. Everywhere today, the institutionalised and consolidated methods, the structuring

---

Watkins 1989. Given their specific training, literary scholars are likely to view the 'junk language' of managerialism ('junk language' is Jameson's term, in a slightly different context) as an insult added to the injury already caused by policies aimed at subordinating universities to contingently defined national and social policy agendas, and about which literary scholars themselves are seldom if ever consulted: 'incentivisation', 'value added', 'quality assurance', 'competitiveness in a knowledge society', 'foresight activities', 'targets of opportunity', etc. In the UK – the national environment in which we ourselves work – the 'Research Excellence Framework' – a top-down, state-imposed scheme, centralised and massively bureaucratic, in which all departments in all universities are obliged to participate – is widely seen to have had deleterious effects on the scope, ambition, originality and independence of humanities scholarship, especially among younger scholars. For further commentary, see Bailey and Freedman 2011; Docherty 2011; Holmwood 2011; Molesworth, Scullion and Nixon 2010; the essays by Gopal, Holmwood and Bhambra, Jarvis, and Power that make up the dossier on 'Assaults on the British University System' in a special 2012 issue of *South Atlantic Quarterly*; and recent writings on this topic by Collini 2010, 2011, 2012, 2013 and Hotson 2011.

4 See also Peter Widdowson, writing at the same time and in the same national context as Williams: 'The "crisis" in English [...] is no longer a debate between criticisms as to which "approach" is best. Nor is it directly, yet, a question of English Departments being closed down along with other economically unproductive (and ideologically unsound) areas [...] Rather it is a question, posed from within, as to what English *is*, where it has got to, whether it has a future, whether it *should* have a future as a discrete discipline, and if it does, in what ways it might be reconstituted' (1982: 7).

5 We cite the Cambridge debate as symptomatic, not primary: other contemporary and linked initiatives (above all, perhaps, the development of the Centre for Contemporary Cultural Studies under Stuart Hall's direction at the University of Birmingham) were equally significant, and perhaps even more so.

premises and principles, the coherence of the disciplinary object of study itself, are being challenged and opened up to reconsideration and sometimes searching and fundamental critique. In comparative literature, for instance, the very questions of why it is worthwhile to 'compare' literary texts at all, and what doing so might involve in a world that is both more transparently, plurally and complexly polyglot and – at the same time, and seemingly paradoxically – more deeply dominated by just one language – English – than ever before, are being discussed. In American studies, similarly, there has been a proliferation of new initiatives aimed at combatting the isolationism and nation-centredness of the field in its established modes, in the interests of reconfiguring it along the lines of systemic (global) and comparative rather than exceptionalist perspectives.[6]

One does not have to be a card-carrying Bourdieusian to know that academics are rather given to pronouncing the fields or sub-fields in which they themselves work as moribund or in crisis. The strategic function of this time-honoured gesture is to pave the way for those involved to present their own interventions as being in the nature of decisive departures, corrective reconstructions or new beginnings. The goal is to make enough of a splash to attract attention, for one increases one's own specific capital in a given field by ensuring that one's own position-taking is registered in it.

In these terms, a certain programmatic scepticism might represent a healthy initial reaction to the kind of work, published under such titles as *Death of a Discipline* (Spivak 2003), *Politics and Value in English Studies: A Discipline in Crisis?* (Guy and Small 1993) and 'Beyond Discipline? Globalization and the Future of English' (Jay 2001), that gestures rather apocalyptically to dead ends and fresh starts. One such sceptic is Thomas Docherty, who, having correctly noted that '[t]he talk of crisis in the discipline compels us to think of ourselves as being at the start of something new or at least something refreshed', and having observed that 'institutional forms of literary criticism have a tendency to be complicit with [the] [...] marketisation and homogenisation of our work', proposes and defends the counter-suggestion that 'Comparative Literature is not "in crisis" at all' (2006: 26, 27). Point taken.[7] Yet we believe that there are nevertheless compelling reasons to view the current evocation of disciplinary turmoil as more than a mere internal power play or strategic ruse. If Williams's identification of a crisis in literary studies in 1981 can be taken to mark the emergence of various new initiatives – among them, postcolonial,

---

6 'The notion of American exceptionalism is in many ways the foundation of the discipline of American studies', Michael Denning notes: 'whether the answers are cast in terms of the American mind, the national character, American myths and symbols, or American culture, the founding question of the discipline was "What is American?"' (2004: 175). See also Dimock and Buell 2007.

7 See also James F. English, who begins his book *The Global Future of English Studies* by announcing the 'strange news' that 'the academic discipline of English is not in a state of crisis, [and] that its future actually looks pretty bright' (2012: 3).

ethnic and women's studies, cultural studies itself, the epistemological and methodological interventions of poststructuralism, postmodernism and deconstruction – perhaps the current moment is marked by the recognition that these 'new formations' have themselves now passed their sell-by dates. Certainly there appears to be a developing consensus that the literary studies field is going to have to reinvent itself in the years just ahead – not only because, subject to irresistible heteronomous pressures, it is being given no choice, but also because what 'literary studies' is taken to be, to mean and to represent – as well as *where* and *how*, and *by whom* and *to what ends* – have (again) become burning questions to academics in the field.

In this context of disciplinary rethinking and reorientation, the notions of 'world literature' and 'global literature' have emerged as important nodes of discussion and research. A relatively minor difference in the sub-disciplinary provenance of these two linked initiatives might be registered quickly. It is clear that the thought-figure of 'globalisation' is fundamental to them both.[8] But where 'global literature' might be understood as in the first instance an extension of postcolonial studies – *as postcolonial studies under the sign of 'globalisation theory'*, in fact – 'world literature' is in the first instance an extension of comparative literature, and might be understood *as the remaking of comparative literature after the multicultural debates and the disciplinary critique of Eurocentrism*. The term 'global' is typically deployed in discussion of contemporary social processes bearing on the modes of production, circulation and reception of literature (and culture, more generally) – hence the significance accorded, as in cultural studies generally, to such concepts as transnationalism, deterritorialisation, diaspora, homogenisation, (post-)modernity, cosmopolitanism, citizenship, and so on.[9] Discussants of the new version of 'world literature',

---

8 The underlying premises of this thought-figure are clearly identified by Hirst and Thompson in the opening sentences of their invaluable dissenting study *Globalization in Question*: '[I]t is widely asserted that we live in an era in which the greater part of social life is determined by global processes, in which national cultures, national economies and national borders are dissolving. Central to this perception is the notion of a rapid and recent process of economic globalization. A truly global economy is claimed to have emerged or to be in the process of emerging, in which distinct national economies and, therefore, domestic strategies of national economic management are increasingly irrelevant. The world economy has internationalized in its basic dynamics, it is dominated by uncontrollable market forces, and it has as its principal economic actors and major agents of change truly transnational corporations, that owe allegiance to no nation state and locate wherever in the globe market advantage dictates' (1996: 1).

9 See for instance Amireh and Majaj 2000; Apter 1999; Barnard 2009; Connell and Marsh 2011; Ganguly 2008; Gupta 2008; Jay 2010; Moses 1995; Mudimbe-Boyi 2002; and Mufti 2005. For the wider context in the study of culture and globalisation, see Appadurai 1996; Breckenridge et al. 2002; Fludernik 2003; Howes 1996; King 1997; Lash and Lury 2006; and the essays by Mignolo, Subramani, Kapur and Paik in Jameson and Miyoshi 1998.

by contrast, typically treat 'globalisation' not directly but as an underlying determinant at a certain remove – as the sociological pretext or warrant for a fresh engagement with questions of comparative literary method (which is what really characterises the new discussion of 'world literature'). We might say, in these terms, that 'world literature' is what happens to comparative literature when – having, however belatedly, engaged the task of 'unthinking' Eurocentrism – it 'goes global' (a phrase that one encounters quite frequently, along with the idea of 'an age of globalisation'). A handy illustration is provided by the advertisement for David Damrosch's *How to Read World Literature* in the 2008 Wiley-Blackwell literature catalogue. Damrosch's book, the catalogue tells us, 'addresses the unique challenges faced in confronting foreign literature – reading across time and cultures, translated works, and considering the emerging global perspective'; it 'offers readers the tools to think creatively and in an organized way about the great literary works produced around our world'.

We can readily see the 'postcolonialist' origins of the discussion of 'global literature' in Frederick Buell's early, but representative, study *National Culture and the New Global System* (1994).[10] Similarly, we can see the 'comparativist' origins of the discussion of 'world literature' in Emily Apter's equally emblematic work *The Translation Zone: A New Comparative Literature* (2006) – one of whose staple arguments we consider in detail below.[11] Today, however, the discussions of 'global literature' and 'world literature' are not only often conjoined, they are also pan-disciplinary, extending beyond 'postcolonial studies' and 'comparative literature' narrowly conceived.[12] Indeed, it is clear that, since the beginning of the new century, the old idea of *Weltliteratur* – whose specific genealogy can be sketched, as in John Pizer's succinct survey, from Goethe through Marx and Engels to Auerbach, Said and such contemporary scholars as Sarah Lawall[13] – has been reformulated quite self-consciously to carry the banner for a new, maximally encompassing project that transcends and supersedes the inherited (sub-)disciplinary formations, whether of comparative literature or postcolonial studies or the various 'national' literatures ('English', 'French', 'Russian', 'Japanese', etc.). Premised on the assumption that the 'world' is one, integrated if not of course united – an assumption that had been discouraged during the Cold War, when the opposition between 'East' and 'West' had prevailed; and not really overturned even by the 'Three Worlds Theory' that arose during the

---

10 See also Bhambra 2007; Dirlik 2002; Gikandi 2001; Krishnaswamy and Hawley 2008; McCallum and Faith 2005; and the essays by Behdad and Cooppan in Loomba et al. 2005. A critical commentary is provided by Brennan 2004.
11 See also Cooppan 2001; Damrosch 2006; Kadir 2004; and many of the essays in Saussy 2006.
12 Exemplary in this regard are Annesley 2006; Dimock and Buell 2007; Gupta 2008; Israel 2004; and Walkowitz 2007.
13 Pizer 2000. See also Hoesel-Ihlig 2004.

Cold War era to challenge that dominant construction[14] – 'global'/'world' literature in its pre-eminent contemporary formulation pushes intrinsically in the directions of commerce and commonality, linkage and connection, articulation and integration, network and system. It thereby distances itself, explicitly or implicitly, from the antecedent lexicon of 'post-'theory, which had been disposed to emphasise not comparison but incommensurability, not commonality but difference, not system but untotalisable fragment, not the potential of translation but rather its relative impossibility, and not antagonism but agonism.

Our ambition in this book is to resituate the problem of 'world literature', considered as a revived category of theoretical enquiry, by pursuing the literary-cultural implications of the theory of combined and uneven development. This theory has a long pedigree in Marxist sociology and political economy and continues to stimulate debate across the social sciences.[15] But the *cultural* aspects of Trotsky's initiating formulation concerning the 'amalgam of archaic with more contemporary forms' (1967: 432) has received less attention, even as what it highlights draws attention to a central – perhaps *the* central – arc or trajectory of modern(ist) production in literature and the other arts worldwide; and this aesthetic dynamic is, in turn, complexly related to histories and conceptions of social and political practice. It is in the conjuncture of combined and uneven development, on the one hand, and the recently interrogated and expanded categories of 'world literature' and 'modernism', on the other, that our project looks for its specific contours. All three of these terms, it seems to us, need to be thought together.

Powerful challenges to traditional ways of doing comparative business have been forthcoming recently from critics such as Pascale Casanova, with her Bourdieu-inflected study of a 'world republic of letters' structured by asymmetries of circulation and exchange, and Franco Moretti, whose insistence on the systematicity of world literature borrows explicitly from the language of combined and uneven development as redeployed by world-systems theory. Casanova's study stresses aesthetic *autonomy* as a foundational precondition of the literary field; Moretti's emphasises the *heteronomy* of literary production to world-economic relations. But both approaches pose a challenge to the received scholarship in the sociology of literature: synthesising the insights of these two lines of thought might enable us to open up a northwest passage in world-literary studies. Certainly, the continuing debates over the cultural implications of globalisation serve as a backdrop for the arguments of both,

14 See Denning 2004 and Brennan 1997, 2001.
15 See, for example, Allinson and Anievas 2009; Ashman 2009; Barker 2006; Davidson 2006b; Löwy 2010; Shilliam 2009; and Smith 1990.

and may suggest why, in the early years of the twenty-first century, the relatively old notions of *Weltliteratur* and combined and uneven development should have emerged as ways of seeking a new materialist basis for a revivified literary comparativism.

One of the landmarks guiding our thinking has been Moretti's firecracker of an article 'Conjectures on World Literature' – witty, down-to-earth, erudite and terrifically 'good to think' – which has been scattering sparks and setting off flares ever since it first appeared in *New Left Review* in 2000. So incendiary has Moretti's intervention proved, indeed (not only in this single article, of course, but across his recent work as a whole), that it has provoked any number of self-appointed Red Adairs in comparative literature to rush to the scene in an attempt to quiet the conflagration – thus far to little effect (and, *necessarily so*, we like to think). 'I will borrow [...] [my] initial hypothesis from the world-system school of economic history,' Moretti wrote in 'Conjectures',

> for which international capitalism is a system that is simultaneously *one*, and *unequal*; with a core, and a periphery (and a semi-periphery) that are bound together in a relationship of growing inequality. One, and unequal: *one* literature (*Weltliteratur*, singular, as in Goethe and Marx), or, perhaps better, one world literary system (of inter-related literatures); but a system which is different from what Goethe and Marx had hoped for, because it's profoundly unequal. (2004: 149–50)

Moretti's recent work provides us with a rich array of things to discuss: the terms of his appropriation of world-systems theory, for instance; the centrality of narrative *prose* in what he says about world *literature* (in general); his promotion of 'distant reading' and wilful corollary disavowal of 'close reading' (which we suppose is in any event more in the nature of an *emphasis* – tactical and contingent – than of any categorical argument whose propositions are to be construed *in principle*). But the formulation just cited strikes us as being indispensable in two immediate respects: insofar as it grasps 'world literature' as neither a canon of masterworks nor a mode of reading,[16] but as a *system*; and insofar as it proposes that this system is structured not on *difference* but on *inequality*.

---

16 Compare Moretti in this respect with Damrosch, who, while rejecting the idea that 'world literature' is 'a set canon of texts', argues that it is to be understood precisely as 'a mode of reading': 'a form of detached engagement with worlds beyond our own place and time' (2003: 281). Damrosch's three-part definition of 'world literature' also includes the propositions that 'world literature is an elliptical refraction of national literatures' and that 'world literature is writing that gains in translation'. See also Vilashini Cooppan: '[w]orld literature, as I tell my students, is not something you are given in full or get by proxy. Not a pre-packaged canon that differs from the traditional one only in its inclusion of a handful of unfamiliar names. Rather, world literature is a way you learn to think, a mode in which you learn to read, and a collective agreement you make to lose something in translation in order to gain something in transformation' (2004: 30).

The idea of 'system' is then one of the primary building blocks of our theory. The term is not treated in Raymond Williams's *Keywords*, where the associated term, 'structure', is explored instead – primarily a noun of process in the fifteenth century, Williams explains, but already by the eighteenth century marked by its emphasis on 'a particular and complex organization of relations, often at very deep levels' (1976: 253–59). But we construe 'system' similarly, as being characterised by vertical and horizontal integration, connection and interconnection, structurality and organisation, internal differentiation, a hierarchy of constitutive elements governed by specific 'logics' of determination and relationality. '*World*-system' represents a further elaboration on this. Following Braudel (1985), Wallerstein (1974, 1980, 1989), and others, we use the term to indicate a bounded social universe – whose functioning is more or less (that is to say, relatively) autonomous, more or less integrated. In general, 'world-systems', in these terms, are not coexistent with the 'world' as such, and are hence not 'global' or 'globally dispersed' systems. The significant exception is the modern capitalist 'world-system', one of the indices of whose historical unprecedentedness consists precisely in the fact that it is a *world-system* that is also, uniquely and for the first time, a *world* system.

We propose, in these terms, to define 'world literature' as *the literature of the world-system* – of the modern capitalist world-system, that is. That, baldly, is our hypothesis, stated in the form of a *lex parsimoniae*. Perhaps, therefore, we should begin to speak of 'world-literature' with a hyphen, derived from that of 'world-system'. The protocol commits us to arguing for a *single* world-literary system, rather than for world-literary *systems*. Here too we follow Moretti – but also Fredric Jameson, whose argument for a 'singular modernity' is – for reasons that we will discuss below – to be vastly preferred over the various theorisations, especially in the field of postcolonial studies, of 'alternative modernities'. Also relevant in this context is Casanova's preference for the terms 'world republic of letters' and 'international literary space' over that of 'world literature', since she wants to make clear that what is at issue in her mobilisation of the category of 'world' is not simply all the literary writing that happens to exist in the world. To think of 'world literature' as the corpus of all the literature in the world would be strictly nugatory or useless. Moretti had written that

> World literature cannot be literature, bigger; what we are already doing, just more of it. It has to be different. The *categories* have to be different. 'It is not the "actual" interconnection of "things",' Max Weber wrote, 'but the *conceptual* interconnection of *problems* which define the scope of the various sciences. A new "science" emerges where a new problem is pursued by a new method'. That's the point: world literature is not an object, it's a *problem*, and a problem that asks for a new critical method; and no-one has ever found a method by just reading more texts. That's not how theories come into being; they need a leap, a wager – a hypothesis – to get started. (2004: 149)

Casanova adds to this: in raising the question of 'world literature', she writes,

> it is not enough to geographically enlarge the corpus of works needing to be studied, or to import economic theories of globalization into the literary universe – still less to try to provide an impossibly exhaustive enumeration of the whole of world literary production. It is necessary instead to change our ordinary way of looking at literary phenomena. (2004: xi)

The 'central hypothesis' of her own book, she then proposes,

> is that there exists a 'literature-world,' a literary universe relatively independent of the everyday world and its political divisions, whose boundaries and operational laws are not reducible to those of ordinary political space. Exerted within this *international literary space* are relations of force and a violence peculiar to them – in short, a *literary domination* whose forms I have tried to describe while taking care not to confuse this domination with the forms of political domination, even though it may in many respects be dependent on them. (2004: xii)

Casanova is here building on Bourdieu's resonant observation, at the beginning of *Distinction*, that '[t]here is an economy of cultural goods, but it has a specific logic' (Bourdieu 1984: 1). This insight needs to be followed where it leads, and Casanova duly goes down this road in *The World Republic of Letters*, as such other Bourdieu-inspired theorists as Sarah Brouillette, Anna Boschetti, Gisèle Sapiro and Michel Hockx have also been doing in their recent work.[17]

Our own approach to the question of world-literature is posed slightly differently from this. Casanova is careful to note that the 'literature-world's' independence from 'the everyday world and its political divisions' is only relative. '[I]nternational forms of literary dependency are to some extent correlated with the structure of international political domination', she acknowledges; 'literary relations of power are forms of political relations of power' (2004: 81). But she nevertheless seems to us to abstract too strongly from the world of politics: she tends to treat the 'literature-world' and the 'everyday world' a little too much as parallel universes, with the result that questions concerning their *intersection* – questions as to the terms of their *relationship* – find themselves being deferred in her study. Since we are suggesting that world-literature be conceived precisely through its mediation by and registration of the modern world-system, our focus falls more directly than Casanova's on such questions. But our approach differs also from the work (much of it, again, enormously important) of scholars working on the political economy of culture, who have sought to identify the encroaching capitalisation of cultural production – that is to say, the commodification of culture, as product, especially intensive in the latter half of the twentieth century – the tendency to monopoly in all sectors of the culture industry,

---

17 See Brouillette 2007 and the articles by Boschetti, Hockx and Sapiro in a special 2012 issue of *Paragraph*, devoted to field theory in literature.

and also the dynamics of cultural imperialism (of what has been called 'Coca-colonisation'), in terms of which not only monopoly products but also regimes of production and patterns of consumption hegemonic in the core capitalist zones are imposed elsewhere, across the international division of labour.[18]

To describe the world literary system as 'one, and unequal' is to reactivate the theory of combined and uneven development. The theory originated in the work of Engels, Lenin and, especially, Trotsky, although it is Fredric Jameson's more recent deployment of it that Moretti evidently has in mind. An appreciation of the 'complex and differential temporality' of the capitalist mode of production, 'in which episodes or eras were discontinuous from each other, and heterogeneous within themselves', is, as Perry Anderson has argued (1984: 101), already observable in Marx's mature writings from the late 1840s onwards.[19] In these writings there is an awareness of the fact that even within capitalist or capitalising social formations, vast rural populations continued to ground the persistence not only of earlier economic conditions, but also of social relations, cultural practices and psychic dispositions.

This identification of unevenness, a staple of Marx's and Lenin's work, is then amplified in Trotsky's writings of the 1930s, in which, on the basis of his consideration first of conditions in Russia in 1905 and subsequently of those in China in 1925–27, he formulated an elaborated theory of 'uneven and combined development', by way of analysing the effects of the imposition of capitalism on cultures and societies hitherto un- or only sectorally capitalised. In these contexts – properly understood as imperialist, as Trotsky noted – the imposed capitalist forces of production and class relations tend not to supplant (or are not allowed to supplant) but to be conjoined forcibly

---

18 See Calabrese and Sparks 2004, whose edited volume features work by several of the best-known scholars in this particular branch of the sociology of culture.

19 In this sense, the famous passages from the *Communist Manifesto* that seem to evoke a transformation that is as abrupt as it is total are potentially misleading: 'All fixed, fast-frozen relations, with their train of ancient prejudices and opinions are swept aside, all new-formed ones become antiquated before they can ossify. All that is solid melts into air', etc. (Marx and Engels 1998: 38). But just as readings of such passages in the *Manifesto* as being infused with enthusiasm for capitalism typically 'forget' that the writings of Marx and Engels are notable also for recording and protesting the violence of expropriation, the systematised misery and servitude that the imposition of capitalist social relations visited on populations everywhere, so too it is necessary to insist that the authors were well aware of the fact that the 'capitalist revolution' was not a once-and-for-all event, but rather a sprawling, bloody and erratic historical process, protracted over centuries.

with pre-existing forces and relations. The outcome, he wrote, is a contradictory 'amalgam of archaic with more contemporary forms' – an urban proletariat working in technologically advanced industries existing side by side with a rural population engaged in subsistence farming; industrial plants built alongside 'villages of wood and straw'; and peasants 'thrown into the factory cauldron snatched directly from the plow' (1967: 432). The theory of 'combined and uneven development' was therefore devised to describe a situation in which capitalist forms and relations exist alongside 'archaic forms of economic life' and pre-existing social and class relations.

This general idea has, inevitably, been important to socialist and left liberation movements since the 1930s, as well as underpinning a sizeable sociological literature.[20] Thus Liu Kang (1998, 2000), who argues, in writing about the imposition of capitalism on China in the nineteenth century, that even as the latest techniques in capitalist production, transport, commerce and finance were being introduced in centres like Shanghai and Beijing, over which the Euro-American powers exercised military and political control, the agents of imperialist intervention were actively propping up an archaic landholding system, and supporting landlords, officials, militarists and comprador elites in prolonging prior forms of social organisation. In discussing colonialism in sub-Saharan Africa, similarly, Mahmood Mamdani (1996) points out that while the colonial powers coercively imposed new modes of production and capitalist social relations, they typically sought at the same time to buttress traditional hierarchies, forms and outlooks, and to encourage the survival of ethnically based local power, 'tribal' divisions and those indigenous cultural habits deemed conducive to promoting social 'stability'.[21] And in their analyses of South Asia, a long line of historians have identified the dynamics of British imperial policy in the Victorian era as consisting precisely in simultaneous and contradictory investment in industrial 'modernisation' and 'archaic' feudal (or semi-feudal) political and social structures.[22]

The significance of the theory of combined and uneven development has been less often registered in the humanities than in the social sciences. But it receives a powerful revisionary elaboration in the work of Fredric Jameson, where it appears as nothing less than a template for *any* consideration of modern culture, whether in the metropoles or at the peripheries of the world-system. Insisting that it can only be conceptualised adequately through reference to world-wide capitalism (2002: 13), Jameson understands modernity

---

20 In addition to the material cited in fn. 15, above, see especially the work of Justin Rosenberg (1996, 2005, 2006, 2007), who revisits and reconstructs Trotsky's conception, partly by way of debunking 'globalisation theory'. See also Rosenberg's exchange with Alex Callinicos in Callinicos and Rosenberg 2008.
21 On the invention of 'tribe' as a means of colonial governance, see Mamdani 2013.
22 See Kaiwar: 'In the colonies, vestiges of older social relations were maintained to ensure a degree of dispersed social control and governance on the cheap, whose main aim was resource removal and market monopolisation' (2014: 41).

as representing something like the time-space sensorium corresponding to capitalist *modernisation*. In this sense, it is, like the capitalist world-system itself, a singular phenomenon. But far from implying that modernity therefore assumes the same form everywhere, as Jameson has sometimes mistakenly taken it to suggest, this formulation in fact implies that it is everywhere irreducibly specific. Modernity might be understood as the way in which capitalist social relations are 'lived' – different in every given instance for the simple reason that no two social instances are the same.

Jameson emphasises both the *singularity* of modernity as a social form and its *simultaneity*. In the idea of *singularity* we hear the echo of a hundred years of dialectical materialist discussion of totality, system and universality – as, for example, in Henri Lefebvre's great essay 'What Is Modernity?' Explicitly evoking the theory of combined and uneven development, Lefebvre 'insist[s] upon the need for a general concept of modernity which would be valid for all countries, social and political regimes, and cultures', while distinguishing between 'the *general* and the *worldwide*' (1995: 188) – the former tendential, the latter empirical, we take it. The concept of *simultaneity*, meanwhile, Jameson derives from Ernst Bloch's ostensibly oxymoronic formula *Gleichzeitigkeit des Ungleichzeitigen* ['simultaneity of the nonsimultaneous'].[23] Modernity is to be understood as governed always – that is to say, definitionally – by *unevenness*, the historically determinate 'coexistence', in any given place and time, 'of realities from radically different moments of history – handicrafts alongside the great cartels, peasant fields with the Krupp factories or the Ford plant in the distance' (1995: 307). The multiple modes in and through which this 'coexistence' manifests itself – the multiple forms of appearance of unevenness – are to be understood as being connected, as being governed by a socio-historical logic of combination, rather than as being contingent and asystematic.

Jameson speaks then of the singularity of modernity, of modernity as a globally dispersed general 'situation'. 'Modernity' does not mark the relationship between some formations (that are 'modern') and others (that are not 'modern', or not yet so). So it is not a matter of pitting France against Mali, say, or New York City against Elk City, Oklahoma. Uneven development is not a characteristic of 'backward' formations only. Middlesbrough and North East Lincolnshire are in the United Kingdom as well as London and the Home Counties – and London itself, of course, is among the more radically unevenly developed cities in the world. To grasp the nettle here involves recognising that capitalist development does not smooth away but rather *produces* unevenness, systematically and as a matter of course. Combined *and* uneven: the face of modernity is not worn exclusively by the 'futuristic' skyline of the Pudong District in Shanghai or the Shard and Gherkin buildings

---

23 Bloch originally developed his concept of *Ungleichzeitigkeit* in *Erbschaft dieser Zeit* (1935); the English translation is *Heritage of Our Times* (Bloch 1991). See also Bloch 1977, and the commentaries in Brennan 2006: 47ff and Durst 2004: esp. 1–32.

in London; just as emblematic of modernity as these are the favelas of Rocinha and Jacarezinho in Rio and the slums of Dharavi in Bombay and Makoko in Lagos, the ship graveyards of Nouadhibou and the Aral Sea, the vast, deindustrialised wastelands north, east, south and west, and the impoverished and exhausted rural hinterlands. These constitute the necessary flipside of the mirroring opacities of a postmodern topos like the Portman Bonaventura Hotel, famously analysed by Jameson in his 'Postmodernism' essay. One liability of this otherwise continuingly suggestive survey – or at least of its reception – has been a tendency to conflate its analysis of a dominant cultural logic with a descriptive account of 'culture' in general. The result has been to encourage acceptance or dismissal of its synoptic generalisations without reference to the second half of Jameson's argument, its dialectical complement as it were, in his widely deprecated essay 'Third-World Literature in the Era of Multinational Capitalism'. Unless these torn halves are brought into relation, Jameson's theses lose their crucial emphasis on the structural connectedness between a cultural dominant expressive of the completed triumph of commodity logic and a condition in which this triumph is not only incomplete but arrested in a kind of freeze frame. Modernity is neither a chronological nor a geographical category. It is not something that happens – or even that happens *first* – in 'the west' and to which others can subsequently gain access; or that happens in cities rather than in the countryside; or that, on the basis of a deep-set sexual division of labour, men tend to exemplify in their social practice rather than women. Capitalist modernisation entails development, yes – but this 'development' takes the forms also of the development of underdevelopment, of maldevelopment and dependent development.[24] If urbanisation, for instance, is clearly part of the story, what happens in the countryside as a result is equally so. The idea of some sort of 'achieved' modernity, in which unevenness would have been superseded, harmonised, vanquished or ironed out is radically unhistorical. Capitalism, as Harry Harootunian has written,

> has no really normal state but one of constant expansion; and expansion requires the permanent production of excess, surplus, in order for it to survive. Part of the price paid for continual expansion is the production of permanent unevenness, permanent imbalance between various sectors of the social formations, the process by which some areas must be sacrificed for the development of others, such as the countryside for the city [...] the colony for the metropole, or even one city for another. (2000b: xv)[25]

24 Thus Claudio Lomnitz, who – writing with reference to Latin America's 'unusually long history of national independence' – observes that the subcontinent's 'long republican history made the tension among capitalist development, modernization, and modernity especially evident, and indeed it led the dependency theorists of the 1960s to puncture the development narrative being promoted on the capitalist side of the Cold War divide, by insisting that *underdevelopment* was not a lack of development but rather a specific *kind* of development' (2012: 349).
25 See the commentary in Pratt 2002 and Young 2012.

This formulation stands as a compelling repudiation of the various recent attempts to pluralise the concept of modernity through the evocation of 'alternative' modernities.²⁶ Inasmuch as these invariably derive from an initial assumption as to the 'western' provenance of modernity – rather than situating it in the context of *capitalism as a world-system* – they are both misguided and unnecessary. Of course, if one believes that modernity is a 'western' phenomenon, it is only possible to understand its global dispersal in terms of the 'universalisation' of 'the west' – to be celebrated or, as in the avowedly anti-Eurocentric conception currently so influential in postcolonial studies, deplored as imperialistic.²⁷ As Harootunian has argued in outlining his own opposition to such 'fashionable descriptions' as '"alternative modernities", "divergent modernities", "competing modernities," and "retroactive modernities,"' to postulate 'the existence of an "original" that was formulated in the "West"' is inevitably to suppose that the form of appearance of 'modernity' elsewhere must be both belated and derivative – 'a series of "copies" and lesser inflections' (2000a: 163). No wonder then that theorists who view modernity in these terms and yet are committed to the critique of Eurocentrism should want to argue for 'alternative' modernities!

Against this postcolonialist line of thought – which seeks to make an end run around the orthodox Eurocentric conception of modernity as a gift to be given or withheld by the capitalist homelands, but succeeds only in ratifying this baleful conception – however, the account elaborated by Jameson (and Harootunian) emphasises modernity's singularity and global simultaneity, while insisting that singularity here does not obviate internal heterogeneity and that simultaneity does not preclude unevenness or marked difference. Harootunian speaks, thus, of 'modernity as a specific cultural form and consciousness of lived historical time that differs according to social forms and practices', an idea that allows for 'differing inflections of the modern' (2000a: 62). In these terms, the specific modes of appearance of modernity in different times and places, or the representations of them in works of literature – St Petersburg in the 1870s, say, Dublin in 1904, rural Mississippi in the 1930s, a village on a bend in the Nile in the Sudan in the 1960s, Bombay in 1975, Glasgow in the 1990s – ought to be thought about not as 'alternative' but as 'coeval or, better yet, peripheral modernities (as long as peripheral is understood only as a relationship to the centers of capitalism[...]), in which all societies shared a common reference provided by global capital and its requirements' (2000a: 62–63). If modernity is understood as the way in which capitalism is 'lived' – *wherever* in the world-system it is lived – then 'however a society develops', its modernity is coeval with other modernities, 'is simply

---

26 The case for 'alternative' modernities has been advanced most notably by Gaonkar 1999. See also Gaonkar 2001. For a critique, see Lazarus and Varma 2008.
27 This line of thought is represented in the work of Dipesh Chakrabarty, Ashis Nandy, Timothy Mitchell, David Scott and Tsenay Serequeberhan, among others. Powerful critiques are marshalled in Chibber 2013 and Kaiwar 2014.

taking place at the same time as other modernities' (Harootunian 2000b: xvi). This should also challenge our uncritical habit of conflating epistemological and chronological primacy ('modernity happened in Europe first and best, and then in other places', etc.), and get us into the habit of systemic thinking in terms of non-linear conjunctions. Additionally, such a view suggests that the only plausible usage of the idea of 'alternative modernity' is to signify a future, post-capitalist (i.e., socialist) modernity (a case for which is made in Liu Kang 1998).[28]

We take our cue, in this book, from this reconceptualisation of the notion of modernity, which involves de-linking it from the idea of the 'west' and yoking it to that of the capitalist world-system. However, our central concern lies less with the politico-philosophical category of modernity as such than with its literary correlates – we are chiefly interested in the *literary* registration and encoding of modernity as a social logic. We are operating therefore with a preliminary tripartite conceptualisation – modern world-system/modernity/world-literature – in terms of which the latter is understood in the broadest sense as *the literature of the modern capitalist world-system*. We understand capitalism to be the substrate of world-literature (or, to borrow the phrase that Nicholas Brown uses as the subtitle of his 2005 study *Utopian Generations*, its 'political horizon'); and we understand modernity to constitute world-literature's subject and form – modernity is both what world-literature indexes or is 'about' and what gives world-literature its distinguishing formal characteristics. Questions of periodisation inevitably arise here. If we follow Wallerstein and others in speaking of the instantiation of capitalism as a world-system around 1500, it nevertheless seems clear that it is only in the 'long' nineteenth century, and then as the direct result of British and European colonialism, that we can speak both of the *capitalisation* of the world and of the full *worlding* of capital. World-literature, as we plan to deploy the concept, would then presumably be understood as a development of the past 200 years, though its formal conditions of possibility would have begun to be established some three centuries earlier.

28 'To understand China's modernity or its alternative modernity, overdetermined by complex and multiple structural relations, the centrality of revolution and political struggle in the field of cultural production must be acknowledged. China's alternative modernity can be best grasped as an ongoing process replete with contradictions: its revolution aiming at constructing socialism in a Third World, unindustrialized economy is alternative to the Western capitalist modernity in political and economic senses, and its emphasis on cultural revolution is also alternative in a cultural sense. But Chinese revolution is an integral part of modernity that is at once fragmentary and unifying, heterogeneous and homogenizing. Its project of modernity is as incomplete as its vision is unfulfilled' (Liu 1998: 168).

Later in this book we will explore a selection of modern-era fictions in which the potential of our method of comparativism seems to us to be most dramatically highlighted. In our analysis, we will treat the novel paradigmatically, not exemplarily, as a literary form in which combined and uneven development is manifested with particular salience, due in no small part to its fundamental association with the rise of capitalism and its status in peripheral and semi-peripheral societies as an import which is in Jameson's words 'as much a component of modernization as the importation of automobiles' (2012: 476). The peculiar plasticity and hybridity of the novel form enables it to incorporate not only multiple literary levels, genres and modes, but also other non-literary and archaic cultural forms – so that, for example, realist elements might be mixed with more experimental modes of narration, or older literary devices might be reactivated in juxtaposition with more contemporary frames, in order to register a bifurcated or ruptured sensorium of the space-time of the (semi-)periphery. A brilliant summary instance of such patterning is to be found in an early passage from *South of Nowhere*, a novel by the Portuguese author António Lobo Antunes, which ought to be as well known as Coetzee's *Dusklands*, but isn't, just as Multatuli's *Max Havelaar* ought to be as well known as Conrad's *Lord Jim* or *Heart of Darkness*, but isn't. 'Understand', writes Antunes's narrator,

> I am a man from a narrow old country, from a stifling city shimmering in the reflections of its tile façades. Even the sky is cluttered with flocks of pigeons. My sense of space here is also determined by a view of the river flowing into the sea but pressed in by two wedges of land. I was born and raised in a dwarfed crochet universe [...] This universe forbade me the eroticism of the ninth canto of the *Lusiads* and taught me daintily to wave good-bye with my handkerchief instead of simply taking my leave. It policed my spirit, in sum, and reduced my concerns to the problems of spindles, to the hourly calculations of the office clerk whose flight to the Indies went only so far as licking stamps at the Formica-topped tables of the post office. (Antunes 1983: 28)

In light of the novel's adeptness at mixing and repurposing narrative modalities, familiar from the analyses of Lukács and Bakhtin, we can draw attention to a further contemporary crisis pressing the case for a reconsideration of world-literature: that of cultural forms. By this we refer not to the historical opposition between mass, popular and elite cultures, terms now outmoded by the completed triumph of cultural commodification everywhere. Instead, the very processes driving the changes in the contemporary world-system have led to a breakdown of traditional boundaries demarcating genres and media, such that world-literary space is now characterised by new forms of convergence, synergy, competition and displacement. We want to suggest that the novel, and particularly the experience of reading and writing novels, has changed irrevocably within an altered mediascape in which diverse cultural forms, including new and newly recalibrated media, compete for representational space and power. The consequence has been that hybrid genres and interactive platforms have retrospectively altered our understanding of the historical development of the novel, prompting reappraisal of its strategies and affinities in light of an expanding communicational economy.

To grasp world-literature as the literary registration of modernity under the sign of combined and uneven development, we must attend to its modes of spatio-temporal compression, its juxtaposition of asynchronous orders and levels of historical experience, its barometric indications of invisible forces acting from a distance on the local and familiar – as these manifest themselves in literary forms, genres and aesthetic strategies. Any typology of combined and uneven development will offer a catalogue of effects or motifs at the level of narrative form: discrepant encounters, alienation effects, surreal cross-linkages, unidentified freakish objects, unlikely likenesses across barriers of language, period, territory – the equivalent of umbrellas meeting sewing machines on (animated) dissecting tables. These are, in essence, dialectical images of combined unevenness requiring not just simple decoding but creative application. Consider the opening lines of Earl Lovelace's *Salt*:

> Two months after they hanged his brother Gregoire, king of the Dreadnoughts band, and Louis and Nanton and Man Man, the other three leaders of African secret societies, who Hislop the governor claimed to be ringleaders of an insurrection that had a plan, according to the testimony of a mad white woman, to use the cover of the festivities of Christmas day to massacre the white and free coloured people of the island, Jo-Jo's great-grandfather, Guinea John, with his black jacket on and a price of two hundred pounds sterling on his head, made his way to the East Coast, mounted the cliff at Manzanilla, put two corn cobs under his armpits and flew away to Africa, taking with him the mysteries of levitation and flight, leaving the rest of his family still in captivity mourning over his selfishness, everybody putting in their mouth and saying, 'You see! You see! That is why Blackpeople children doomed to suffer: their own parents refuse to pass on the knowledge that they know to them.' (1996: 3)

We might then see the 'accordionising' or 'telescoping' function of combined and uneven development as a form of time travel within the same space, a spatial bridging of unlike times – in Lefebvre's sense, the production of *untimely* space – that leads from the classic forms of nineteenth-century realism to the speculative methodologies of today's global science fiction.

Our play with the Jamesonian triptych of modernisation/modernity/modernism leads us to believe that the temporal parameters of its third term, *modernism*, whose relation to world-literature it must be part of our work to specify, need to be set back rather earlier than they conventionally are, to incorporate the great wave of writing from the mid-nineteenth century onwards that is construable precisely – as in Marshall Berman's reading (1983), for instance – as an encoding of the capitalisation of the world, its tangible transformation at both of the levels – 'economic civilization' and 'material civilization' – specified by Braudel in his magisterial study *Civilization and Capitalism, 15th–18th Century* (1985).[29] We need to do away once and for all with the still-dominant understandings of modernism that situate it both in terms of writerly technique (self-conscious, anti- or at least post-realist, etc.) and as a Western European phenomenon, whose claims to being *the* literature of modernity are underscored precisely by this geo-political provenance. The discussion of *later* and *differently situated* modernisms is of course well under way in contemporary literary scholarship.[30] But we are interested in setting the work written by writers celebrated as 'modernist' alongside coeval and even antecedent work by writers from peripheral and semi-peripheral locations – Pérez Galdós, Machado de Assis, José Rizal, Hristo Botev, Knut Hamsun and Lu Xun, for instance – writers seldom considered in this context because critics have rarely thought through the full implications of the link between modernism, modernity and modernisation.

It is worth stressing that even if the logic of what Marx identified as the commodity form is not solely reducible to the processes of reification and commodification, it lies at the heart of combined and uneven development. We must take stock of the curious salience of the commodity fetish in the work of many metropolitan writers in the mid-nineteenth century, at a point when commodification achieved sufficient density to become the organising principle of society and insinuate itself into the fabric of everyday life to become, for the estranged perspective, visible – perhaps for the first time – as the uncanny coloniser of consciousness and the puzzling substrate of the new bourgeois 'common sense'. There is perhaps a twenty-five-year window, from 1835 to 1860, when this set of problems takes centre stage in such writers and artists as Dickens, Baudelaire, Hoffmann, Hawthorne, Poe, Grandville and Daumier – and then disappears beneath accreted layers of normalised perception. (Perhaps it is this latter development – the normalisation of commodity logic – that determines the emergence of naturalism?) We might then speculate that this 'window' reappears whenever and wherever commodification installs itself as an unfamiliar logic – especially if we bear in mind Wallerstein's repeated emphasis (1996) that the production of capital entails 'the commodification of everything': 'commodification' is a never-ending

---

29 '[M]any works written around the First World War struck me as being part of a much more extensive history (from, say, 1800 to 2000), of which they constituted merely one moment. A moment of great inventiveness and complexity, to be sure – the high point of the whole process, if you like – but no longer an autonomous, coherent reality demanding a specific category' (Moretti 1996: 3).
30 See for instance Brown 2005; Doyle 2010; Friedman 2001, 2010; GoGwilt 2011; Mejías-López 2009; Ramazani 2009.

rather than a once-and-for-all process; it ramifies both *extensively* – through the ceaseless development and conquering of new markets – and *intensively* – through the equally ceaseless quantification of quality. So – again – this is not a story that moves from 'west' to 'east': what is normalised as commodity logic in the time of Dickens finds itself being estranged by the new eco-semiotic regimes of subsequent eras.

In these terms our project involves remappings of both the history of modernism and the intertwined trajectories of world-literary wave formations. Theodor Adorno has already given us a reading of modernism as the (modern) culture that says 'no' to modernity. His argument, more precisely, is that modernism ought to be conceptualised as a cultural formulation of resistance to the prevailing – indeed, the hegemonic – modes of capitalist modernisation in late nineteenth- and early twentieth-century Europe. Hence the 'modernisms' of, for example, Ibsen and Dostoevsky, Breton and Woolf, Kafka and MacDiarmid – all hostile, in their various ways, to 'industrial civilisation' and its objectifying (or desubjectifying) social thrust. Provided we are prepared, for the sake of argument, to abstract from the precise determinants, contours and coordinates of this 'modernist' projection, the Adornian conception is relatively elastic. It can readily be extended forwards in time to apply to such writers of the latter half of the twentieth century as Lorine Niedecker and Geoffrey Hill, John Berger and Gloria Naylor, Elfrieda Jelinek and Jose Saramago, Roberto Bolaño and Nadine Gordimer, and also backwards – certainly as far as Romanticism, say, and such obvious figures as Percy and Mary Shelley, Hölderlin, Heine and Mickiewicz.[31] But it can also, and notwithstanding Adorno's own deep-seated Eurocentrism, be extended geographically – or rather geo-politically – to incorporate such writers as Lu Xun and Lao She, Aimé Césaire, Gabriela Mistral and Miguel Asturias, Saadat Hasan Manto, Ismat Chughtai and Mahasweta Devi, Ngugi wa Thiong'o, Nawal El Saadawi and Abdelrahman Munif, in whose work the dissenting registration of capitalist modernisation takes the historically unforgoable form of a critique of imperialism.

Certainly it is the case, as Nicholas Brown has pointed out in his consideration of the relation between modernist (that is to say, 'Euro-modernist') and independence-era African literatures, that both of these formations revolve around and are animated by the same world-historical process. 'The mere fact that European imperialism names a key moment in the spread of capitalism as a global economic system already implies a certain baseline of universality', Brown writes, before cogently drawing the key implication that 'there can be no question of merely applying the methodological norms developed for [the] one literature ['Euro-modernist'] to the texts of the other [African]'. Rather, what is required is to 'reconstellate [...] modernism and African literature in such a way as to make them both comprehensible within a single framework within which neither will look the same. This framework

---

31 In this connection, see Löwy and Sayre 2001.

will hinge neither on "literary history" nor abstract "universal history" but on each text's relation to history itself' (2005: 2–3).³²

Adorno understood modernism as being imbued with a (more or less explicit, more or less self-conscious) *criticality*. But his emphasis on dissidence – the identification of modernism with resistance – is too categorical for us to adapt without qualification to our thinking about world-literature. The Adornian conception issues in a hyper-canon, comprising expressionism, serialism, Beckett's drama and hardly anything else: it notoriously ignores the celebratory wing of fascist modernism (as in Marinetti) and the contradictory juxtapositions of reactionary plots and vanguard formal structures (as in *The Waste Land*, for instance). In proposing a definition of world-literature as literature that 'registers' the (modern capitalist) world-system, we, by contrast, are not suggesting that only those works that self-consciously define themselves in opposition to capitalist modernity be considered world-literary – nor even that world-literary works are those that stage a coded or formally mediated resistance to capitalist modernity. As we understand it, the literary 'registration' of the world-system does not (necessarily) involve criticality or dissent. Our assumption is rather that the effectivity of the world-system will *necessarily* be discernible in any modern literary work, since the world-system exists unforgoably as the matrix within which all modern literature takes shape and comes into being. Obviously this 'registration' of the world-system will be more self-evidently marked, more transparently at issue, in some works than in others. The fictions that we have selected for analysis below, for instance, seem to us to plot with particular clarity and resonance the landscape of the world-system: its hills and valleys, nodes and contours, lines and textures, balance and compaction. But it would be possible to elucidate the world-literary dimensions of any modern work, even one that set out

32 In a subsequent passage, Brown notes that such a 'reconstellation' would involve a deconstructive demystification of the very ideas of 'western' and 'non-western' literature: 'The question', as he puts it, 'would not be whether the most vital writing of the second half of the twentieth century was produced by Third World writers: it was. The question is rather what we mean by "literature" and what we mean by "West," what agendas reside in those words and whether they have any meaning at all [...] What we usually call "non-Western" literature is rarely the expression [...] of some other culture, if by that we understand some other set of norms and rules that has developed along its own internal logic; rather, it must be thought of in terms of the positions that economically, ethnically, sexually, and geographically differentiated subjects occupy within the single culture of global capitalism that has more or less ruthlessly subsumed what was once a genuinely multicultural globe.

All of this should be obvious, even if our entire mainstream multicultural discourse is built around its explicit denial. But the recognition of what multiculturalism denies should not be taken to signify a celebration of, or acquiescence to, the power of some henceforth inescapable "Western' tradition. Indeed, the capitalist monoculture dissimulated in multicultural discourse is not strictly speaking "Western" at all' (2005: 6).

very purposefully (as does Ian McEwan's *On Chesil Beach*, for example) to chart strictly private and socially incommensurable consciousness, experience or memory.

Here, too, Fredric Jameson's work is particularly important to us, since he has been concerned centrally with the relations between capitalist modernity and literary form. Thus while his essay on Third World literature has regrettably received attention only because of its claims about 'national allegory'[33] – claims which in our view have been tendentiously misunderstood – we find remarkable and illuminating his commentary in that essay on the 'crisis of representation' in non-metropolitan cultures that were, and remain, 'locked in a life-and-death struggle with first-world cultural imperialism [...] a cultural struggle that is itself a reflection of the economic situation of such areas in their penetration by various stages of capitalism, or as it is sometimes euphemistically termed, of modernization' (1986a: 68).[34] The proposition that the violence entailed in the imposition of capitalism in such societies made for the 'generic discontinuities' of the literatures subsequently produced (83) receives elaboration also in 'On Magic Realism in Film', another of Jameson's essays addressing Third World cultures – published, like the 'Third-World Literature' essay, in 1986 – in which he provisionally proposes that magic realism be considered as 'a formal mode [...] constituently dependent on a type of historical raw material in which disjunction is structurally present', and in which the content

> betrays the overlap or the coexistence of precapitalist with nascent capitalist or technological features. In such a view [...] the organizing category of magic realist film [...] is one of modes of production, and in particular, of a mode of production still locked in conflict with traces of the older mode [...] [T]he articulated superposition of whole layers of the past within the present (Indian or pre-Columbian realities, the colonial era [...]) is the formal precondition for the emergence of this new narrative style. (1986b: 311)[35]

---

33 The paradigmatic critique of Jameson's essay remains Ahmad 1987. For a counter-critique of Ahmad and corresponding defence of Jameson, see Lazarus 2011, and also Buchanan 2002, 2003; Lazarus 2004; McGonegal 2005; and Szeman 2003.
34 We take it that the 'crisis of representation' to which Jameson refers here is that of working simultaneously *within* and *against* imposed cultural forms, of deploying these without thereby subordinating oneself to their received ideological valences: in taking up the form of the novel, for instance, 'Third World' writers sought to appropriate it, to make it over or 'refunction' it, by way of turning it into an instrument through which their own very distinct cultural and political aspirations could be expressed.
35 See also the argument in the concluding section of Jameson's book on postmodernism that modernism itself must be seen as 'uniquely corresponding to an uneven moment of social development', in which there is a 'peculiar overlap of future and past', such that 'the resistance of archaic feudal structures to irresistible modernizing tendencies' is evident (1995: 307, 309). Jameson illustrates this

Our contention is that the features of 'combined unevenness' that Jameson identifies in magical realism are evident also (although not in quite the same ways) in other modern(ist) literary forms: primitivism, early surrealism, Kafka's supernatural naturalism, even critical realism. In a footnote to the 'Third-World Literature' essay, Jameson furthermore suggests – decisively, for our purposes – that this way of thinking about combined unevenness demands a new type of literary comparativism: namely the 'comparison, not of the individual texts, which are formally and culturally very different from each other, but of the concrete situations from which such texts spring and to which they constitute distinct responses' (1986a: 86–87, fn. 5).[36]

The premise of 'combined unevenness' developed here repudiates at a stroke the idea – linked, presumably, to the political mantra that 'globalisation' is a tide lifting all boats – that the 'world' of world-literature is a 'level playing field', a more or less free space in which texts from around the globe can circulate, intersect and converse with one another. It is remarkable how pervasive this idea of a 'level playing field' is in contemporary literary critical discourse. Particularly among those committed to a reconstructed model of comparative literature there is discernible a tendency to suppose that 'after' the multiculturalism debates and the disciplinary critiques of Eurocentrism and Orientalism, comparative literature was now finally free to become genuinely, authentically comparative – a supposition perfectly encapsulated in the title of an article by Jonathan Culler: 'Comparative Literature, at Last' (2006). Thus Gayatri Chakravorty Spivak, who writes that it has been her 'long-standing sense that the logical consequences of our loosely defined discipline [i.e., comparative literature] were, surely, to include the open-ended possibility of studying all literatures, with linguistic rigor and historical savvy. A level playing field, so to speak' (2003: 13). Inasmuch as it has elsewhere been one of Spivak's signature gestures to deconstruct particularisms that masquerade as universalisms, and to draw out their ideological presuppositions, it is difficult to appreciate the grounds on which, here, she chooses to subscribe to the idealist fantasy that a 'level playing field' is a 'logical consequence' of

---

argument through reference to Kafka's *The Trial*, focusing on the juxtaposition in the novel of a thoroughly modernised economic order and an older, indeed archaic, legal bureaucracy and political order deriving from the Austro-Hungarian Empire. See also, in these terms, David Durst's discussion of the 'structure of feeling' of what he calls 'Weimar Modernism' (Durst 2004).

36 He adds that comparative analysis of this kind 'would necessarily include such features as the interrelationship of social classes, the role of intellectuals, the dynamics of language and writing, the configuration of traditional forms, the relationship to western influences, the development of urban experience and money, and so forth' (Jameson 1986a: 86–87, fn. 5).

comparative literature as a discipline. In our view, comparative literature – in the Euro-American academy, at least – has pretty much always commenced from an unalloyed and irrevocable Eurocentric particularism.[37] In *Death of a Discipline*, however, Spivak holds out an olive branch to the discipline. What she is 'advocating', she says, is not 'the politicization of the discipline', but 'a depoliticization of the politics of hostility toward a politics of friendship to come'. To the extent that we understand them, we view these tactics as deeply misconceived. For it seems to us that what is called for is precisely *not* the 'depoliticization of the politics of hostility toward a politics of friendship to come', but, on the contrary, the active *politicisation* of the discussion on the basis of a steady and thoroughgoing *critique* of comparative literature as a disciplinary projection, both in the past and as it continues to exist today.

Some contemporary comparativists have wanted to project the 'level playing field' gesture backwards in time, to propose that the deepest intrinsic tendency of comparative literature was always 'global' or 'universalistic' in this sense.[38] Emily Apter, for instance, argues that 'Comparative literature was in principle global from its inception, even if its institutional establishment in the postwar period assigned Europe the lion's share of critical attention and short-changed non-Western literatures' (2006: 41). She attempts to defend this empirically counter-intuitive thesis by redrawing the lines of the received

---

37 Elsewhere – in South Asia, Latin America, China and the Arab world, for instance – literary comparativism has often had a very different critical underpinning.
38 A splendid and somewhat whimsical example of the 'orthodox' Eurocentrism of comparative literature is to be found in Hazel S. Alberson's 1959 article 'Non-Western Literature in the World Literature Program'. We write 'whimsical', because the exoticisation of 'non-western' culture appears despite Alberson's best intentions and most earnest aspirations, in an essay explicitly directed against cultural arrogance and condescension. 'The pressures upon all of us to become acquainted with non-western countries are more urgent and more vital than in Goethe's time', she writes, at the high point of the Cold War. 'Today we are faced with a ONE WORLD. No longer can we hide behind the façade of our ignorance and our provincialism, no longer can we be indifferent to those parts of the world we do not know. Today the reality of the Orient with its varied cultures, its different orientations, its problems, is here, not to be made over in our image but to be understood and to be accommodated. It always seems to me that there should have been a Fifth Freedom – Freedom from Contempt which comes with ignorance' (Alberson 1960: 45–46). All this is deeply humane, and rather affecting. Alberson believes that 'in exploring [literary works from the "non-West"] with our general knowledge of literatures and our comparative approach we can introduce the East within the perspective of the West, arouse a respect for the traditions of the East, erase some of the contempt that springs from ignorance and promote a larger tolerance' (49). But she gives the game away, betraying in the process also the narrow and strictly time-bound provincialism of her own cultural formation, when she adds: 'I will admit that at times the literature of the Orient can seem like its foods – highly spiced, exotic, with strange flavours – but they are usually concocted on the basis of staples with which we are are quite familiar, just as is their literature' (49).

history of comparative literature, such that Leo Spitzer's period of residence in Istanbul is afforded exemplary significance, rather than – as in most accounts – Erich Auerbach's. Her point is that where the manifestly Eurocentric Auerbach claimed to feel himself in the wilderness in Istanbul, cast out of 'Europe' and hence adrift of the civilised world, and made no attempt to learn Turkish (Apter suggests that his rather self-pitying accounts were ungenerous at least, and in fact inaccurate), Spitzer made himself rather more at home in the city, learning Turkish and setting up a school of philology that published actively. Apter's speculation is that Spitzer's example 'might have significant bearing on attempts to redefine comparative literature today as a "worlded," minoritarian comparativism', inasmuch as it might be taken to signify that 'early comparative literature was always and already globalized' (45–46). Thus she reproduces the table of contents of the 1937 issue of the *Publications de la faculté des lettres de l'Université d'Istanbul* – which featured ten articles: four in German, three in French, one in English and two in Turkish – and argues that the multilingualism of this issue 'attests to a policy of *non-translation* adopted without apology' which '[i]t is tempting to read [...] as the in vitro paradigm of a genuinely globalized comparative literature, as evidence of critical reading practices that bring the globe inside the text' (54–55, 61). For Apter, Spitzer's philology 'affords its micrological counterpart as close reading with a worldview: word histories as world histories; stylistics and metrics in diaspora' (64). It is this 'worlded' model – 'always already' spectrally present within comparative literature as a promise to be redeemed – that she sees as having resurfaced over the course of the past decade in literary studies overall – hence her bold claim that '[i]n many ways, the rush to globalize the literary canon in recent years may be viewed as the "comp-lit-ization" of national literatures throughout the humanities' (41).

All of this strikes us as deeply unconvincing. Let us note in passing that, whatever might be said in this respect about, say, 'French' or 'German' or 'Spanish' as sub-disciplinary formations, Apter's purported defence of comparative literature against 'national literature' programmes fails to hit the mark against English. For 'English' has never been 'national' in the sense evidently imagined by Apter. On the contrary, it has always, and for any number of reasons (not all of which do it credit, to be sure), been deeply invested in the worldliness of language and literature, in their political instrumentality and social power. It is for this reason, for example, that it has been within departments of English that materialist, feminist, anti-racist and anti-imperialist criticism has found room to breathe in recent decades. It is true that these progressive tendencies have often led minority existences in English departments, which have mostly been given over to distinctly orthodox, if nevertheless very varied, work. But criticism of this kind could neither have arisen nor have sustained itself in the chill formalist climate of the established comparative literary scholarship.

More substantially, Apter's emphasis on translation, multilingualism and philology not only fails to challenge, but in fact reinscribes the idealist version of comparativism central to comparative literature in its dominant institutional form. Although she refers repeatedly to 'globalisation' in thinking about what comparative literature does, and how it does it, Apter's failure to say anything at all about the structure of the world-system renders moot her claims for the universalism inherent in the discipline. It is all very well to call for 'critical reading practices that bring the globe inside the text', but it is difficult to see how the referencing of 'globality' here differs from the orthodox construction of 'the world' in comparative literature as a virtual universe of circulating languages and literatures, cultures and values.

Against 'national' particularism, Apter advocates 'a paradigm of *translatio* [...] that emphasizes the critical role of multilingualism within transnational humanism' (61). One problem here is that comparative literature has always been disposed to uphold a merely *quantitative* notion of multilingual competence, to celebrate multilinguisticality as though it in itself conduced to social harmony and equality.[39] The fact that the ten articles in the Istanbul literary review are written in four different languages seems to have blinded Apter to such other, less congenial, facts as that eight of these ten articles are in the hegemonic languages of metropolitan northwestern Europe and that, with only one exception, they all tackle problems to do with these languages or the literatures written in them.[40] Apter speaks of 'close reading with a worldview', but the evidence that she adduces in support of her contention that the 'worldview' in question here is no longer Eurocentric but genuinely globalised is thin, to say the least. As Apter herself knows very well, a daunting number of colonial administrators and Orientalist scholars were fluent in Farsi or Arabic or Zulu or Urdu without in the least feeling the need to question their Eurocentrism. *Their* 'multilingualism' was 'critical' not to 'transnational humanism' but to what they saw as 'the pacification of primitive tribes'!

---

39 Compare Rey Chow, who makes the excellent point that, although she 'deeply appreciate[s] the intellectual and personal benefits of knowing multiple languages, it appears problematic [...] to equate comparison with multilingualism per se. In that equation, so often voiced in the decision-making processes of hiring committees and other professional situations, language has come to be viewed as a stand-in for method, and the ability to use a particular language, more or less as the equivalent of having knowledge itself – indeed, as a privileged – because nativist – way into a culture, a key that opens all doors' (2004: 290). We will consider Chow's own critique of comparative literature below.

40 The multilinguisticity of this particular issue of the *Publications de la faculté des lettres de l'Université d'Istanbul* also seems less portentous when considered against the backdrop of the vibrant cosmopolitanism of Turkish (and especially Istanbul) intellectualism generally in the period. See Kendall, for instance, who points out that of the 47 journals appearing in Istanbul in 1876, 'only 13 were in Turkish: the others were in mainly Greek, Armenian, and French' (2002: 331). 'Western' literature and culture were actively debated by Turkish writers, journalists and intellectuals from the second half of the nineteenth century onwards. See also Konuk 2010 for a splendid contextualising analysis of Turkish intellectual life during World War II.

The argument has been made, by Lawrence Venuti (1998), among others, with respect to translation, and Louis-Jean Calvet (2006), with respect to the 'ecology' of languages themselves, that languages, literary forms and literary productions never enter the world on their own terms. A fundamental inequality – not intrinsic, but fully social – marks their capacities as representational practices; and this inequality is then overdetermined by the social logistics of translation, publication, reading, pedagogy, and so on.[41]

Moreover, the idea of 'close reading with a worldview' is itself unconvincing to us in its apparent assumption as to the ideological neutrality of critical method. Whatever might be said about Moretti's injunction to scrap 'close reading' altogether in favour of 'distant reading' (and Apter is writing with Moretti's provocation firmly in mind), it is surely a mistake, given its irrecuperable formalism, to attempt to defend the received disciplinary practice of 'close reading' in any strict sense. For the price of the rigorous examination of language and literature in institutionalised 'close reading' has invariably been abstraction from their social determinants and structuring conditions of existence.

It is of course necessary to acknowledge that translation – a mediating social practice, after all – is inextricably bound up with cultural misrepresentation, linguistic domination and social inequality. It might seem, in these terms, that comparative literature's refusal of translation and its commitment to reading in original languages is a culturally progressive gesture. But as Chow has argued very convincingly, 'language as such tends to be viewed as a neutral fact' by literary comparativists:

> seldom is it pointed out in discussions of comparative literature, that languages and cultures rarely enter the world stage and encounter one

---

41 Thus Calvet: 'even if to the linguist's eye all languages are equal (the most widely spoken languages and those that are in the process of disappearing, those languages in which hundreds of thousands of books have been written and those that have not been transcribed), the world's languages are in fact fundamentally unequal. To be sure, absolutely any dialect form of a little-spoken language of the Amazon basin or Africa deserves to be analysed just as much as English, Chinese or French and, so long as one undertakes the necessary labour of coining new words, everything can be said, written or taught in absolutely any language. But the fact remains that a discourse which would represent English and Breton, or French and Bobo, as socially equivalent would be both unrealistic and ideological: all languages do not have the same value, and their inequality is at the heart of the way they are organized across the world. To maintain the contrary would be an act of blindness or a sort of demagogy, granting the same importance to a mosquito as to an elephant, to a human being as to a butterfly: there are "elephant languages" and "mosquito languages" which it is difficult to consider on the same level, except of course from the point of view of the science which describes them. This comes down to saying that "elephant languages" and "mosquito languages" are all languages, a remark that borders on tautology' (2006: 4).

another on an equal footing, that "languages embed relations of dominance," and that the notion of parity embedded in comparison as it currently stands would need to be recognized perhaps as a form of utopianism that tends to run aground in practice. (2004: 296)[42]

Comparative literature's insistence on multilinguisticality is more often the leading edge of an unambiguous fetishism of language (and hence of the authority of professional experience) than of any commitment to cultural dialogue or social mutuality.[43] Behind it we typically encounter thoroughly idealist assumptions as to the ineffability, universality and timelessness of literature – the gamut of assumptions that Terry Eagleton once addressed under the rubric of 'the ideology of the aesthetic' (1990).

An enabling counter to the doxic position on the impossibility and undesirability of translation is provided in Andrés Neuman's novel *Traveller of the Century*, which features an extended discussion of translation in the contexts of core/periphery social relations. At a literary salon, the traditionalist Professor Mieter puts forward the comparativist position as typified by Apter, arguing against translation on the grounds that literature is ineffable and that translation does violence to its integrity. 'You must all agree', he contends, 'as discerning readers of poetry, that each poem possesses an untransmissible essence, a distinctive sound, precise forms and connotations that are impossible to adapt to another language with a similar perfection' (Neuman 2012: 330). The response given to this statement by Hans, one of the novel's protagonists, and himself a translator, strikes us as being full of consequence: 'I think being faithful is a contradiction', he suggests,

> because the moment another text emerges, faithfulness is no longer achievable, the poem has been transformed, it has become a different poem. We have to take as a given the impossibility of rewriting anything literally, not even a single word. Some translators are wary of this transformation, seeing it as a betrayal rather than a variation. But if it is well done, if the job of interpretation gives the right result, the text may even be improved, or at least become a poem as worthy as its predecessor. And I would go further – I think it is the translator's duty to offer the reader an authentic poem in

---

42 See also Gupta 2008: 147ff.
43 In her recent work *Against World Literature*, Apter makes her case against 'translatability' (and, implicitly, for the continued relevance of a comparative literary studies powered by 'high theory') even more starkly: 'I have been left uneasy in the face of the entrepreneurial, bulimic drive to anthologize and curricularize the world's cultural resources, as evinced in projects sponsored by some proponents of World Literature [...] A primary argument of this book is that many recent efforts to revive World Literature rely on a translatability assumption. As a result, incommensurability and what has been called the Untranslatable are insufficiently built into the literary heuristic' (2013: 3). It is striking that this argument, which links the predatory spread of 'World Literature' to the homogenising tendencies of globalized capital, is never extended to the 'translatability' of Theory itself; it may be that Apter takes the latter's ineffability for granted.

> his own language precisely in order to remain faithful to the poetic nature of the original [...] Let us not deceive ourselves – even an original poem has no single interpretation, to read a poem is also to translate it, we can never be completely sure of what a poem is saying even in our own language. As I see it, a translation is not made of an authorial voice and one that obeys it, rather it is more akin to a meeting of two literary wills. In the end, there is always a third person – isn't there? – who is a third discordant voice, which turns out to be that of the reader. (331)

What Hans introduces here is the idea of a continuum – something approaching an identity, in fact – between the acts of reading and translating. If to read is already to 'translate', then the seeds are already sown for the view that, even if translation is by definition a 'political' act, something may be gained by it, not merely something lost.[44] We are further enjoined by this insight to grasp reading and translating as themselves social rather than solitary processes, and thereby to attend to the full range of social practices implicated: writing as commodity labour, the making of books, publishing and marketing, the social 'fate' of a publication (reviews, criticism, the search for, creation and cultivation of a readership, etc.). As Hans puts it in *Traveller of the Century*,

> [a] work doesn't begin and end with its author, it forms part of a much broader group, a kind of writing collective that includes translators. Translation is neither a betrayal nor a substitute, it is another contribution, a further push to something that is already in motion, like when someone jumps into a moving carriage [...] No good translation can ever distort the translated work – it simply exaggerates the mechanisms of reading itself. (334)

'Efforts to rethink the study of world literature will continue', Sarah Lawall has written, 'as long as there is a discrepancy between the lively expectations generated by the term "world" and the pinched reality elicited by conventional approaches' (quoted in Damrosch 2003: 129). We would like to construe this thought-provoking formulation along materialist lines. Across the full range of disciplinary literary studies, the structurality of the capitalist world-system is typically misrecognised, if it is not ignored (or even denied) altogether. The misprision generally takes the form of an idealist recasting of capitalism – and/or of imperialism and modernity – in civilisational terms as 'the west'.

---

44 See Eliot Weinberger 2001: 'Translation liberates the translation-language. Because a translation will always be read as a translation, as something foreign, it is freed from many of the constraints of the currently accepted norms and conventions in the national literature' ('Anonymous Sources: A Talk on Translators and Translation', http://www.fascicle.com/issue01/Poets/weinberger1.htm). Accessed 10 April 2010.

The effect of this idealism is to undermine, in our view fatally, contemporary efforts to rethink the object of disciplinary literary studies. Let us examine briefly three instances of this idealism in operation, and consider their implications: Edward Said's *Culture and Imperialism* (1993) and two representative and ground-clearing articles by Susan Bassnett (2006) and Rey Chow (2004), respectively. These three pieces come from very different points on the literary critical spectrum, both methodologically and ideologically: Said stands significantly, of course, at the disciplinary crossroads between 'English', 'comparative literature' and 'postcolonial studies'; Bassnett offers an endorsement of comparative literature in the wake of the disciplinary critique of Eurocentrism; and Chow argues that this critique has been cosmetic only, and that comparative literature remains fundamentally Eurocentric. Our argument will be that despite the stark differences between them in almost every other respect, Said, Bassnett and Chow all demonstrate the same tendency to substitute the civilisational category of 'the west' for the category of capitalist modernity as the object of their analysis – a substitution that has the inevitable effect of dematerialisation.[45]

In *Culture and Imperialism*, Said proposes that it has been the belated discovery on the part of contemporary scholars of 'the enormously exciting, varied post-colonial literature produced in resistance to the imperialist expansion of Europe and the United States in the past two centuries' that has served most decisively to throw the received paradigms of literary scholarship into question (1993: 71). He mobilises the category of the 'post-colonial' here following Ashcroft, Griffiths and Tiffin, who had used the term 'to cover all the culture affected by the imperial process from the moment of colonization to the present day' (1989: 2). Said tends to speak in this context of *contrapuntalism*, as in his characteristic identification, in *Culture and Imperialism*, of 'overlapping territories, intertwined histories common to men and women, whites and non-whites, dwellers in the metropolis and on the peripheries, past as well as present and future' (1993: 72).

The larger point that he is concerned to make is that *imperialism* is the 'major, I would say determining, political horizon of modern Western culture' (1993: 70). His argument, in fact, is two-edged. On the one hand, he suggests that imperialism is fundamental to modern 'western' culture – is, in fact, that culture's very substrate or grounding instance. On the other hand, he suggests that precisely this truth, or reality, has been ignored, systematically and symptomatically, within 'western' culture itself: within literary studies, a 'massive avoidance' – which, were it a matter of consciousness, rather than of ideology or, better, of epistemic 'atmosphere', might be said to amount to the mother of all conspiracies – 'has sustained a canonical inclusion and exclusion: you include the Rousseaus, the Nietzsches, the Wordsworths, the Dickenses, Flauberts, and so on, and at the same time you exclude their relationships with the protracted, complex, and striated work of empire' (70).

---

45 See also Lazarus 2002.

Writing at the end of the 1980s and the beginning of the 1990s, Said argues that 'the relationship between empire and culture' has only just begun to find registration in literary studies (1993: 71). We have been quoting thus far from the chapter in *Culture and Imperialism* significantly entitled 'Connecting Empire to Secular Interpretation'. The contention in this chapter is that from the mid-eighteenth century to the time of his own writing in the late twentieth, the literary field has been blind to its own enabling conditions, modes of operation and ideological effects. The thrust of literary scholarship during this period has sometimes been nation-centred (and occasionally narrowly chauvinistic) and sometimes (as in Goethe or Auerbach, for instance) comparativist and even universalist in its rhetoric. But even in its more expansive, comparativist guises, which Said himself vastly prefers, the scholarship has been constitutively Eurocentric: the field has been organised 'epistemologically [...] as a sort of hierarchy, with Europe and its Latin Christian literatures at its centre and top' (52).

The fundamental task that Said therefore enjoins upon his colleagues in the literary field is to 'unthink Eurocentrism'.[46] This is partly a matter of opening oneself to the existing archives and burgeoning new literary production from the world outside the 'west', for he argues, surveying the scholarship of the past 200 years, that '[w]ithout significant exception, the universalizing discourses of modern Europe and the United States assume the silence, willing or otherwise, of the non-European world. There is incorporation; there is inclusion; there is direct rule; there is coercion. But there is only infrequently an acknowledgement that the colonized people should be heard from, their ideas known' (58). But 'unthinking Eurocentrism' also involves revising our construction of 'western' culture itself. We cannot simply add or assimilate new material to an otherwise unchanged canon in accordance with unaltered modes of disciplinary practice. The constitutive Eurocentrism of old-style 'Victorian studies' for example, would not be transformed were we merely, so to speak, to 'add colonialism and stir'. Said enjoins us instead to

> reinterpret the Western cultural archive as if fractured geographically by the activated imperial divide, to do a rather different kind of reading and interpretation. In the first place, the history of such fields as comparative literature, English studies, cultural analysis, anthropology can be seen as affiliated with the empire and, in a manner of speaking, even contributing to its methods for maintaining Western ascendancy over non-Western natives [...] And in the second place our interpretive change of perspective allows us to challenge the sovereign and unchallenged authority of the allegedly detached Western observer. (1993: 59)

This injunction – it would be more accurate, perhaps, to understand it, as Raymond Williams has taught us, as a dispersed and historically specific political imperative, rather than through reference to a single scholar, no matter

---

46 See Shohat and Stam 1994.

how influential – has been at the heart of much of the work produced across the full range of literary studies over the course of the past quarter-century.[47] Said's identification of the inextricability of 'culture' from 'imperialism'[48] – the 'integration and connections between the past and the present, between imperializer and imperialized, between culture and imperialism' (1993: 72) – strikes us as being of indispensable importance. But we need to register a major weakness in his understanding of the key concept of imperialism. This weakness has already been addressed and explored in some of the criticism directed at Said by his materialist followers and interlocutors in postcolonial studies.[49] There are various ways of registering the problem in shorthand. One of them is simply to point out that while the terms 'empire' and 'imperialism' run like a rich dye through all of Said's work, there are far fewer references to the term 'capitalism'. Another is to observe the anomalousness of his repudiation of Marxism: as Benita Parry has pointed out, we can scarcely fail to remark on the fact that Said's work on culture and imperialism 'neglected that very analysis which has done most to explain modern colonialism and imperialism as integral to capitalism's beginnings, expansion, and ultimate global entrenchment' (Parry 2013: 107).[50]

The main problem is that Said presents imperialism as a *political* dispensation rather than as a *process of accumulation on a world scale*, under conditions of capitalist monopoly. Imperialism for him implicates military conquest,

---

47 A mere recitation of some key titles might be sufficient to demonstrate this: *Rule of Darkness: British Literature and Imperialism, 1830–1914* (Brantlinger 1988); *Gender, Race, Renaissance Drama* (Loomba 1989); *The Masks of Conquest: Literary Study and British Rule in India* (Viswanathan 1989); *Critical Terrains: French and British Orientalisms* (Lowe 1991); *The Poetics of Imperialism: Translation and Colonization from 'The Tempest' to 'Tarzan'* (Cheyfitz 1991); *Macropolitics of Nineteenth-Century Literature: Nationalism, Exoticism, Imperialism* (Arac and Ritvo 1991); *Civilising Subjects: Metropole and Colony in the English Imagination 1830–1867* (Hall 2002); *Colonial Encounters: Europe and the Native Caribbean, 1492–1797* (Hulme 1992); *Imperial Eyes: Travel Writing and Transculturation* (Pratt 1992); *Cultures of United States Imperialism* (Kaplan and Pease 1993); *Imperial Leather: Race, Gender and Sexuality in the Colonial Contest* (McClintock 1995); *Out of Place: Englishness, Empire, and the Locations of Identity* (Baucom 1999); *Literary Culture and US Imperialism: From the American Revolution to World War II* (Rowe 2000); *Fabulous Orients: Fictions of the East in England 1662–1785* (Ballaster 2005).
48 Said presents his argument here as a break from the dominant forms of aesthetic philosophy since Kant: 'Cultural experience or indeed every cultural form is radically quintessentially hybrid, and if it has been the practice in the West since Immanuel Kant to isolate cultural and aesthetic realms from the worldly domain, it is now time to rejoin them' (1993: 68).
49 See for example Brennan 2013; Lazarus 2011: 183–203; Parry 1992, 2006, 2013; San Juan, Jr. 2006, 2008.
50 Parry continues: 'Because his focus is exclusively on colonialist exploitation, Said's writing [...] neglects the ubiquity of class inequality and the assaults visited on workers and the poor in the core capitalist countries and the semi-peripheries as well as the peripheries' (2013: 107).

alien governance, systematised top-down violence, social asymmetry, cultural and symbolic domination, and Eurocentrism as a set of deeply patterned 'structures of attitude and reference'. It is characteristically about domination rather than about exploitation or class struggle or the imposition of a mode of production. The tendential severing of imperialism from capitalism leads Said to neglect the structuring dynamics, agencies and vectors of modern historical development. Situating imperialism in civilisational terms as an 'ongoing contest between north and south, metropolis and periphery, white and native' (1993: 59), he typically refers us to 'the west' as its originating force – as when, in *Orientalism*, he speaks of 'a Western style for dominating, restructuring, and having authority over the Orient' (1979: 3).[51] In the absence of a materialist conception of imperialism, 'the west' in Said's work comes to stand in for the socio-historical process that it tacitly references, but at the price of mystification.

A second liability of Said's conceptualisation follows directly from this first. A further consequence of his conflation of imperialism and 'the west' is that the latter instance tends to suffer homogenisation: both historically and geo-politically, its internal divisions and differences, the trajectories of its development, are flattened out and disregarded. It is not only that between the categories of 'the west' and 'Europe', no significant difference is registered – such that, for example, the United States is presented as a more or less organic outgrowth of 'Europe', merely with a broader geo-strategic base. Also observable in *Culture and Imperialism* is a steady if reductive progression from 'England', 'France' and 'the United States', to the 'major metropolitan' formations, and thence to 'the west' itself. The fact, as Lucia Boldrini has pointed out, that '[m]any European countries have no imperial history if not a passive one, having themselves been "colonised", subjugated or controlled by other political powers' (2006: 15–16), is never taken into account by Said. Although Boldrini's complaint about the 'continuing identification of Europe on the one hand with *some* Western European countries and, on the other, with "the west" and therefore with colonial history – of the reduction, that is to say, of Europe to the colonial history of some of its states' (15), is not directed at Said's work, it is easy to see its relevance to any appraisal of Said.

It is because Said's work both homogenises 'the west' and construes it as the agent of imperialist domination that he has sometimes been accused, by critics to his left and to his right, of 'Third-Worldism'. There is no need to rehearse this dispute here. What can be noted, however, is that the

---

51 For an interesting critique of Said's 'civilisational' understanding of imperialism, suggesting its affinities with Max Weber, see Farris 2010.

tendency to essentialise 'the west' has become a staple ingredient, across the range of literary scholarship, of much of the work that – following Said's injunction – has been directed to 'unthinking Eurocentrism'.[52] We can see this very clearly, for instance, in Rey Chow's influential call for a 'post-European' perspective in comparative literature, to which we will turn shortly. Before doing so, however, it will behove us to look at Susan Bassnett's 'Reflections on Comparative Literature in the Twenty-First Century', since it is to the kind of thought exemplified in Bassnett's essay that Chow is evidently responding.

Bassnett wants to take stock of comparative literature *after* the disciplinary critique of Eurocentrism. This critique is taken to have been levelled, absorbed and appropriately acted upon. '[W]e have come a long way in three decades', Bassnett writes airily, *en route* to a restatement of the value and vitality of the 'western' literary canon and the tradition that it inscribes and memorialises.[53] She readily concedes that it was important for scholars of literature generally to take to heart the central argument brought against mainstream scholarship by the critics of Eurocentrism – which argument she introduces under the rubric of 'plurivocality': the call for multiple voices to be attended to, 'rather than one single dominant voice' (4). (It is worth registering in passing here the distance between this concept of 'plurivocality' and the Saidian notion of 'contrapuntalism'. For all that might be said against it, the latter, as we have seen, identified 'overlapping territories' and 'intertwined histories' which, according to Said, it was necessary to think *together*, as registrations of a vast social experience binding all its participants, even if antagonistically and unequally.[54] 'Plurivocality', by contrast, identifies only the multiplicity of discourses; it has nothing to say about their interrelations.) But in a passage directed explicitly at Gayatri Spivak, Bassnett suggests that while a comparativist approach to literature governed by this model of plurivocality 'works for anyone approaching the great literary traditions of the northern hemisphere from elsewhere', it is not

> particularly helpful for those of us who have as a starting point one or other of those great traditions. The question remains as to what new directions

---

52 See the analysis of the 'fetishism' of 'the West' in postcolonial theory in Lazarus 2002.
53 '[T]here is a need now to look again at the idea of the canon, not least because of the way in which Western foundation texts have found their way into other literatures – think of the impact of naturalism on southern Indian literatures, of the extraordinarily creative use of Homer and the epic tradition by the St. Lucian Nobel laureate Derek Walcott, of the current translation boom in China, as Western writing is translated, imitated and rewritten in exciting new ways. A fundamental question that comparative literature now needs to address concerns the role and status of the canonical and foundation texts that appear to be more highly valued outside Europe and North America than by a generation of scholars uneasy about their own history of colonialism and imperialism' (Bassnett 2006: 5).
54 See the dedication to Nayantara Sahgal's 1985 novel *Rich Like Us*: 'To the Indo-British Experience and what its sharers have learned from each other'.

in comparative literature there can be for the European scholar whose intellectual formation has been shaped by classical Greek and Latin, by the Bible, by the Germanic epic, by Dante and Petrarch, by Shakespeare and Cervantes, by Rousseau, Voltaire and the Enlightenment, by Romanticism and post-Romanticism, by the European novelists of the nineteenth and twentieth centuries, by generations of writers who have borrowed, translated, plagiarized and plundered, but whose works run inexorably to some degree through the consciousness of anyone writing today. (4–5)

Some of the implications of this deeply tendentious formulation are worth exploring in detail.[55] We can start by noting the conceptual muddle entailed in the internal slippage from 'northern hemisphere' to 'Europe' – and compounded elsewhere in the essay, when Bassnett mobilises in addition the category of the 'west' (as in 'Western foundation texts' and 'Western writing'). She deploys these three terms – 'Europe', 'northern hemisphere' and 'west' – in her essay as strict synonyms, all naming the same thing. That thing is, evidently, a (singular) trans-national (but not global) 'culture' or 'civilisation'. 'No single European literature can be studied in isolation', Bassnett writes, evidently meaning thereby to challenge national(ist) literary scholarship; but nor, she adds, 'should European scholars shrink from reassessing the legacy they have inherited. There is a great deal to learn from the perspectives of Southern hemisphere scholars, principle [sic] of which is the shift in perspective that their views inevitably incite, but it is important not to lose sight of where we, as Europeans, stand in relation to our own literary history' (10). While 'Europe' comes into focus as a civilisational unity for Bassnett, the premise of a *world*-system is denied or disregarded. 'No single European literature can be studied in isolation', she writes; but *European* literature evidently can – indeed, must – be studied in isolation from 'non-European' (or 'southern hemisphere') literatures. No 'contrapuntalism' for Bassnett, evidently. Instead, we must assume that she conceives of the world as the ensemble of plural, more or less discrete, *civilisations*.[56]

---

55 The tendentiousness of Bassnett's argument can be exposed merely through counter-citation of Sophie Bessis's elegant demolition of its general premises. Bessis writes of Eurocentric evocations of a 'Greco-Roman tradition': 'In fact, since Petrarch and others gave it an initial form in the fourteenth century, the founding myth of an exclusive Greco-Roman source has functioned as an implacable machine for the expulsion of oriental or non-Christian sources from European civilization. Erased: the Babylonian, Chaldean, Egyptian and Indian influences on Greece, from the pre-Socratics to the late descendants of Alexander. Disregarded: the huge prestige that Egypt always enjoyed within the Greek world, whose literary figures happily recognized what they owed to its sciences and its religion. Obscured: the crucial dimension of the Hellenistic era, that hybrid of Hellenism and the East. Passed over in silence: the cultural pluralism of a Roman empire for which the barbarians were men from the North, not the familiar peoples along the southern shores of the Mediterranean' (2003: 13).

56 In which case, one would want to know the grounds on which Bassnett's idealist

What Bassnett proposes as a bedrock – the cord that supposedly binds together and unites into a single 'Great Tradition' the various micro-traditions of the constituent cultures, nations and peoples of 'Europe'/'the northern hemisphere'/'the west' – is in our view a strictly ideological construction, which it would be better to construe as a *post facto* justification for the currently prevailing global dispensation.[57] The problem is not only that Bassnett's presentation tends to erase the violence structurally entailed in 'inter-cultural' relations in the contexts of colonialism and capitalist modernity – specifically, the relations between 'Europe' and the world beyond its historically porous and often shifting boundaries. (What she terms 'interconnectedness', in this respect, and sees as a positive good might with greater historical warrant be described as Conrad described it in *Heart of Darkness*: 'robbery with violence, aggravated murder on a great scale' [2007: 8].) Just as important is the fact that her essentialism serves to mystify the history of Europe itself. It is worth reminding ourselves that, far from representing any intrinsic civilisational unity or 'community of values', the 'making of Europe' involved (and continues to involve) conflict, division, violence and mutual animosity. The 'Europe' that would come to impose itself on the rest of the world in the modern era – and that would present itself in civilisational terms in doing so – was, as Robert Bartlett has argued very eloquently, itself the product of 'internal' conquest, colonisation and enforced cultural change:

> Conquest, colonization, Christianization: the techniques of settling in a new land, the ability to maintain cultural identity through legal forms and nurtured attitudes, the institutions and outlook required to confront the strange or abhorrent, to repress it and live with it, the law and religion as well as the guns and ships. The European Christians who sailed to the coasts of the Americas, Asia and Africa in the fifteenth and sixteenth centuries came from a society that was already a colonizing society. Europe, the initiator of one of the world's major processes of conquest, colonization and cultural transformation, was also the product of one. (1994: 313–14)

---

positioning of the 'inter-connection' between these 'civilisations' is to be preferred over Samuel Huntington's rather grimmer, 'realist' theory of a 'clash of civilisations'.

57 In fact, Bassnett's argument is in places so definitively Eurocentric (in the restricted sense of 'Europe-centred') as to render implausible even her own conflation of 'Europe' with 'the west' and 'the northern hemisphere'. It is difficult to know, for instance, how North American or Russian readers are to position themselves in relation to the advice that 'it is important not to lose sight of where we, as Europeans, stand in relation to our own literary history'. The facts that significant sections of the Russian intelligentsia have consistently defined themselves in explicit opposition to the category of 'the west' (while insisting on their fidelity to 'Europe') and that significant sections of the US intelligentsia have consistently defined themselves in explicit opposition to the category of 'Europe' (while insisting on their fidelity to 'the west') have evidently not given Bassnett pause.

Reciting the names of Dante and Shakespeare and Cervantes, evoking Latin and the Bible and the Enlightenment, Bassnett conjures up the image of a literary tradition freely available, as something like a family inheritance, to all 'Europeans' – but not, evidently, to 'non-Europeans'.[58] (Her thesis is made more convoluted still – not to say, more untenable – by the fact that on her reading the category of 'Europeans' would include [some? most? all?] North Americans, Australians, etc.) One could play Bassnett's game in reverse here, and recite other names that point in a completely different direction: Andalusian Arabic, Bulgar, Drevani, Muromian, Curonian and Pomeranian, for instance – now extinct 'European' languages, obliterated (and along with them the cultural identity of the people who spoke them) in the long march of 'Europeanisation'; or Cornish, Welsh, Occitan, Breton, Livonian and Sardinian – dominated and/or sub-national languages that still survive in Europe despite the fierce pressures exerted upon them by hegemonising forces (often trans- or super-national cultures and languages), whose imposition it has proved impossible to resist. It takes nothing away from Shakespeare and Cervantes, the epic and the Bible, English and German, surely, to recognise that it has often been precisely in the name of the selective tradition identified through reference to them (and such as them) that politically dominant forces in Europe have rained violence and terror upon their neighbours, by way of subduing and subordinating them – a process involving first deculturation and then enforced acculturation. It is not only in extra-European theatres that English, French, German, Italian and Russian have been imposed on speakers of other languages, by way of breaking their resistance and undermining their cultural integrity.

Bassnett's article is written partly by way of attempting to re-energise comparative literature after the critique of Eurocentrism – a critique which, for all its indispensability, is seen to have left the discipline somewhat demoralised. Hence her suggestion that 'the perspectives of Southern hemisphere scholars' are 'not particularly helpful for those of us who have as a starting point' the Great Tradition represented by the 'western' canon. Her argument is clearly predicated on an assumption as to the distinctiveness and the internal unity of 'Europe'/'the northern hemisphere'/'the west' as a civilisational bloc

---

58 We are reminded here of what Karl Heinz Bohrer has written recently of Ernst Robert Curtius: 'Curtius's conception of Europe [was] as a delightful garden in which major writers and thinkers meet, from Virgil to Goethe, from Balzac to Miguel de Unamuno, from Ortega y Gasset to T.S. Eliot and Jean Cocteau' (2012: 591). However, Bohrer identifies this idealism in Curtius as a compensatory utopianism – an historically specific determination that is quite obviously different from that animating Bassnett's understanding: 'Curtius's idea that the different national writers belonged together in the spiritual present of European literature was utopian in the sense that it responded to the two wars and the state of continental Europe as a landscape in ruins. It was the anticipation of a longed-for alternative, the illusion that ideas could literally move mountains, the mountains in question being the borders separating countries' (591).

irreducibly different from, if not necessarily in opposition to, other civilisational blocs (e.g., that represented by 'the southern hemisphere'). We have attempted to demonstrate that, because of its essentialism, this construction of 'Europe' mystifies the history of Europe, as well as, of course, the relations between Europe and the rest of the world.

It might be worthwhile here to place Bassnett's argument in relation to the debate about European 'identity' sparked off by Jürgen Habermas's call for the development and projection of a European presence capable of counter-balancing 'the hegemonic unilateralism of the United States' (2005: 6). Writing in May 2003, in the shadow of the US-sponsored invasion of Iraq, Habermas asked whether there were 'historical experiences, traditions, and achievements offering European citizens the consciousness of a shared political fate *that can be shaped together*' (7). He answered in the affirmative, but only after rejecting firmly the civilisational idea of Europe evoked by thinkers like Bassnett. For Habermas, that idea would be merely the corollary of the particularist chauvinism sponsoring the 'bellicose past' that 'once entangled all European nations in bloody conflicts' (12). He proposed instead an idea of 'Europe' predicated precisely on a break from this past through the reflexive creation of 'new, supranational forms of cooperation' (12). A similar argument is proffered by the Swiss writer Adolf Muschg, who writes, in dialogue with Habermas, that

> What holds Europe together and what divides it are at heart the same thing: common memories and habits, acquired step by step through the process of distancing oneself from fatal habits. Europe is what Europe is becoming. It is neither the Occident nor the cradle of civilization; it does not have a monopoly on science, enlightenment, and modernity. It shouldn't attempt to ground its identity in any other way than through its own experiences: any claims for exclusivity can only lead into the same delusion and pretension through which Europe of the nineteenth century believed itself to represent the rest of the world, and entitled to dominate it. (2005: 25)

The idea here is of Europe as a counter-hegemonic work in progress – a strictly contemporary project negatively motivated by recognition that the effects of all of the previous projections of 'Europe' – which took themselves to be gestures of civilisational self-assertion – have been catastrophic.[59] Yet even this carefully historicised and radically contingent construction[60] is

---

59 See also Bauman 2004 and Todorov 2005.
60 Or one could describe it as deconstructive. Habermas's manifesto actually appeared under the joint signatures of himself and Jacques Derrida. Derrida was too ill at the time to contribute directly, and managed to append only a short preface. But he indicated that he wished to have Habermas's piece appear under his own name also. The manifesto – 'both an analysis and an appeal' (Habermas 2005: 3) – duly appeared simultaneously in the *Frankfurter Allgemeine Zeitung* and *Libération*. See Levy, Pensky and Torpey 2005: xi–xxix.

susceptible to criticism on the grounds that it generalises unwarrantedly from the modern experience of the historically dominant European nations to all of Europe. A latent essentialism lurks in the background of Habermas's refunctioning of the category of 'core Europe' ('*Kerneuropa*') and his suggestion that this 'avant-gardist core of Europe' must play the role of 'locomotive', powering the generation of a new, pan-European consciousness and politics (2005: 5–6). While we certainly appreciate the necessity of defending France and Germany – whose governments opposed the rush to war against Iraq – from the wrath of the Bush administration, the assumption that avant-gardism or progressive values are to be found in 'core' or 'old' Europe[61] seems to us both impolitic and high-handed.[62] Hence, presumably, the anger directed at Habermas's manifesto by certain commentators – not only in 'east' and 'central' Europe, but also in Scandinavia and the Iberian peninsula – unwilling to accept his apparent marginalisation of them as 'non-core' Europeans.[63]

61 Habermas was responding to the then-US Secretary of Defense, Donald Rumsfeld, who had infamously castigated France and Germany as 'old Europe', praising instead the 'new Europe' of Poland, Hungary and the Czech Republic, among others, whose leaders supported – or at least refrained from publicly disavowing – the American-led offensive.

62 See also the discussion of the Habermas/Derrida intervention in Rita Felski's introduction to a special issue of *New Literary History* devoted to 'rethinking Europe' (Felski 2012).

63 See for example the dissenting pieces by Esterházy, Stasiuk, Krzeminski and Keel in Levy, Pensky and Torpey 2005. Esterházy begins his piece with the witty observation that 'Once, I was an Eastern European; then I was promoted to the rank of Central European. Those were great times (even if not necessarily for me personally), there were Central European dreams, visions, and images of the future; in short, everything (everything one needs for a round table, but that is spoken in haste and unfairly). Then a few months ago, I became a New European. But before I had the chance to get used to this status – even before I could have refused it – I have now become a non-core European' (2005: 74). Stasiuk, too, protests that Habermas's idea of 'core Europe' is not only truncating but falsifying, beginning his article with a cascading list of peoples evidently relegated by Habermas to the status of non-core Europeans: 'Albanians, Bosnians, Bulgarians, Estonians, Croatians, Lithuanians, Macedonians, Moldavians, Montenegrins, Poles, Romanians, Serbs, Slovaks, Slovenians, Czechs, Ukrainians, White Russians'. And he adds: 'And just so it doesn't appear too simple, let's add the "belt of mixed population" – as Hannah Arendt calls the diverse, amorphous areas somewhere between Germany and Russia – that is, small heaps of Germans and Russians scattered here and there. To this, we can add, for example, the Gagausians and Aromunians, the restless international Sinti, the Crimeans and the Turks who didn't get back to their native lands on the Bosporus before it unexpectedly shrank' (2005: 103). For his part, Keel, self-consciously writing from 'the Scandinavian perspective', takes the opportunity to remind Habermas that if Danes in the modern era have participated in the 'bellicose past' that Habermas sees as having 'entangled all European nations in bloody conflicts', 'it has not been exclusively as instigators but also as subjects struggling against German domination: 'Around the year 1700', he writes, 'some 20 per cent of Copenhagen's

Rey Chow's article 'The Old/New Question of Comparison in Literary Studies: A Post-European Perspective' appeared two years before Bassnett's, and so does not, of course, address the latter directly. But Chow writes self-consciously from what Bassnett calls the 'perspective of the Southern hemisphere': indeed, she might be seen as offering a 'Third-Worldist' critique of precisely the model of comparative literary scholarship that Bassnett both champions and seeks to represent. Chow begins, thus, by identifying the performative contradiction represented by comparative literature's 'cosmopolitanism' or 'universalism' whenever the focus is shifted from the European to the world stage. On the one hand, the commitment to comparativism in the discipline gestures towards inter-cultural reciprocity:

> As part of a cluster of concepts that sees linguistic cosmopolitanism and the peaceful coexistence of national and cultural traditions as its telos, comparison in comparative literature is understandably grounded, as the etymology of the word suggests, in the notion of parity – in the possibility of peer-like equality and mutuality among those being compared [...] Hence [...] comparative literature often proceeds with investigating multiple literary traditions on the assumption that there ought to be a degree of commonality and equivalence – and thus comparability – among them; that they are, somehow, on a par with one another despite their obvious differences. (2004: 290)

On the other hand, this 'mutuality' proves to be highly selective. It operates only between (some) 'European' literatures and cultures, never between 'Europe and its Others'. Chow quotes as exemplary in this respect Wellek and Warren's formulation, in their *Theory of Literature* (1949), of the basic predicate of comparative literature as a discipline:

> it is important to think of literature as a totality and to trace the growth and development of literature without regard to linguistic distinctions [...] Western literature, at least, forms a unity, a whole [...] and, without minimizing the importance of Oriental influences, especially that of the Bible, one must recognize a close unity which includes all Europe, Russia, the United States, and the Latin American literatures. (Quoted in Chow 2004: 294)

One might have expected Chow to criticise the essentialism evident in Wellek and Warren's statement – their insistence on the singularity and specificity of what they call 'western' culture. But she does not. Nor does she comment on the fact that their formulation is altogether blind to the radically

---

population was German-speaking, and Herder still regarded Copenhagen as "the Danish end of Germany". Up until the end of the eighteenth century, German was the native tongue of the Danish royal family. It was only in 1773 that Danish became the official language of the army' (2005: 81–82).

discrepant and incongruent histories of the ideas of 'Europe' and 'the west'. She focuses instead on Wellek and Warren's bracketing of the 'non-West' and the implications that derive – in her view, inevitably – from it:

> Wellek and Warren's formulation of comparison, which may be named 'Europe and Its Others,' remains a common norm of comparative literary studies in North America today. In this formulation, the rationale for comparing hinges on the conjunction *and*; the *and*, moreover [...] signals a form of supplementation that authorizes the first term, Europe, as the grid of reference, to which may be added others in a subsequent and subordinate fashion [...] The *and* thus instigates not only comparison but also a politics of comparison: on the one side, the infinite opening of histories, cultures, languages in their internal vicissitudes in such a manner as to enable their studies to become ever more nuanced and refined; on the other side, a crude lumping together of other histories, cultures, and languages with scant regard to exactly the same kinds of details and internal dynamics of thought that, theoretically speaking, should be part of the study of any tradition. These other histories, cultures, and languages remain by default undifferentiated – and thus never genuinely on a par with Europe – within an ostensibly comparative framework. (Chow 2004: 294–95)

Proposing that Eurocentrism is, as it were, 'hard-wired' into the disciplinary machinery of comparative literature, Chow calls not for a revision of the discipline, but for the generation of an entirely new notion of comparativism, implicating a new form of critical practice: 'The incommensurability between what scholars might want to uphold as the ethical as well as theoretical ideal of an inclusive world literature, on the one hand, and the actual events that take place in the name of comparison, on the other, requires us to conceive of a radically different set of terms for comparative literary studies' (297).

There is much in this proposal – and in Chow's general critique – that we find attractive and congenial. We echo her call for a new form of comparative critical practice. The problem, however, is that she mis-identifies both the nature and the historical dynamic of the dominant social instance that she wishes to counter and oppose. Linking her project explicitly to Dipesh Chakrabarty's influential campaign to 'provincialise Europe' – an agenda as thoroughly 'Third-Worldist' as her own, and for pretty much the same reasons – Chow promotes a 'post-European perspective' in literary studies. However, the persistent slippage in her commentary between geo-historical and ideological categories – 'European' on the one hand, 'Eurocentric' on the other – fatally undermines her argument, transforming a potentially compelling ideological critique into an ineffectual complaint about 'European' civilisation, which, she supposes, has always, or at least throughout modern history, presented itself as 'culturally superior'.

Thus 'the dominance of *European* conceptual models' (emphasis added) – not 'Eurocentric models' – is deplored, and 'Europe' is incoherently identified not merely as the 'source' but as the very *form* of domination on the world stage.

This way of putting things has the effect of homogenising 'Europe', mystifying its 'internal' history and flattening out the unevenness of its 'internal' development. (It's a bit rich for Chow to complain that her antagonists are guilty of 'a crude lumping together of [...] histories, cultures, and languages with scant regard to exactly the [...] kinds of details and internal dynamics of thought that, theoretically speaking, should be part of the study of any tradition' [77], when this exactly describes her own commentary on 'Europe'.) In this respect, what Paulo de Medeiros has written in general of contemporary attempts to unthink Eurocentrism pertains directly to Chow:

> Within the general attack on Eurocentrism [...] there are two related flaws: first, the amalgamation of everything European into a fictive unity that, even if it might have some correspondence to the dream of homogeneity, has no real counterpart in a fragmented and divided Europe, more often than not torn against itself and amongst its constituent members; second the forgetting exactly of those parts of Europe that 'Europe' itself tends to forget, its own, anything but central, dominated others. (1996: 43)

Chow's 'Third-Worldism' also leads to a dehistoricisation and dematerialisation of the dynamics of 'modernity'. Her suggestions that 'comparison' in literary scholarship ought to include 'a critique of the uneven distribution of cultural capital among languages themselves' (2004: 303) and that such scholarship ought to take as its object 'a type of discursive situation, involuntarily brought into play by and inextricable from the conditions of modern world politics' (301), for instance, sound very promising, until we realise that, on her understanding, *capitalism* evidently plays no part in 'modern world politics'. Instead, the latter are evidently to be thought of as being about the encounter between civilisational blocs: 'Europe' (including the United States, of course) and its various 'others'. Even when 'imperialism' is named, the term is inevitably prefixed by the qualifier 'European', thus making it clear that what is centrally at issue for Chow is the imposition of 'European' culture upon other cultures.

Fredric Jameson has urged us to take on board the implications of the fact that 'the United States is not just one country, or one culture, among others, any more than English is just one language among others. There is a fundamental dissymmetry in the relationship between the United States and every other country in the world, not only third-world countries, but even Japan and those of Western Europe' (1998: 58). Chow is deaf to this suggestion. She proceeds as though it were possible to achieve the 'provincialisation' of 'Europe' in the absence of any plausible account or understanding of what has grounded and enabled 'European' dominance over the course of the past five hundred years. The fact that this idealist understanding is counter-posed to the dominant understanding, equally idealist, does not in our view make it more compelling. We would argue that the idea of a new comparativism in literary studies only makes sense in the context of an overarching theory of the (capitalist) world-system.

We can pursue the critique we are making further by turning our attention for a moment to the belated 'worlding' of American literature. Where US writing is concerned, the liabilities of nationalist exceptionalism are widely recognised today. But if the contemporary desire, as Lawrence Buell reminds us, is to think '"against" or "beyond" nationness', critical practice has tended to lag behind this desire; for many of the '[d]iscourses that aspire self-consciously to transnational or global reach [...] end up recontained by nation-centered mentalities' (Buell 2007: 227–28). The converse is also true: the search for larger frameworks often leads to a decisive underestimation of the roles played by nation-states in the trajectory of the world-system. Even when it is accompanied by protestations of sympathy for the wretched of the earth, this sort of underestimation characteristically bespeaks unquestioned privilege. That is to say, it is only those citizens inhabiting the privileged spaces of dominant nation-states in the contemporary world system who tend to speak confidently of their ability and desire to transcend nations. While the desire to escape from what Buell, drawing on Casanova,[64] calls the 'Herderian imperative' to situate nation-ness as the generative matrix of all aesthetic production is readily understandable, a premature dismissal of the material effectivity of the nation paves the way, in some contemporary criticism, for the adoption of an even less plausible analytical framework: a militantly idealist transcendentalism that glories in literature for its civilisational (that is to say, community-building) capabilities, across, athwart and, indeed, in defiance of the boundaries (historical as well as geographical) of any actually existing social order. Often encountered in such contemporary slogans as 'planetarity' and 'epochal time', this new form of transcendentalism avows to release literary and cultural studies from concerns about not simply nation-statism, but capitalist modernity also.

The tendency is notably exemplified in Wai Chee Dimock's *Through Other Continents: American Literature Across Deep Time* (2006). Dimock seeks to emancipate US writing and culture from nationalist exceptionalism by recourse to more expansive geographic and temporal registers. Concepts borrowed from the disciplines of astronomy and geology are metaphorised and pressed into service to provide the justification for a literary critical practice involving epochal loops of time and the tectonic collision of textual elements, such that (very) distant times and places are conjoined and juxtaposed. 'Literature is the home of nonstandard space and time', Dimock writes: 'Against the official borders of the nation and against the fixed intervals of the clock, what flourishes here is irregular duration and extension, some extending for thousands of years or thousands of miles, each occasioned by a different tie and varying with that tie, and each loosening up the chronology and geography of the nation' (2006: 4). Dimock's move from history and geography to the discourse of 'deep time' testifies to a pronounced animus towards the

---

64 See the discussion of 'the Herderian Revolution' and 'the Herderian effect' in Casanova 2004: 75–81.

social sciences. Her substitution of a geological for a geographical cartography and her conjuring of maximally suprahuman time-frames function alike to render literature – the final object of her enquiry – irrecuperable to historicist methodologies of any stripe. Literature, on her reading, is not amenable to analysis through reference to temporally or spatially bounded power relations. It eludes explication through these means. She cites the 'large-scale model' that is Wallerstein's world-system, but only to propose, '[w]ithout disagreeing with him' (!), that 'there are other phenomena, not reducible to capitalism, that also unfold against long durations, requiring scale enlargement for their analysis' (5). These 'other phenomena' include 'world religions' – which 'invite us to think of the world's population as a locally inflected and yet globally connected unit'; the 'morphology of language' – which 'presents us with an array of vernaculars, creolized forms developed through centuries and spread across continents'; certain 'categories of experience, such as beauty or death, that seem not entirely predicated on the temporal and spatial boundaries of the nation-state'; 'long-lasting genres, such as epic and novel', likewise demanding expanded frames of reference; and 'the concept of a global civil society', whose purview is for Dimock both global (requiring us to think at the level of planetarity) and pan-historical, reaching back centuries (5).

It is difficult to know what to make of this inventory. So far as we know, nobody has ever proposed either that the categories of beauty or death are 'entirely predicated on the temporal and spatial boundaries of the nation-state', or that the development and dispersion of 'world' religions are 'reducible to capitalism'. But Dimock seems to want to infer from the statement that the development and dispersion of 'world' religions are not *reducible to capitalism* (whatever that might possibly mean) that capitalism has not been a powerful *determinant* of this development and dispersion. This inference is unwarranted. By the same token, to recognise that the categories of beauty or death are not 'entirely predicated on the temporal and spatial boundaries of the nation-state' is not to demonstrate that these categories ought to be analysed without reference to the nation-state (and/or, indeed, to other historical forms of bounded sociality). Dimock seems determined to delegitimate any investigation into the ways in which capitalist modernity has distinctively restructured linguistic, phenomenological, socio-cultural and demographic patterns. *Through Other Continents* conflates the individual, the particularistic and the local with the species, the universal and the geo-galactic so as to elide the registers of the national *and* of the international, and all mediating registers of time-space – whether economic or cultural – that might open onto a conversation about transformation or social change. The catechistic fusion in her study of the human (or of the literary work as aestheticised 'more-than-human') and the ineffable (time-space beyond human comprehension) works to silence questions directed to conflict, domination, exploitation and temporal rupture or discontinuity.

Dimock sets out to disarticulate American nation-statism – 'the temporal and spatial boundaries of the nation' – from 'other expressive domains', most particularly the literary. The problem, as she puts it, is that when we use the term 'American' to describe literary work, 'we limit ourselves, with or without explicit acknowledgement, to an analytic domain foreclosed by definition, a kind of scholarly unilateralism. Literature here is the product of one nation and one nation alone, analyzable within its confines' (2006: 3). But her would-be revisionary initiative – to 'bind [...] America to the rest of the world', to 'thread America texts into the topical events of other cultures, while also threading the long durations of those cultures into the short chronology of the United States', to 'bind [...] continents and millennia into many loops of relations' (3) – has three main weaknesses. Ironically, each of these, in its own way, bears witness to the persistence in Dimock's thought of the elitist (and exceptionalist) Americanism that, at the level of political self-consciousness, she rightly seeks to problematise and move beyond.

Dimock's initial problem is that her nomination of literature as an instance of 'global civil society' remains blind to the materiality of literature as a social institution. She wants us to think of reading – and of literary culture more generally – as communicative action, whose effect is to thread together the 'single reader, doing his reading in one particular locale' (9) and the planetary and trans-historical – that is to say, the *individual* on the one hand, and *all times* and *all places*, on the other. Thus she refers us to Robert Pogue Harrison's proposition 'that we think of literary culture [...] as a "lexical" civil society, made up of strings of words, nuances, and etymologies reflecting the long histories of linguistic usage, and weaving our lives into a semantic network, at once endlessly localized and endlessly extended' (8). The problem here, of course, is that this virtuality is construed as an actuality, as a substantive effect of literary culture as an actually existing domain of action. Seeking to construe the literary field in analogy with Michael Walzer's formulation of global civil society, Dimock asks us to entertain the idea of a

> playing field called 'literary culture' brought into being by that most minute, most intimate of acts, the act of reading. This act, pursued within the compass of a word, a phrase, a sentence, generates relational ties that can nonetheless extend for thousands of miles and thousands of years. It is an NGO of sorts, an NGO *avant la lettre*, an unusually fine-grained as well as long-lasting one, operating on a scale both too small and too large to be policed by the nation-state. (8)

That we are cued to think of this 'playing field' as 'level' directs us immediately to the idealism underlying Dimock's thought experiment. She imagines literary culture to constitute a 'low-skill, low-stakes, low-level playing field, where people of no particular consequence can become momentarily consequential, can have some say, can take it upon themselves to step forward and "propose, debate, and decide"' (8). The image put before us is explicitly of literary culture in analogy with a non-governmental organisation such as Amnesty International. Yet the effect of Dimock's historically particular mobilisation of the NGO as a model here is to reinscribe an 'aid mechanism' according to which metropolitan elites administer resource allocations to and for peripheralised regions outside of these localities' own state apparatuses and electoral procedures – a mechanism that has been rightly and extensively criticised by participants, activists and scholars of 'aid and development'. Literature on this reading becomes a self-credentialising mechanism that structures the development of underdevelopment as classically theorised by Samir Amin and Andre Gunder Frank. Prioritising the literate over the non- or weakly literate hinterlands, and the individual over the communal or the collective, Dimock imagines literary culture as a settled field, as trans-historical as the various geological formations and as aloof from dissension, competition and dispute. While we might harbour some reservations about Casanova's notion of a world republic of letters, for reasons that we have already discussed, her theory might be evoked here as a powerful and plausible counterstatement to Dimock: for Casanova rightly insists that unequal power relations are constitutive of the literary field and structure it in all of its aspects and dimensions. Hence her rousing proclamations, early in *The World Republic of Letters*, that literature comprises 'a world of rivalry, struggle and inequality' (2004: 4), and that '[i]ts history is one of incessant struggle and competition over the very nature of literature itself – an endless succession of literary manifestos, movements, assaults, and revolutions. These rivalries are what have created world literature' (12).

The second problem for Dimock is that her fusion of esoteric deep time and place marks a return to an old variant of cultural anthropology. 'To accept the earth as an astronomical object', she writes, in a commentary on Gary Snyder, 'is to embrace a religion affirming the primacy and equality of matter, a primacy and equality that cross the boundaries between species, even as they cross the boundaries between the animate and the inanimate' (2006: 174). Along with its surface preference for the 'new materialism' studies over historical materialism, this stance suggests a benign version of the romantic conceit that, before the arrival of Europeans, aboriginal peoples lived in musicalised content, in harmony with the natural world, free from fear of the unknown or the need to block greed through taboo. Those who espouse 'humanness' in these terms and propose that the 'archaic past redefines species membership itself' are disinclined to attend to the trans-historicality of secular cycles of war, environmental mismanagement and epidemics, or to register the record of the vast translocations of populations resulting from their desperate search for survival in the face of scarcity or locally engendered ecological disruption, or their flight to escape capture and domination as bound, coerced labour by neighbouring factions, groups or peoples. Dimock calls for a 'science-inspired humanities' and, counter-posing 'science' and 'social science' as paradigmatically at odds with one another, suggests that '[n]on-Western cultures would especially benefit from [the] elongated field' corresponding to the 'scientific' problematic: 'not just Buddhism, but all ancient cultures with a time frame asymmetrical to the shape of European history, and crucial to the fate of the earth if modernity is to be saved from being a runaway locomotive'

(175). In dissenting from Dimock's programme, we might refer here to Adam Curtis's telling argument that the ideology of the ('resilient') self-harmonising ecosystem developed alongside the neoliberal ideology of deregulation of public resources and the rise of an extreme version of *laissez-faire* economics. However unwittingly, Dimock's New Age-influenced eco-spirituality mirrors neoliberal attacks on statal forms of regional self-determination in the 'Third World'. When literary culture is presented as a vegetational concept (under the rubric of astrologic and geologic paradigms), the now extra-human speech act, freed from time and space, primordial and external to consciousness, is deprived of the means to function as an agent of political engagement.

A third weakness in *Through Other Continents* is revealed in the way that Dimock frames her initial example, Thoreau's *Walden*. Her suggestion is that, in and through its referencing of the *Bhagavad Gita*, Thoreau's text — conceived in Concord, Massachusetts — finds itself 'irrigated' by that 'ancient text from Asia'. 'Swept by that text and its torrents of time, *Walden* in turn flows outward, circumnavigating the globe, gliding past Europe and Africa on its way back to India' (2006: 9). Two problems arise simultaneously here. The first is that Dimock's identification of a subterranean affinity between a contemporary American text and an ancient Asian one squares all too comfortably with a philosophy of history that sees the modern west in precisely civilisational terms as the trustee of the world's cultural heritage: the 'concord' between *Walden* and the *Bhagavad Gita* stands conspicuously in place of conversation between Thoreau and any South Asian intellectuals of his own time. One way of making this point might be to observe that *Walden* was published in 1854, twenty years after the publication of 'Macaulay's Minute' and three years prior to the onset of the 'Indian Mutiny' in 1857; another would be to note that respect, even reverence, towards such 'treasures' as Petra, the pyramids, Chichen Itza or Angkor Wat was a marked feature of colonial discourse throughout the nineteenth century and the first half of the twentieth. Eager to promote her argument that literary culture contributes to humanisation, Dimock forgets that supremacist, racist and imperialist ideologies have often gone hand in hand with fervid and learned commitment to the glories of the ancient past.[65] The appropriate

---

65 Dimock begins *In Other Continents* with an account of the ransacking of the Iraqi National Library and the Islamic library in the Religious Ministry in Baghdad by American Marines in April 2003. 'Operating under a military timetable, and under the short chronology of a young nation', she writes, the Marines 'were largely indifferent to the history of the world' (2006: 1). The implication that the action of the Marines was in some sense attributable to their status as representatives of a 'young nation' with a 'short chronology' is immediately belied by Dimock's own reference to a prior sacking of Baghdad and despoliation of its archives at the hands of a Mongol expeditionary force in 1258. Meanwhile, the fact that they were operating under the long chronology of an ancient nation scarcely caused those who ordered the destruction of the Babri Masjid in 1992 or the Buddhas of Bamiyan in 2001 to scruple.

counter-statement to Dimock is provided by Susan Buck-Morss, who writes, in a forum addressed to her book *Hegel, Haiti, and Universal History* (2009), that '[w]ithin the existing model, universal history is cosmopolitanism for the privileged. The past is considered universalized when UNESCO incorporates it into the project of World Heritage, declaring historical sites as cultural treasures – "masterpieces of creative genius" – that remain the property of the state on whose territory they are located, and whose past greatness they display' (2010: 184).

A second problem here is that Dimock's postulation of a virtual universe in which ancient and contemporary texts roam freely in mutual recognition operates as a kind of secularised creationism, a humans-walking-with-dinosaurs imaginary. The metonymic drift from one text to another, one moment of communion to another, one world to another (through these communicating texts) very obviously flattens out historical specificities, gradations and differences. So what is ignored here is precisely the question of the specificity of the mode of this communication and exchange – *how do they meet and through whom do they talk?*[66] In many ways – especially in its mistaking of evidentiary material as interpretive method – Dimock's project resuscitates Cold War models of the field. The centrality of the New England Transcendentalists (Emerson, Thoreau, Fuller) and their regional followers (Lowell, Henry James) to *Through Other Continents* would hardly disturb a Cold War Americanist. By combining these elite nineteenth-century regional writers with New Age ecosystemic claims, Dimock has forged a means of reconsecrating a canon whose self-evident centrality has otherwise long been under attack. It is striking, moreover, how the questions raised by the particular conjunctions of ancient and modern in her examples, themselves expressions of combined and uneven development, go unasked. Her account is unsurprisingly silent concerning the specific forms and means of importing classical Vedic texts to antebellum New England, and the role they might play in its cultural economy; nor does she explore how the uses to which they were put differ across national and regional boundaries. Rather than analyse how particular transportation and communication networks developed in mid-nineteenth-century America in relation to those elsewhere, Dimock implies that non-American texts are primarily interesting inasmuch as they provide 'ec-centric' cultural prestige to core texts that continue to feature prominently on undergraduate syllabi. In this way, landmarks of world culture are made to give themselves up for symbolic exploitation, to the extent that

---

66 As Mark McGurl has noted, 'Faced with arguments that leap from Margaret Fuller to ancient Egypt, and from Gilgamesh to Henry James, a contemporary media theorist might be compelled to note how tenuously materialized Dimock's connections across deep time appear to be. What about the media of transmission from Hafez to Emerson and from Emerson to us? What about the long chain of objects, institutions, and techniques that may have had their own agendas in that meeting of minds? What story does this hardware tell?' (2012: 535).

their antiquity is used to illumine and revivify, however fleetingly, the glory of the familiar canon.

As this selective overview of recent efforts to renew the project of comparativism indicates, the challenge of 'world literature' excites expectation and arouses anxiety in equal measure; and this anxiety frequently manifests itself at the level of methodology as a swerve towards civilisational categories in place of historical and materialist ones. The question remains: if 'the way we imagine comparative literature is a mirror of how we see the world', what 'world' does world-literature demand be made visible? What methodology might substitute for the persistent forms of misrecognition that characterise extant comparative approaches? If literature as a form of knowing is to retain its specificity, what knowledge can it convey of the irreducibly conflictual terrain of interrelations that is the modern world-system?

CHAPTER TWO

The Question of Peripheral Realism

I

A single but radically uneven world-system; a singular modernity, combined and uneven; and a literature that variously registers this combined unevenness in both its form and its content to reveal itself as, properly speaking, world-literature – these propositions sum up the kernel of our argument. 'World-literature', as we understand it, is an analytical category, not one centred in aesthetic judgement.[1] We find unconvincing those writings that seek to position the 'world' in 'world literature' in value terms, as signifying 'world-class' – as though 'world literature' were to be thought in analogy to

---

1 See Fredric Jameson, who distinguishes between 'taste', 'analysis' and 'evaluation'. The former, he writes, 'correspond[s] to what used to be nobly and philosophically designated as "aesthetic judgment"'. 'Analysis' is then construed, by contrast, as 'that peculiar and rigorous conjuncture of formal and historical analysis that constitutes the specific task of literary and cultural study: to describe this further as the investigation of the historical conditions of possibility of specific forms may perhaps convey the way in which these twin perspectives (often thought to be irreconcilable or incommensurable in the past) can be said to constitute their object and thereby to be inseparable'. And Jameson then goes on to distinguish 'evaluation', in turn, from both 'taste' and 'analysis': 'Analysis in this sense can be seen to be a very different set of operations from a cultural journalism oriented around taste and opinion; what it would now be important to secure is the difference between such journalism – with its indispensable reviewing functions – and what I will call "evaluation," which no longer turns on whether a work is "good" (after the fashion of an older aesthetic judgment), but rather tries to keep alive (or to reinvent) assessments of a socio-political kind that interrogate the quality of social life itself by way of the text or individual work of art, or hazard an assessment of the political effects of cultural currents or movements with less utilitarianism and a greater sympathy for the dynamics of everyday life than the imprimaturs and indexes of earlier traditions' (1995: 298).

those imaginary teams that sport enthusiasts love to argue about, in which the best players from everywhere and from all time are 'selected' to play together in some fantasy match or tournament: the *Iliad*, the *Upanishads*, *Gilgamesh*, the *Divine Comedy*, *King Lear*, *Dream of the Red Chamber*, *Faust*, *Anna Karenina*, *One Hundred Years of Solitude* and *Things Fall Apart*, for example. It is equally nugatory to think of 'world literature' as a kind of summit conference of great writers: exercises of this nature, as Bourdieu has pointed out, are both derealising (of time and place) and intellectualist.[2] When we argue that it makes good sense to read, say, *Wieland*, *Max Havelaar*, *Noli Me Tangere*, *Rickshaw* and *The Lost Steps* together, we are not proposing any abstract connectivity linking them across time and space: our suggestion, rather, is that these texts should be considered together because they all bear testimony – in their own distinct ways, and in both their form and their content – to the 'shock of the new', the massive rupture effected at the levels of space-time continuum, lifeworld, experience and human sensorium by capitalist modernisation.

'World-literature' as we understand it is therefore a creature of modernity. Our definition differs obviously from that of Damrosch, who takes the category 'to encompass all literary works that circulate beyond their culture of origin, either in translation or in their original language' (2003: 4). Damrosch's formulation is self-consciously indifferent to historicity. Virgil's work circulates beyond its culture of origin; but so too do Petrarch's, Proust's and Murakami's. All four authors are therefore exemplars of 'world literature' for Damrosch. For us, by contrast, the 'world' identified in 'world-literature' is that of the modern world-system. It is of course true that work produced in earlier times continues to circulate and to exercise profound influence in modernity – but neither its dispersal nor its durability suffices to render it 'world-literature' as we understand this term.[3]

We prefer to speak then not of literary forms spreading or unfolding across empty time (and hence of literary history as being divided into sequential 'periods' – classicism, realism, modernism, postmodernism, etc.), but of forms

---

2 See Bourdieu: 'Ignorance of everything which goes to make up the "mood of the age" produces a derealization of works: stripped of everything which attached them to the most concrete debates of their time (I am thinking in particular of the connotations of words), they are impoverished and transformed in the direction of intellectualism or an empty humanism. This is particularly true in the history of ideas, and especially of philosophy. Here the ordinary effects of derealization and intellectualization are intensified by the representation of philosophical activity as a summit conference between "great philosophers"; in fact, what circulates between contemporary philosophers, or those of different epochs, are not only canonical texts, but a whole philosophical doxa carried along by intellectual rumour – labels of schools, truncated quotations, functioning as slogans in celebration or polemics – by academic routine and perhaps above all by school manuals (an unmentionable reference), which perhaps do more than anything else to constitute the "common sense" of an intellectual generation' (1993: 32).
3 See in this connection the arguments made by Beecroft 2008 and Hayot 2012.

that are brought into being (and often into collision with other, pre-existing forms) through the long waves of the capitalisation of the world – not of *modernism* (or even *modernisms*) but of the *dialectics of core and periphery* that underpin all cultural production in the modern era. In the chapters that follow, we present some case studies in order to exemplify and test our method: we look at Tayeb Salih's *Season of Migration to the North* (Sudan, 1969), Victor Pelevin's *The Sacred Book of the Werewolf* (Russia, 2005), Peter Pist'anek's *Rivers of Babylon* (Slovakia, 1991), Pio Baroja's *The Quest* (Spain, 1922), Halldor Laxness's *The Atom Station* (Iceland, 1948), James Kelman's *The Busconductor Hines* (Scotland, 1984) and Ivan Vladislavic's *Portrait with Keys* (South Africa, 2006), among others. Our selection of texts is not meant to suggest the chronological or geographical limits of what we take world-literature to be. We have already identified as the time-frame of the world-literary system the entire span of the two-hundred-plus years from the early nineteenth century or even the late eighteenth. While the texts we examine in this book are all products of the twentieth century, our argument could have been advanced with equal plausibility, we believe, through reference to works by such authors as, say, Whitman, Heine, Gaskell, Multatuli, Schreiner or Machado de Assis. Nor does the fact that the works we have chosen to comment on derive mostly from (semi-)peripheral Europe and Africa – and, in this chapter, from Latin America and the Caribbean – indicate that these regions are somehow exceptional in their characteristics. It is worth re-emphasising, perhaps, that the modern world-system is, uniquely, a *world* system, and that combined and uneven development is a defining feature of this system as such. Our aim is less to illustrate the geo-historical reach of our methodological framework than to test out its plausibility and explanatory potential. We are concerned to show *how* the idea of combined and uneven development works in the literary realm, and to consider whether it bears out our thesis on world-literature. We think that if what we propose can be shown to work in and through our chosen sample of works, it will hold relevance also for other works and cultural forms in which the modern world-system looms as a conceptual horizon. Indeed, this is precisely what we hope to show in our subsequent (collective and individual) projects.

For now we want to show that the texts we have selected for examination – produced at different times and places across the span of the century – share not only common themes, plots and subjects, but also a range of formal features that we propose to call 'irrealist'. Of course, anti-linear plot lines, meta-narratorial devices, un-rounded characters, unreliable narrators, contradictory points of view, and so on, have all been identified as the techniques and devices characteristic of the distinctive (and restricted) Euro-American literary formation typically addressed under the name of 'modernism'. But we understand these techniques and devices more broadly as the determinate formal registers of (semi-) peripherality in the world-literary system, discernible wherever literary works are composed that mediate the lived experience of capitalism's bewildering creative destruction (or destructive creation).

Additionally, these formal features appear in the literary texts we examine as a result of their authors' self-conscious conversation with, and deployment of, relevant formal properties of adjacent forms (often non-literary) within their local or regional cultural ecology. Thus Salih's novel, for example, quite explicitly juxtaposes the techniques of the traditional Arabic oral story-telling mode of *hakawati* with that of consecrated literary modernism, in order to signal registration of a (semi-)peripheral social space (and correspondent consciousness).

We should also note in passing that the texts that we have selected can evidently only make reference to the 'world' by articulating the problem of modern imperialism. Theoretical debates currently underway in the fields of history and sociology, among others, concerning the strict conjunction or co-relation between the capitalist world-system and modern imperialism and colonialism do not directly concern us here, although they certainly inform our thinking. But (semi-)peripheral texts' meditations on the world are necessarily performed in the harsh glare of past and present imperial and colonial dispensations, whatever the specific national, trans-national or regional provenance of these dispensations might be: British, French, Spanish, Ottoman, Soviet/Russian, American, and so on.

Building on Nicholas Brown's argument in *Utopian Generations*, Michael Niblett has argued that while the 'interpretive horizon' of capitalism might 'constitute some distant and dimly perceived limit for literatures from the core, marking a totality that, where it is not repressed, may be posited as unrepresentable or mystified as a static Absolute, for peripheral literatures the situation is somewhat different. On the other side of the international division of labour this horizon is more immediate and pressing, its historical character more apparent' (Niblett 2012b: 20). Jameson also has suggested that the representation of class-based social relations often appears more vividly in the margins and peripheries of the world-systems: 'Not only must history (the history of the classes) be surprised in the least likely places', he writes, but

> we must also have the instruments of registration ready to seize it; and those may not be old-fashioned stories of individuals at all, but we also may not have the right ones. This is the sense in which I would like to maintain and strengthen the word margins: not as the 'useless eaters' who have been rejected by society, or as the spatial deserts in which no production is to be done or money made – but rather as these 'weak links in the chain,' where the Real may appear without warning, and disappear again if we are not alert to catch it. (2012: 480)

In a similar vein, Franco Moretti distinguishes in *Modern Epic* between texts produced in the core formations of England and France from the late eighteenth century onwards and those produced in (semi-)peripheral regions (including in semi-peripheral Europe: his immediate example is Goethe's Germany). Citing Ernst Bloch on the 'nonsynchronism' of Germany – 'Germany in general, which did not accomplish a bourgeois revolution until 1918, is, unlike England and much less France, the classical land of nonsynchronism, that is, of unsurmounted remnants of older economic being and consciousness' (Bloch 1991, cited in Moretti 1996: 49–50) – Moretti suggests that we think not only of linked but starkly contrasted economic formations – core and (semi-) periphery – but also of the linked but starkly contrasted aesthetic modes that correspond to these formations:

> England and France on the one hand, Germany on the other. Non-synchronism, Bloch here suggests, is connected with a specific position within the world-system: unknown to the relatively homogeneous states of the core, it is typical of the semi-periphery where, by contrast, combined development prevails. And it is precisely there that we find many of the masterpieces of the modern epic form: in the still divided Germany of Goethe (and of the early Wagner); in Melville's America (the *Pequod*: bloodthirsty hunting, and industrial production); in Joyce's Ireland (a colony, which nevertheless speaks the same language as the occupier); in certain zones of Latin America. All [...] sites of combined development, where historically non-homogeneous social and symbolic forms, often originating in quite disparate places, coexist in a confined space. In this sense, *Faust* is not 'German', just as *Ulysses* is not 'Irish' or *One Hundred Years of Solitude* 'Colombian': they are all world texts, whose geographical frame of reference is no longer the nation-state, but a broader entity – a continent, or the world-system as a whole. (1996: 50)

Moretti is looking for 'a possible geography of literary forms': 'while world texts are concentrated in the semi-periphery, the novel by contrast flourishes in the highly homogeneous cultures of France and England, at the core of the world system' (50). Two points can be made here. The first is to recognise that Moretti's interest in reading literary form under the rubric of world-systems theory is no mere passing fancy or 'accidental' feature of the 'Conjectures' essay, but has long been at the heart of his work. Thus his argument in *Modern Epic* that Goethe's *Faust* allows us to see how the expansion of the capitalist world-economy makes redundant older, 'imperial' ambitions to consolidate power through military force is made through reference to Wallerstein's *The Modern World-System* – and specifically to Wallerstein's argument at the beginning of that book that, in its development, the capitalist world-economy simply out-scaled all hitherto existing political systems.[4] When Moretti speaks,

---

4 Wallerstein begins his book by distinguishing categorically between the capitalist world-system and prior imperial formations: the capitalist world-system is 'different, and new', he writes: 'a kind of social system the world has not really known before [...] an economic but not a political entity, unlike empires, city-states and nation-states. In fact, it precisely encompasses within its bounds (it is hard to speak of boundaries) empires, city-states, and the emerging "nation-states." It is a "world" system, not because it encompasses the whole world, but because it is larger than any juridically-defined political unit. And it is a

therefore – as he often does – of formal 'compromise' or 'incorporation', he is referring not to any 'site of cultural hybridization' or cosmopolitanising gesture, as critics such as Shu-mei Shih have evidently supposed (2013: 263). Still less is he seeking to offer a blueprint for understanding 'non-western' forms. Rather, he is attempting to theorise the mechanisms specific to cultural production through which conflict and struggle between core and (semi-) peripheral positions in the capitalist world-system are encoded.[5]

In his epilogue to *Modern Epic*, Moretti deploys combined and uneven development as an interpretive heuristic, with the formal manoeuvres of García Márquez's 'magical realist' *One Hundred Years of Solitude* as his prime example. Grasped as 'another story of accelerated modernization and of combined development' (239–40) and read through the Blochian lens of the 'heterogeneity of historical time', *One Hundred Years of Solitude* displays for Moretti 'another version of non-contemporaneity' in a novel that, like *Faust* (and, we must assume, a whole host of other semi-peripheral works), 'tells the story of "incorporation": of an isolated community that is caught up in the modern world-system, which subjects it to an unexpected, extremely violent acceleration. It is the novel of uneven and combined development' (243). Evidenced in various technical devices conventionally associated with modernism – digressions, restlessly shifting viewpoints, subversions of conventional causality, chronological disjunction, recursiveness – the form of the novel gestures to the uneven results of forced integration to the modern world-system, exemplifying 'Macondo's role in the international division of labour' (244). The 'compromise' represented by the novel's form registers not the liberally consensual process implied by cultural hybridisation, but, on the contrary, 'enslavement to monoculture'. It embodies the violence of capitalism, the uneven advance of modernity: in *The Bourgeois: Between History*

"world-*economy*" because the basic linkage between the parts of the system is economic, although this was reinforced to some extent by cultural links and eventually [...] by political arrangements and even confederal structures' (1974: 15). He then adds that 'Political empires are a primitive means of economic domination. It is the social achievement of the modern world, if you will, to have invented the technology that makes it possible to increase the flow of the surplus from the lower strata to the upper strata, from the periphery to the center, from the majority to the minority, by eliminating the "waste" of too cumbersome a political superstructure' (15–16).

5 Thus *Faust*'s world ambitions are taken to demonstrate the incorporating tendencies of a multiform world system that is profoundly unequal politically, but unified nonetheless by virtue of its encroaching penetration by capital. This understanding proves revelatory in explanation of the manner in which *Faust*'s ambit (which moves restlessly between magic/archaic and rational/Enlightened situations and guises) becomes extra-national. Crucially, it also accounts for the radically uneven and 'compromising' *formal* dimensions of the text – a characteristic that *Faust* shares with all the other 'modern Epics' discussed by Moretti: in Goethe's play, and perhaps for the first time, 'a symbolic form has been found' for the 'new reality' of the modern world-system (1996: 51).

and Literature, Moretti speaks of 'a sort of cultural double helix, where the spasms of capitalist modernization are matched and reshaped by literary form-giving' (2013: 13–14).

In *Atlas of the European Novel*, Moretti muses that 'one day, who knows, a literary criticism finally transformed into a comparative historical morphology may be able to [...] recognize in the geographical variation and dispersal of forms the power of the center over an enormous periphery' (1999: 195). The second of the points that we would like to make about his recent work is then more critical. While the case studies in our book are intended to demonstrate the fruitfulness of his reading strategy, we think that it is necessary to extend the historical ambit and spatial reach of his conception. In particular, while embracing his idea that (semi-)peripheral symbolic forms register the unevenness of the modern world-system, rather than their own autotelic reality – they are 'world texts' rather than 'national texts' – we object to the starkness of the antinomy that Moretti sometimes tends to set up between a 'European' (English or French) literature conceived too homogeneously in systemic terms as 'core' and other – peripheral or semi-peripheral – literatures, in which the 'marvelous reality' brought about by jagged and heterogeneous modernisation is held to provide the basis for 'marvelous realism' as an aesthetic mode. The opposition between core and (semi-)periphery, including in continental Europe, is clear enough. (It provides the basis for the satire in E.M. Forster's *Where Angels Fear to Tread*, for instance.) But we think that Moretti rather overstates the 'homogeneity' of conditions in the core territories and regions. The processes of 'centralisation' (becoming 'core') and 'peripheralisation' are multi-scalar, playing themselves out at multiple levels – neighbourhood, city, nation, region, macro-region – in addition to that of the world-system itself. Literature originating from (semi-)peripheral nations is very frequently produced by metropolitan writers who inhabit a 'core' relative to a 'periphery' within the (semi-)periphery itself – so, Buenos Aires within the context of Argentina, for instance, or Bombay within the context of India[6] – and within these cities, certain districts that are themselves 'core' in relation to (semi-)peripheral areas. By the same token, some of the most significant literature from the core countries emanates from the semi-peripheries or peripheries of those countries: marginalised class, ethnic or regional positions, as in the case of Faulkner in the US context, for instance, or of Hardy, Lawrence and others in England. In works that seek consciously to map the horizons of the world-system, the differential operations of combined unevenness are often registered multiply in the structure itself; in other works, the local scale is sometimes the most clearly articulated, with the uppermost and overdetermining scales only distantly implied.

We also take issue with the characterisation in 'Conjectures on World Literature' and elsewhere of literary forms as moving uni-directionally from

---

6 For an exemplary account of poetic production in Bombay in just these terms, see Bird 2013.

cores to peripheries. In 'World-Systems, Evolutionary Theory, *Weltliteratur*', for example, an essay published after the debates that followed the appearance of 'Conjectures', Moretti follows Itamar Evan-Zohar in speaking not only of the 'asymmetry' of the world-literary system, but also of the directionality of influence: 'powerful literatures from the core "interfere" all the time with the trajectory of peripheral ones, whereas the reverse almost never happens, making the inequality of the system grow over time' (2011: 70). 'While studying the market for novels in the eighteenth and nineteenth century', Moretti continues,

> I reached very similar conclusions to Evan-Zohar's. Here, the crucial mechanism was that of *diffusion*: books from the core were incessantly exported into the semi-periphery and the periphery, where they were read, admired, imitated, turned into models – thus drawing those literatures into the orbit of core ones, and indeed 'interfering' with the autonomous development. And then, diffusion imposed a stunning *sameness* to the literary system: wave after wave of epistolary fiction, or historical novels, or *mystères*, took off from London and Paris and dominated the scene everywhere – often, like American action films today, even more thoroughly in the smaller peripheral markets than in the French or British core. (70)

In gross terms, the point can perhaps be conceded. This, after all, is a particular variant of what has been generally theorised under the rubric of cultural imperialism.[7] But the broad tendency in terms of which core modes and forms superimpose themselves on or overwrite peripheral ones, 'interfering' with their autonomous development and producing 'sameness' across the core/periphery divide, should not blind us to the existence of a counter-current. The combinatory effect of capitalist development is uneven, yes; but its energy does not flow in one direction only. It is not only that cores do not always remain cores, or peripheries peripheries (the world-system is the site of a ceaseless struggle for power). It is also that in the literary and cultural spheres, at least, 'incorporation' of foreign forms – accommodation, assimilation, even indigenisation – is altogether routine in 'core' sectors also: literary forms and models developed in (semi-)peripheral locations are often pirated by core writers – appropriated, translated, generally 'borne across' – sometimes scoring themselves very significantly into 'core' productions and styles.

Some of the potential of Moretti's work seems to us not to have been tapped as yet. The 'Conjectures' essay has of course given rise to a small library of rejoinders, but most of its readers have failed to accept or to appreciate the significance of Moretti's long-term preoccupation with literary form as corollary to the modern world-system. Nor has this situation been helped by the author's own penchant for detouring into other (contradictory)

---

7 See Tomlinson 1991. For a particular discussion, focused on African popular music, of the dynamics and impact of cultural 'diffusion', 'domination', 'indigenisation' etc. across the international division of labour, see Lazarus 1999: 196–225.

models of mapping, evolutionism, network theory and marketology.[8] Our case studies will suggest that Moretti tends to overlook the possibility that the 'unevenness' characteristic of (semi-)peripheral literature will also be discernible in literature from the core formations that is nonetheless 'peripheralised' by its relatively disprivileged (or provincial) location *within* the highly mobile and scalar 'centre'. For of course the unfolding of combined and uneven development produces unevenness throughout the world capitalist system, and not merely across the divide represented by the international division of labour.

The texts we have selected for examination are all novels, or at least (bearing in mind the undecidability in this respect of Vladislavic's *Portrait with Keys*), all works of narrative prose. We do not mean to suggest through this, however, that poetry or other literary genres, or indeed other forms of cultural production – art, theatre, television, cinema, opera, dance, music – are not as sensitive to the logic of combined and uneven development as is fiction. In one sense, our selection of texts is merely tactical and contingent: we have chosen to examine works that, by virtue of their location within a shared geography of combined and uneven development, allow – and, indeed, oblige – us to identify structural analogies between them. However, within the necessarily circumscribed orbit of these case studies, an emphasis emerges on varieties of numinous narration – including magical realism, irrealism, gothic and fantasy – that seems to suggest that it is easier to explore questions about '(semi-)peripherality' in the world-literary system through reference to 'modernist' and 'experimental' modes than through reference to 'realist' or 'naturalist' ones. The questions of why and to what extent our reading method seems initially to lead us away from 'realism' as conventionally defined and understood necessitate a preliminary discussion of the aesthetics of peripherality.

II

The realism–modernism debate has often been constructed around opposition, with the terms being defined against one another – one of them being identified (and celebrated) as more progressive than the other, as more subversive or inventive or daring or resourceful, and the other being identified, reciprocally, as less so. In particular, the German-language Marxist

---

8 In our opinion, even the 'Conjectures' essay itself does not devote enough time to specifying the theory of capitalist modernity upon which it depends. This is excusable, of course, since the essay is short and intended as a spur to thought. The essay's presentation of arguments around distant reading, markets and canon formation is crucial, but it comes at the cost of any deep engagement with the relationship between world-systems theory and the idea of the world-literary system.

debates of the mid-twentieth century that centred on the forms, meaning and value of contemporary writing tended to calcify into a stark and iron-cast (and, in our view, unhelpful) antinomy between 'modernism' and 'realism'.[9] Adorno's vitriolic polemic, in his essay 'Extorted Reconciliation: On Georg Lukács' *Realism in Our Time*' – the latter a work in which the Hungarian Marxist had criticised 'the attenuation of actuality' in modernist literature (1979: 25) and had affirmed what he took to be the superior power of realism to represent the totality of society – has proved deeply influential in this respect. Accusing Lukács of projecting a dogmatic sclerosis of content, Adorno set out not merely to question Lukács's 'indignation' at the 'worldlessness of modern art' (1991: 225), but to challenge and, indeed, rout the terms of his conception *tout court*:

> Hegel's critique of Kantian formalism in aesthetics is reduced to the oversimplified assertion that in modern art style, form, and technique are vastly overrated [...] What looks like formalism to Lukács aims, through the structuring of the elements in accordance with the work's own formal law, at the same 'immanence of meaning' that Lukács is pursuing, instead of forcing the meaning into the work from the outside by fiat, something he himself considers impossible and yet objectively defends. He willfully misinterprets the form-constitutive moments of modern art as *accidentia*, contingent additions to an inflated subject, instead of recognizing their objective function in the aesthetic substance. The objectivity he misses in modern art and which he expects from the material and its 'perspectivist' treatment devolves upon the methods and techniques he would like to eliminate, which dissolve the purely material aspect and only thereby put it into perspective. (218)

Where Lukács had spoken of the passivity and defeatism of modernist writing in the face of modern social existence, Adorno celebrates modernism for the pertinence of its grasp of contemporary reality. It is 'modernism', he argues, not contemporary 'realism', that voices an immanent negative critique (whether from the left or the right) of the intensification of social misery in capitalist society. 'The great avant-garde works of art cut through [the] [...] illusion of subjectivity both by throwing the frailty of the individual into relief and by grasping the totality in the individual, who is a moment in the totality and yet can know nothing about it' (225). The distinctive features ascribed to European modernist writing from this perspective – its metropolitanism, its 'bracketing out' of the world (225), its deliberated rejection of tradition, its stylistic innovation, its non-representational narration that dispenses with linearity, its rendering of self- or inner consciousness, its obsessive focus on the libidinal horizons of bourgeois subjectivity – all relate to that particular historical moment in the late nineteenth and early twentieth centuries, when changes to experience and lifeworld in the rapidly modernising capitalist

---

9 The definitive collection here is Adorno et al. 1986.

societies of the 'west' are seen as necessitating new cultural forms to mediate or express them.[10] Naming Joyce, Proust, Musil, Kafka and others as exemplars of this kind of modernist literary practice, Adorno turns the tables on Lukács's celebration of Balzac and Dickens, asserting that the works of these latter authors 'are not so realistic after all' (228). This point he elaborates by describing Balzac's novels as 'an imaginative reconstruction of an alienated reality, that is, a reality that can no longer be experienced by the subject', suggesting that in these terms, the difference between the Balzacian conception and that of the modernist authors is not very significant, 'except that Balzac, in accordance with the sense of form in his works, considered his monologues to represent the fullness of the world, whereas the great novelists of the twentieth century enclose the fullness of their worlds within the monologue' (228).[11]

That Lukács's critique of modernism is doctrinaire and often reductive cannot be gainsaid. In this sense, as Michael Löwy has written, the essay

10 This paradigmatic change in the 'structure of experience' constituted, of course, one of the major objects of Walter Benjamin's research. See especially 'On Some Motifs in Baudelaire' (Benjamin 2003). But see also, in this respect, Raymond Williams's commentary on Dickens's style in his 'Notes on English Prose 1780–1950': 'We can then see more clearly what Dickens is doing: altering, transforming a whole way of writing, rather than putting an old style at a new experience. It is not the method of the more formal novelists, including the sounds of measured or occasional speech in a solid frame of analysis and settled exposition. Rather, it is a speaking, persuading, directing voice, of a new kind, which has taken over the narrative, the exposition, the analysis, in a single operation. Here, there, everywhere: the restless production of a seemingly chaotic detail; the hurrying, pressing, miscellaneous clauses, with here a gap to push through, there a restless pushing at repeated obstacles, everywhere a crowding of objects, forcing attention; the prose, in fact, of a new order of experience; the prose of the city. It is not only disturbance; it is also a new kind of settlement' (1991b: 93–94).
11 See also the account of characterisation in Dickens that Adorno gives in his rather remarkable essay on *The Old Curiosity Shop*, which stands somewhat at right angles to his generally critical approach to the English novelist: 'Dickens is currently considered to be one of the founders of the realistic and social novel. Historically, this is correct; but when one examines the form of his work itself, it requires some qualification. For Dickens' fictional work, in which poverty, despair, and death have already been recognized as the fruits of a bourgeois world, a world to which only the traces of human warmth and kindness in individual human relationships can reconcile one – this work also contains the outlines of a completely different sort of view of the world. You may call it prebourgeois; in it the individual has not yet reached full autonomy, nor, therefore, complete isolation, but instead is presented as a bearer of objective factors, of a dark, obscure fate and a starlike consolation that overtake the individual and permeate his life but never follow from the law of the individual, as do, for instance, the fates of the characters in Flaubert's novels. The novels of Dickens contain a fragment of the dispersed baroque that maintains a strange ghostly presence in the nineteenth century' (1992b: 171).

to which Adorno takes such exception 'is probably one of [Lukács's] most unconvincing essays' (Löwy 2007: 213). Even so, we might follow Fredric Jameson and suggest that history itself – the history since World War II – has had the last, or at least the latest, laugh. Reminding us that it would be a mistake to reify the concepts of 'realism' and 'modernism', Jameson points out that even if Adorno clearly had the better of his argument against Lukács in the mid-century, it is, today, some sixty years later, not so easy to ratify the terms of the German theorist's celebration of modernism's irrecuperability – the source, apparently, of its resistance to incorporation – when 'what was once an oppositional and anti-social phenomenon in the early years of the [twentieth] century, has [...] become the dominant style of commodity production and an indispensable component in the machinery of the latter's ever more rapid and demanding reproduction of itself' (1986c: 209). 'Realism' and 'modernism' are not to be grasped as phases in a stably unfolding literary history: Jameson describes modernism, rather, as 'realism's historical counterpart and its dialectical mirror-image' (198);[12] and he draws the conclusion that follows from his contemporary resituating of the mid-twentieth-century Marxist debates 'within the broader context of the crisis of historicity itself' – a conclusion that, if we were thinking of 'realism' and 'modernism' in categorical terms, as counter-posed absolutes, would loom as paradoxical or even inexplicable:

> [Today,] indeed, there is some question whether the ultimate renewal of modernism, the final dialectical subversion of the now automatized conventions of an aesthetics of perceptual revolution, might not simply be ... realism itself! For when modernism and its accompanying techniques of 'estrangement' have become the dominant style whereby the consumer is reconciled with capitalism, the habit of fragmentation itself needs to be 'estranged' and corrected by a more totalizing way of viewing phenomena. In an unexpected dénouement, it may be Lukács – wrong as he might have been in the 1930s – who has some provisional last word for us today. (211–12)

What Jameson finds compelling in Lukács is his dialectical understanding of history, discernible in all of his writing, and in terms of which realism has 'to do with an art whereby the narrative of individuals [is] [...] somehow made to approach historical dynamics as such, [is] [...] organized so as to reveal

---

12 Elsewhere, he writes that the 'concepts of modernism and realism are not on all fours with each other [...] [T]he two terms, whether considered to be concepts or categories, are drawn from two unrelated systems, and like those two well-known lines which, prolonged into infinity, never meet, they are incommensurable with each other. Modernism is an aesthetic category and realism is an epistemological one; the truth claim of the latter is irreconcilable with the formal dynamic of the former. The attempt to combine the two into a single master narrative must therefore necessarily fail, yet its failure produces the more productive problem which is that of the model of innovation which underwrites both' (2002: 124).

its relationship with a history in movement and a future on the point of emergence' (Jameson 2012: 479). We, too, would prefer not to close the door on the Lukács of the mid-twentieth century. His essay 'Dostoevsky', for instance, written in 1943 and first published in 1949, seems to us to demonstrate the workings of a sort of critical apprehension that is far removed from the manifest reductionism of those sections of *The Meaning of Contemporary Realism* that drew Adorno's scorn. This essay on Dostoevsky is of special interest to us because it comes at the question of realism in such a way as to offer what might be extracted as a nascent theory of literary production in the light of combined and uneven development. With a kind of astonished admiration, Lukács heralds Dostoevsky's social location as fundamental to his ability to invent a new form that, by registering the particular dynamics of social life in the Russian semi-periphery in its nineteenth-century moment, gestures towards the actuality of capitalism as an unevenly integrated world-system:

> It is a strange, but often repeated fact that the literary embodiment of a new human type with all its problems comes to the civilized world from a young nation. Thus in the eighteenth century Werther came from Germany and prevailed in England and France: thus in the second half of the nineteenth century Raskolnikov came from far-off, unknown, almost legendary Russia to speak for the whole civilized West [...] 'Suddenly' there appeared from an underdeveloped country, where the troubles and conflicts of contemporary civilization could not yet have been fully unfolded, works that stated – imaginatively – all the problems of human culture at its highest point, stirred up ultimate depths, and presented a totality hitherto never achieved and never since surpassed, embracing the spiritual, moral, and philosophical questions of that age. (1962: 146)

In Dostoevsky, Lukács thinks he sees 'the first and greatest poet of the modern capitalist metropolis', the first to draw 'the mental deformations that are brought about as a social necessity by life in a modern city', the first to recognise and represent 'the dynamics of a future social, moral, and psychological evolution from germs of something barely beginning' (153). When he writes as a journalist, Dostoevsky speaks 'consolingly' and as a political conservative; yet in the delirious, hallucinatory realism of his fiction, a social vision asserts itself over political intentions: 'It is a revolt against that moral and psychic deformation of man which is caused by the evolution of capitalism'. The experimentalism of the novelist's prose is read as 'a desperate attempt to break through the barriers which deform the soul and maim, distort, and dismember life' (156).[13]

13 Compare Marshall Berman's account of a 'modernism of underdevelopment' in Dostoevsky: 'The contrast of Baudelaire and Dostoevsky, and of Paris and Petersburg in the middle of the nineteenth century, should help us see a larger polarity in the world history of modernism. At one pole we can see the modernism of advanced nations, building directly on the materials of economic and political modernization and drawing vision and energy from a modernized reality – Marx's

Two implications deriving from Lukács's observation that there is 'nothing unusual in the fact that a backward country produces powerful works' might be highlighted here. The first is that parts of the world undeveloped by capitalist modernisation – or, indeed, *underdeveloped* by it – are nonetheless coeval contemporaries of the world-system's metropolitan centres. The second, even more important, is that it might well be in these 'backward' locations that the pressures of combined and uneven development find their most pronounced or profound registration – including in the sphere of culture, where new forms are likely to emerge, oriented (and uniquely responsive) to these pressures, which constitute their final determinants.

Dostoevsky is able to parlay the sense of backwardness and incongruity into a source of literary innovation and pre-eminence, processing the co-presence of the archaic and the new into a modern form that has few parallels elsewhere in nineteenth-century literary space. His 'realism' – if it is that – does not register the smoothly commodified and rationalised surfaces of capitalist modernity as experienced by the dominant fractions in the core zones (which have their peripheries and semi-peripheries, also, but in which the ruptures and divisions are more deeply concealed – in key instances self-consciously so, in advertising, publicity, etc. – beneath the second nature of appearances and spectacle). Rather Dostoevsky's 'realism' registers the manifest incongruities, dislocations and forms of unevenness characteristic of the (semi-)periphery.

In these terms, we can understand why literary theorists and historians should sometimes have invoked the Russian situation in attempting to explain the emergence of remarkable and seemingly anomalous forms of writing in contexts far removed from Russia itself. Writing about the great Brazilian novelist Machado de Assis, for instance, Roberto Schwarz refers us to St Petersburg and Dostoevsky in his account of how the 'backwardness' of Brazil in the nineteenth century came to be reworked into a source of literary innovation. Addressing the generic features of the novel as a literary form that did not emerge 'organically' but was imported into Brazil, Schwarz notes 'the dissonance between representations and what, upon consideration, we know to be their context' (1992: 27). The specificity of Brazilian fiction is given to it by its affirmation of European ideas and ideals in local conditions that contradict these ideas and ideals: the consequence is a distinctive aesthetic marked by varieties of unevenness, stylistic mismatches and improbable contiguities.[14] Connecting the stylistics and literary devices of

---

factories and railways, Baudelaire's boulevards – even when it challenges that reality in radical ways. At an opposite pole we find a modernism that arises from backwardness and underdevelopment. This modernism arose first in Russia, most dramatically in St. Petersburg, in the nineteenth century; in our own era, with the spread of modernization – but generally, as in old Russia, a truncated and warped modernization – it has spread throughout the Third World' (1983: 232).

14 See Jameson's reference to Cuban theoreticians of the 1980s, who, instead of decrying the technological underdevelopment of Cuban film, affirmed a 'Third World aesthetic politics' in terms of which Cuba's 'own "imperfect cinema"',

(semi-)peripheral novels in general to their social ground, Schwarz proposes that the forms of these fictions be read in the light of the overdetermined complexity of their material, cultural, social and existential conditions:

> Sustained by its historical backwardness, Russia forced the bourgeois novel to face a more complex reality. The comic figure of the Westernizer, Francophile or Germanophile (frequently under an allegorical or ridiculous name), the ideologies of progress, of liberalism, of reason, all these were ways of bringing into the foreground the modernization that came with Capital. These enlightened men proved themselves to be lunatics, thieves, opportunists, cruel, vain and parasitical. The system of ambiguities growing out of the local use of bourgeois ideas – one of the keys to the Russian novel – is not unlike the one we described for Brazil. The social reasons for this similarity are clear. In Russia, too, modernization would lose itself in the infinite extent of territory and of social inertia, and would clash with serfdom or its vestiges – a clash many felt as a national shame, although it gave others the standard by which to measure the madness of the individualism and progressomania that the West imposed and imposes on the world. The extreme form of this confrontation, in which progress is a disaster and backwardness a shame, is one of the springs of Russian literature. Whatever the difference in stature, there is in Machado [...] something similar, something of Gogol, Dostoyevsky, Goncharov and Chekhov. (1992: 29)

Expanding on these suggestions, Schwarz observes that when the ideas and ideals of European liberalism are affirmed in a Brazil in which social relationships are based on *latifundia* and the unfree labour of slaves, they stand out in bold relief as 'second-degree ideology', incongruous with the circumstances of Brazilian life (50). These affirmations are accordingly always 'improper' (29) – which does not, of course, make them false or lacking in material consequence – and the cultural work that is predicated on these particular social foundations looms (even to its producers and champions) as backward and belated. The novel in Brazil then has to wait 'to discover some arrangement by which these elements, instead of producing an incongruent form, would become part of a regulated system, with its own logic and its own – our own – problems, dealt with on their own appropriate level' (53). It is with Machado, according to Schwarz, that this breakthrough is achieved. In *A Master on the Periphery of Capitalism*, his study of Machado's 1880 novel *The Posthumous Memoirs of Brás Cubas*, Schwarz argues that the work's 'Babel of literary mannerisms' (2001: 17), the heterogeneity and bewildering multiplicity of its juxtapositions of narrative form and style, is to be read neither as inconsistency nor as baroque exhibition, but as a figuration of the contradictoriness of Brazilian sociality, 'slave-owning and bourgeois at

---

consequent on economic constraints, is transformed 'into a strength and a choice, a sign of its own distinct origins and content' (1986b: 316).

the same time' (3). The sheer *volubility* of Machado's prose is itself the point here. Schwarz draws our attention to 'the profusion and crucial nature of the relationships implied in the rhythm of Machado's prose, and the extraordinary contrasts between the voices orchestrated in its truly complex music' (16) in order to suggest that what might seem at first – and especially to a metropolitan reader – excess or superfluity is in fact 'intensified realism' (73), more 'realistic' actually than the Romantic, nationalist endeavours of such contemporaries of Machado's as José de Alencar.[15]

In *A Master on the Periphery of Capitalism*, Schwarz describes his own methodology as an extension to the cultural field of the arguments that had been advanced by the members of a group of scholars of his teachers' generation at the University of São Paulo, who 'used to meet to study *Capital* with a view to understanding Brazil':

> This group had reached the daring conclusion that the classic marks of Brazilian backwardness should be studied not as an archaic leftover but as an integral part of the way modern society reproduces itself, or in other words, as evidence of a perverse form of progress. For the historian of culture and the critic of the arts in countries like ours, ex-colonies, this thesis has an enormous power to stimulate and deprovincialize, for it allows us to inscribe on the present-day international situation, in polemical form, much of what seemed to distance us from it and confine us to irrelevance. (3)

Hence Schwarz's argument that the aesthetic of *The Posthumous Memoirs of Brás Cubas* is not simply *uneven* – 'fractured', its constituent elements uneasily juxtaposed, concatenated, imposed one upon the other – but also *combinatory*, its elements 'telescoped' and 'accordionised'. This marks the difference between Machado and his contemporaries, and also between the early Machado and Machado from the *Memoirs* onwards:

> [W]hen Machado in his first phase retreated from the so-called contemporary terrain and practically excluded the new and critical discourse of individual freedoms and the right to self-fulfillment from his novels, he was fleeing from the false position in which liberal ideology and the conspicuous virtues of progress found themselves in the Brazilian context. Once this position of discernment is established, it will permit him, from the *Memoirs* on, to reintroduce the presumptions of modernity, only now explicitly marked by belittlement and dislocation, as was demanded by the circumstances. (158)

The volubility of the *Memoirs* bespeaks neither marginalisation or restriction nor the pseudo-universality of a dominant discourse that imagines itself unisonant, but rather the 'accordionised' combination of all aspects of Brazilian

---

15 And compare Jameson on Joyce: 'Joyce, in his Irish context, is far more realistic than other contemporaneous strains of a romantic or nationalist Irish culture' (2012: 476).

sociality: the work's volubility 'squeezes' these contradictory aspects, Schwarz writes,

> stretches them, and explores them in every direction, in any way it pleases. In other words, we have a firework display of a caricatured universal culture, a kind of down-market universality, in the best Brazilian tradition, in which Brás Cubas's caprice takes as its province the total experience of humanity and makes itself absolute. *It is no longer a passing tendency, psychological or stylistic, but a rigorous principle, placed above everything else, and that therefore is exposed, and can be appreciated all along the line.* This universalization establishes the axis that gives ideological power to the *Memoirs*. (18)

No wonder, then, that a novel of the 1880s can appear to a present-day reader as anticipating the dislocated and absurd worlds of Eastern and Central Europe conjured up in the writing of the early decades of the twentieth century by such authors as Kafka and Musil.

Yet, if Machado's aesthetic seems to anticipate Kafka and Musil, his novel's form also looks backward to the eighteenth century in modelling itself partly on *Tristram Shandy*, another fictional work that could be considered authored by a semi-peripheral author, and whose narratorial experimentalism, as Terry Eagleton has written, 'strikingly prefigures Irish literary modernism' almost a century and a half before its debut (Eagleton 1995: 147). Sterne's biography renders him a liminal figure in Irish literature: he was born into an Anglo-Irish family in County Wicklow, but lived for most of his life in England. He can be understood, as such, as an intellectual born in the semi-periphery but resident in the imperial centre. In his prologue to the third edition of *Memoirs*, Machado cites his narrator's description of his autobiography as 'a scattered work where I, Brás Cubas, have adopted the free form of a Sterne or a Xavier de Maistre', and goes on to note that '[a]ll those people traveled: Xavier de Maistre around his room [...] Sterne in other people's lands' (Machado 1998: 3). Eagleton notes that while 'reality is not disowned in Irish writing', there is in the tradition from Sterne to Beckett a 'calculatedly [...] ironic rift between [reality's] own meagerness and the self-consciously elaborate languages used to record it. This bathetic gap between form and content [...] is then among other things an index of the condition of the colonial writer, wryly conscious of the discrepancy between the exuberance of the signifier and the meanness of the referent' (1995: 150). Given Machado's appropriation of Sterne's form, we might take more seriously Viktor Shklovsky's provocative declaration that '*Tristram Shandy* is the most typical novel of world literature' (2006: 52). For Shklovsky is referring, we take it, to the way in which Sterne's novel represents – and indeed embodies – a fundamental dissonance in the structure of reality, and therefore also in the way in which reality is experienced.[16]

---

16 Perhaps, indeed, the form of Machado's novel might be traced backwards, through an alternative route, not to the eighteenth century world that produced *Tristram Shandy*, but to the seventeenth century world that produced *Don Quixote*.

III

Our intention here is not to repeat the disciplinary privileging of 'modernist' over 'realist' writing. '[W]e all know what precedes modernism', Jameson writes, in characterisation of the prevailing viewpoint – 'or at least we say we know (and we think we know): it can be none other than realism, about which it is surely obvious that it constitutes the raw material that modernism cancels and surcharges' (2002: 119–20). Rather, we seek an explanation for the apparent proliferation of forms of irrealist narrative and catachresis at particular moments of systemic crisis, above all as experienced in the (semi-) peripheries of the world-system.

To unfold the full implications of Lukács's assessment of Dostoevsky and Schwarz's of Machado requires us to think beyond the received constructions of modernism. Adorno's insight that '[m]odernity is a qualitative, not a chronological, category' (Adorno 1985: 218) already allows us to recognise that 'modernism' is not to be thought of as 'coming after' 'realism', as 'succeeding' or finally 'displacing' it. For what is at stake in Adorno's defence of modernist literature is paradoxically (its) *realism*: the various modernist techniques are affirmed not for their own sake but because they are taken to register and resonate with the systemic crisis of European modernity in the late nineteenth and early twentieth centuries. (Stripped of any reference to society, the Poundian injunction to 'make it new' would not have interested Adorno.) Adorno's defence of modernism is thus a defence of modernism's realism.

The inverse holds true, too: the defence of realism will take the form of an identification of its *modernism*. It is not only, as Jameson observes, that 'each genuinely new realism denounces its predecessors as unrealistic'. It is also that 'genuine realism, taken at the moment of its emergence, is a discovery process, which, with its emphasis on the new and the hitherto unreported, unrepresented, and unseen, and its notorious subversion of inherited ideas and genres (the *Quijote*!), is in fact itself a kind of modernism, if not the latter's first form' (Jameson 2012: 476).

Of course, the Adornian insight needs to be complemented by an analogous

---

'Cervantes lived his age', Carlos Fuentes has written, in describing the 'revolutionary' political implications of the 'uncertainty' upon which his novel is premised: 'the decadent Spain of the last Hapsburgs, Philip III and the devaluation of money, the fall of the economy due to the successive expulsions of the industrious Jewish and Arab populations, the compulsion to disguise Hebrew or Moorish origins leading to a society of brittle masks, the lack of efficient administrators for a far-flung empire, the flight of the gold and silver of the Indies to the mercantile powerhouses of northern Europe. A Spain of urchins and beggars, hollow gestures, cruel aristocrats, ruined roads, shabby inns, and broken-down gentlemen who, in another, more vigorous age, might have conquered Mexico and sailed the Caribbean and brought the first universities and the first printing presses to the New World: the fabulous energy of Spain in the invention of America' (Fuentes 2006: 615).

spatial awareness: 'modernity is a qualitative, not a *chronological*, category'; but it is also a qualitative, not a *geographical* (or *geopolitical*) category. Even Jameson's lexicon of 'modernistic realisms' and 'realistic modernisms' only becomes fully serviceable when it is yoked to a politics of space as well as a politics of time, in circumstances in which it can be deployed to characterise the relationship between literary form and a (changing) social landscape. 'The fruitful idea of "estranging estrangement" might well be raised here, in the context of a text that uses and then questions the experimental; and a modernist realism would begin to emerge when the traditional methods of narrative representation (novelistic realism) are used and then undermined', Jameson writes (2012: 479). He might have written 'when *or where*', for as he himself shows us in much of his work, one of the paradigmatic sites of emergence of a 'modernist realism' such as is here under review is the world of the semi-periphery, in which 'local' and 'global' forces come together in conflictual and unsteady flux.

To read modernist literature in the light of combined and uneven development is then to read it with one eye to its realism. Such a reading cuts against the grain of the received literary histories, which, throughout the twentieth century, have sought to drive a wedge between these two modes. On the political left, of course, and in the 'Third World', realism, as Jameson notes, has continued to 'be saluted as a conquest of reality and a weapon in cognitive struggle' (2012: 476). But these are exceptions that prove the rule, since – for those gazing out from the citadels of cultural hegemony and the various cathedrals of learning – developments on the political left or in the 'Third World' are frequently assumed to be residual if not quite anachronistic. If socialist and 'Third World' writers continue to insist on 'realism' – well, that just goes to confirm their belatedness. Closer to home, meanwhile, the many varieties of peripheral and semi-peripheral realism are typically stigmatised or marginalised in critical discourse, or taken to be fatally compromised by the reductionism that derives, supposedly inevitably, from their class consciousness. The further from 'realism' one travels, the more likely it is that one will be lionised for one's 'modernism'.

Thus within postcolonial studies, to provide just one disciplinary example, we can discern a pronounced tendency to privilege writings that reject narratives of nation and nationalism and that stylistically inscribe the techniques of hybridity, pastiche, irony and defamiliarisation. A very large number of works have gone largely ignored by practitioners in the field because their 'realism' has been taken, programmatically, to testify to a secret or explicit accommodationism. Meanwhile, the actual 'realism' of many of the works that *have* been read widely has typically been misrecognised, their 'irrealism' being misunderstood as existing in stark opposition to any aesthetics of representation. So we find Yambo Ouologuem's once notorious novel *Bound to Violence*, for instance, being celebrated (by no less influential a reader than Anthony Appiah) as a work that 'seeks to delegitimate the forms of the realist African novel'. The suggestion is that realism itself has become obsolete: an historically discredited idiom, it has now been categorically eclipsed. Realism seeks 'to naturalize [...] a nationalism that, by 1968, had plainly failed' (Appiah 1991: 349). Appiah's characterisation of Ouologuem's novel as 'postrealist' simply reiterates the orthodox (self-)understanding of modernism. The same structure of interpretation governs the contemporary reception of Roberto Bolaño's *2666* – again, a work widely celebrated for its 'post-postmodernism', that is to say its definitive post-realism. We would want, in opposing ourselves to such readings, to draw attention instead to what is registered, formally and as content, in the narrative arc of Bolaño's novel: the self-conscious incorporation of the problematic of imperialism, cultural and otherwise; the attention to the starkest manifestations of inequality in the social and economic realm – the 'deathworld' epitomised by the serial killings of female workers in the maquiladoras on the US–Mexican border; the sustained and extended critique of a system that engenders moral and psychological deformation. In a recent article, Joe Cleary emphasises that 'most of the great modernist epics' arose in the cultural context of 'a turbulent and changing world-system' (2012: 260). '[H]owever conceived', Cleary writes, modernism 'was essentially the literature of an interregnum between the dissolution of one kind of European world-ordering imperialism and the consolidation of a new kind of US-Soviet imperialism in its place' (261).

In these terms we might suggest that the value of literary-world systems theory lies in the fact that it enables comparison of discrepant literary subunits and social formations of the world-system, both at the same point in chronological time and at congruent conjunctures in the recurring rhythmic cycles of capitalism – Russian and Brazilian novels of the 1880s, for instance, or those from the Austro-Hungarian empire and Ireland in the early twentieth century, and so forth. It is surely possible to pay attention to the irrealist aesthetics of (semi-)peripheral literatures without stumbling into either of the complementary pitfalls: on the one hand, of subscribing to stagist accounts of realism and modernism as periodic categories; on the other, of losing sight of the historical specificity of mutations in literary form (and their correspondence to particular social developments).

IV

We are proposing that something of an elective affinity exists between the general situation(s) of peripherality and irrealist aesthetics. Our suggestion is that the work of literary representation in (semi-)peripheral contexts seems to require a supplementation or heightening of what, following Michael Löwy (from whom we have derived the term 'irrealism' in the first instance), we might call the 'ideal-type' of realism (2007: 195). It might then be worthwhile to spell out here some of the structural factors that underlie the evident need of (semi-)peripheral writers to look beyond 'ideal-type' realism.

It is by now widely understood that the current crisis of the world-system was preceded (and indeed heralded) by a shift in the core capitalist zones, from material production to credit and speculation (financialisation). This shift has been actively registered in any number of recent works of fiction: without looking beyond the English language or the social terrain of Anglo-America, we can immediately name such works as Franzen's *The Twenty-Seventh City* (1988), Haslett's *Union Atlantic* (2009), Faulks's *A Week in December* (2010) and Lanchester's *Capital* (2012), for instance. Less widely commented on, however, is the fact that shifts of exactly this kind – from 'real' to 'fictitious' capital[17] – have been a symptomatic feature of historical contexts in which a fundamental transformation takes place in the balance of power between core states, regions or sectors in the world-system. Marx spoke, for example, of 'the sudden emergence of [...] [a] brood of bankocrats, financiers, *rentiers*, brokers, stock-jobbers, etc.' at the end of the seventeenth century and the beginning of the eighteenth, decades that bore witness to the founding of the Bank of England and to the 'South Sea Bubble' (1990: 920). And in *The Long Twentieth Century* (1994), Giovanni Arrighi makes a similar observation about shifts in the prevailing forms of capitalisation, with reference not merely to the recent 'bubble' of the 1980s, but to the pre-Crash years of the 1920s also.[18]

It is certainly interesting to reflect on the fact that the shift to fictitious capital is a tendential feature of capitalist development on the world scale, and not – as many contemporary commentators seem to imagine – one that is historically without precedent and unique to the conjuncture of the late twentieth and early twenty-first centuries. But what is key to our purposes here is not this fact alone, but a corollary one. For inasmuch as they create (and themselves respond to) imbalances and ruptures in the world-economy, these tendential shifts in forms of capitalisation typically become the occasion also for new cycles of material despoliation, violence and expropriation on a world scale, as imperialist powers compete with one another for relative advantage. In his chapter 'Primitive Accumulation' in *Capital*, Marx famously argued that 'it is a notorious fact that conquest, enslavement, robbery, murder, in short, force, play the greatest part' in capitalist development (1990: 874). What he called 'primitive accumulation' (*ursprünglich*, 'original' or 'originating') – and which should not be understood in stagist terms as an *early* form of accumulation, one progressively eclipsed and left behind as capitalism 'matures' or 'advances' – David Harvey (2005: 137–82) has more recently theorised

---

17 These are Marx's terms: see Chapter 29 ('Banking Capital's Component Parts') of Part Five of the third volume of *Capital* (Marx 1991: 594–606).
18 Among the more important works of fiction registering – and, typically, deploring – the growth of speculation and fictitious capital in the contexts of earlier crises, we might cite Zola's *L'Argent* (*Money*, 2007 [1891]), Trollope's *The Way We Live Now* (1991 [1873]), Sinclair's *The Moneychangers* (2006 [1908]) and Dreiser's *The Financier* (2008 [1912]).

as 'accumulation by dispossession' and Jason Moore (2012) as 'plunder and productivity'.[19]

The appearance and growth of fictitious capital, the most virtual or immaterial form of capitalisation, and primitive accumulation, the most bloody and material, are interlinked. The two forms depend on each other. One cannot separate the history of credit from the wider history of capitalist imperialism. The simultaneity of material and immaterial regimes of production – of spilled blood and evanescent credit, to put it sloganistically – which is a pervasive and conspicuous feature of peripheral social formations, especially, does not readily lend itself to representation through the relative facticity of realist forms of the 'ideal-type'. The in-mixing of the imaginary and the factual that characterises 'irrealist' writing is arguably more sensitive to this simultaneity, to the seemingly incongruous conjunction of 'abstract' and 'scarring' modes of capitalisation. Irrealist aesthetics might then be presented as corresponding not to any depreciation of realism, but to a refinement of it, under the specific circumstances of combined and uneven development.

Of course, even the canonical texts of nineteenth-century realism are marked by a degree of this 'in-mixing' – one thinks of the spectre of the Megalosaurus, 'forty foot long or so, waddling like an elephantine lizard up Holborn Hill' in the opening sentences of Dickens's *Bleak House* (2001 [1852–53]: 3); or of the 'aleatory realism' of the parable of the pier-glass in George Eliot's *Middlemarch*, which Matthew Beaumont has used as the basis for a thoroughgoing and very welcome critique of 'the simplistic conception of realism sponsored by postmodernist thought' (2011: 11). It is also the case that, precisely because core countries have their own peripheries and semi-peripheries, we often encounter a subdued or mediated registration of combined unevenness in these sectors as well.[20] This is discernible even within

---

19 Among other things, these formulations are important inasmuch as they make clear that the history of modern European colonialism cannot be separated from the wider history of capitalism. This argument has long been a staple of materialist criticism within postcolonial studies (see Lazarus 2002 and several of the essays in Parry 2004, for example, and also the discussion of Edward Said in Chapter One, above), but has recently been forcefully restated in Chibber 2013.

20 See Jameson, who points out that canonical approaches to the 'great works of the West' for the most part exclude not only the 'realities of the rest of the world', but even 'their own "peripheries"' (2012: 484). Consider also Casanova's astute observation that Faulkner's writing has exerted so much influence over writers from the global south – particularly in the southern hemisphere of the Americas – precisely because he has been taken as 'the precursor and inventor of a specific – narrative, technical, formal – solution that made it possible to reconcile the most modern aesthetics with the most archaic social structures and landscapes' (2004: 345). The famous axiom in *Requiem for a Nun*, 'The past is never dead. It's not even past' (Faulkner 1973 [1953]: 81), powerfully evokes the ways in which social situations corresponding to residual formations such as the archaic plantocracy in the post-bellum South might linger in combined form in the peripheral regions of industrialised cores. With the rise of multiculturalist

the metropoles of the core countries, whose populations have long since been divorced from and have forgotten their agrarian cultural roots. Stripped of – or liberated from – direct contact with non-urban and residual modes of sociality, metropolitan writers often resuscitate other forms of 'obsolete' culture in their work. What then emerges are peculiarly metropolitan variants of irrealism or magical realism. In graphic novels, for instance, of both the 'serious' and the 'superhero' or horror kinds, an uncanny form of realism is developed with its roots in fanciful childhood modes of narration and representation but its branches in the unforgiving salt air of the present.[21] Speculative fiction similarly displaces 'ideal-type' realism backwards and forwards: a particularly vivid example can be found in Kim Stanley Robinson's *2312*, which explicitly describes late capitalism as riven by unevenness – an unstable formation that rocks between residuality and emergence – and sets out to map 'the combination and battleground of its residual element, feudalism, and its emergent element – what?' (2012: 126) by aligning the techniques of science fiction, with its emphasis on the revenant and the numinous, to the collage techniques employed in an earlier SF novel, John Brunner's *Stand on Zanzibar*, which had itself been inspired by the experimental realist *U.S.A.* trilogy by John Dos Passos.[22] Here we have a writer mining

---

politics, this registration of combined unevenness in the work of writers from core countries has, unfortunately, often been co-opted or redirected, producing an emphasis on 'minoritarianism' and 'hyphenation' and a corresponding focus on questions of identity. Writers who have been positioned as 'multicultural' – Maxine Hong Kingston, Amy Tan, Toni Morrison, Gloria Anzaldúa, Jhumpa Lahiri, even Ishmael Reed, for example – have typically been read in the light of a substantialist cultural politics that works, in Jameson's words, to 'secure an appearance of multiculturalism at odds with economic, existential and class realities' (2012: 481).

21 See, for example, the body-horror allegorisation of teenage alienation and social caste in Charles Burns's *Black Hole* (2005), or the more nuanced depiction of reified consumerist identity in Daniel Clowes's *Ghost World* (2001).

22 Asked in an interview about the 'collage structure' of *2312*, Robinson responds as follows: 'The book was clearly going to have a big information load, and as I was planning it, Jerad Walters of Centipede Press asked me to write introductions for new editions of John Brunner's novels *Stand on Zanzibar* and *The Sheep Look Up*, classics from 1968 and 1973. I agreed to do that, and rediscovered the way Brunner had portrayed a complex global culture, which was by adapting the technique invented by John Dos Passos for his great *U.S.A.* trilogy of the 1930s. So I finally actually read the Dos Passos trilogy, which had been sitting on my shelf for thirty years, and I was amazed at how good it is – truly one of the great American novels. I decided to follow Brunner's example and adapt the Dos Passos method, which in essence is a weave or collage of different kinds of writing, including songs, newspaper articles, stream-of-consciousness passages, impressionist pocket biographies of famous Americans, and so on. My lists, extracts, planet biographies, and quantum walks are my variations on the Dos Passos technique'. Interview with Kim Stanley Robinson: http://blogs.publishersweekly.com/blogs/genreville/?p=1789. Accessed 19 August 2013.

or reactivating the techniques of not just one but two writers from earlier moments, and projecting them into a narrative future, precisely in order to portray the 'unstable mix of past and future systems' that characterise contemporary capitalism (126).

When pre-existing social unities are violently destroyed, the relative stability – or, as Jameson has put it, the 'conviction as to the massive weight and persistence of the present as such' (2007: 263) – required by realist representation of the 'ideal type' disappears with it. In the work of writers from peripheral and semi-peripheral formations, the registration of combined and uneven development through deployment of an aesthetics of anamorphosis is characteristically pronounced and intensified. Of course, not every work from the peripheries will consciously encode disjunction and amalgamation as literary innovations in the manner of a Machado or a Dostoevsky or a Faulkner or a Salih; but there is very characteristically a propensity to reactivate archaic and residual forms, to use these to challenge, disrupt, compound, supplement and supersede the dominant (often imposed) forms, in order to convey the palimpsestic, combinatory and contradictory 'order' of peripheral experience.[23] Even the narratives of (semi-)peripheral authors who hew quite closely to the line of the dominant realist traditions display irrealist or catachrestic features when registering the temporal and spatial dislocations and the abrupt juxtapositions of different modes of life engendered by imperial conquest, or the violent reorganisation of social relations engendered by cyclical crisis.

In (semi-)peripheral aesthetics, the 'shock' of combined unevenness is registered with particular intensity and resonance. Insofar as the mode of representation is (ir)realist, the writing will take the present social order as its object. But the *epistemology* of irrealist representation is quite often historicist: the attempt will be made to peer back into the past, by way of recovering both the specific history of the present and the alternative histories that might have been but were not, yet that (paradoxically) still might be. Wilson Harris's fiction, for example, typically reads the present through the past, searching for the moment or moments when the structurality of the present order was first concretised and set in place. In his discussion of Harris's *Palace of the Peacock*, Niblett cites the Glissantian formulation of a 'point of entanglement, from which we were forcefully turned away' – a formulation that he then glosses as follows:

> The point of entanglement for Glissant as much as for Harris is the point of contact between diverse histories and modes of existence. It is a dynamic conflictual site; Glissant calls it the point 'where our problems lay in wait

---

23 Representative examples might include Argueta's *Little Red Riding Hood in the Red Light District* (1998 [1977, rev. 1996]), Carpentier's *Kingdom of this World* (1989 [1949]), Chamoiseau's *Texaco* (1998 [1992]), Ngugi's *Wizard of the Crow* (2006), Pepetela's *The Return of the Water Spirit* (2002 [1995]) and Yi Mun-Yol's *The Poet* (2001 [1992]).

for us', and Harris views it as simultaneously constituting the problem (the colonial conquest, for example) and containing within itself the seeds of a radically different future to the one that was materialized under imperialism. This unfulfilled potential – a potential Harris elsewhere refers to as a 'phenomenal legacy' – is represented by the folk in *Palace of the Peacock* and must be uncovered to rethink history: as a past that did not come to fruition, it must be brought into and concretized in the present so as to transform the future. (Niblett 2012a: 65)[24]

We might emphasise the relative singularity of a specifically *colonialist* violence here. As Benita Parry has cautioned, it is surely necessary to take the measure of

> the extent and degree of the coercions visited on those societies that were seized for their natural and labour resources, or invaded for both material and political reasons. Such determinants inflected the singular accents of the modernisms in these locations, registering a consciousness of a violent imperialism that we will not expect to find in Eastern Europe or Portugal. (2009: 29)

The key point here, as Niblett elaborates it in a recent essay, is that while in such specifically colonial theatres as the Caribbean, 'colonial conquest involved the near complete destruction of pre-existing social formations', in other regions – semi-peripheral Europe, for instance, or 'territories subject to informal colonialism' – 'the penetration of capitalist modes and structures has occurred in less extreme or abrupt fashion' (2012b: 23). As Niblett explains, this difference in the intensities of social violence accompanying the forced incorporation of particular territories (as peripheries) into the world-system has potentially decisive implications for culture. For '[i]f irrealism comes to the fore in those periods when "all that is solid melts into air"', we might suppose that it would 'wane as an aesthetic strategy once the emergent conditions have been stabilized and new socio-ecological unities created' (23). And this stabilisation is more likely to occur in the 'economically driven' circumstances of capitalist globalisation, for instance, than in the more 'politically driven' circumstances of the colonial project.

Niblett refers us to Sylvia Wynter's seminal analysis of the relation between the form of the novel and the plantation system in the Caribbean – the latter 'inseparable from external domination, its systematic extraction of surplus value and natural wealth fostering economic and environmental underdevelopment'. In Wynter's analysis, 'the rise of the capitalist world-economy, as both cause and effect of the region's plantation-societies, marked "a change of such

---

24 The internal quotations here are from Glissant 1989: 26, 25; and Harris 1981: 45. See also Niblett 2013, which discusses the 'conflicting ecologies' of sugar and cassava in *The Guyana Quartet*: the former 'mediating the impact of plantation capitalism on Guyana', the latter underpinning 'an aesthetic of the socio-ecological totality' (148).

world-historical magnitude that we [in the Caribbean today] are all, without exception, still 'enchanted', imprisoned, deformed and schizophrenic in its bewitched reality'" (Niblett 2012b: 22).[25] Because it is impossible in existing circumstances to imagine the Caribbean as free of external domination, Niblett speculates, 'the irrealist current in the corresponding literary texts [...] is also likely to be a constant narrative tendency' (23). This 'irrealist current' he finds not only in the forms of writing where it is widely recognised as existing, such as in the 'marvellous realism' of the 1950s or in the work of such subsequent authors as Harris, Chamoiseau and Wynter herself, but equally in a whole array of so-called 'realist' fictions, all the way from the barracks-yard novels of prominent representatives of the 'Trinidad Awakening' of the 1930s (James, Mendes, etc.), through the 'West Indian' generation of the 1950s (Selvon, Lamming, etc.), to such contemporary authors as Lovelace and Kempadoo.[26]

V

Sociological studies suggest that one prerequisite of the consolidation and rise to prominence of literary realism in nineteenth-century Europe was the prior emergence of bureaucracies (state and para-state, public and private) charged with the task of collecting, storing and disseminating 'value-free' and 'objective' data, and legitimated by their success in doing so. The crisis of absolutism that lay behind the development of the modern state form saw an army of professionals being newly created to produce normative, analytical data: about population, the economy, jurisprudence, social deviance, social migration, the movement of 'masterless men' from the country to the city, and so on (Bauman 1987: 38–50). The accumulated information produced by this corps of professionals – increasingly, experts in the collection and classification of particular forms of knowledge, and trained in their fields of specialisation – would come in time to constitute the 'raw material' from which the realist novel would itself be processed. The epistemo-political basis upon which is erected the work of such nineteenth-century writers as, say, Flaubert, Eliot, Howells, Fontane and Prus is altogether different from that underlying the work – variously 'sentimental', 'picaresque' or 'romantic' – of writers who had preceded them by only fifty years or so.

Let us briefly consider Marx's *Capital* itself, in terms of its 'realist' project. While the text has been influentially read by S.S. Prawer (1976) as a signal contribution to 'world literature', and celebrated as such for its erudite intertextuality and virtuosic incorporation of the tropology of the gothic

---

25 The internal quotation here is from Wynter 1971.
26 Even the work of Naipaul warrants (re-)consideration in these terms. See the interesting discussion in Krishnan 2012 of the registration of what he calls 'historical derangement' in Naipaul's writing.

novel, it is also one of the first great achievements of the realist impulse. Without the data collected in the *Blue Books*, for example, or the existence of a more or less open reading room in the British Library, *Capital* would not have been possible. The work's extraordinary scholarship is dependent on the existence of a set of bureaucratic institutions devoted to the production and dissemination of knowledge: it was the accumulation and concentration of work produced, in multiple spheres, by dedicated professionals and experts that allowed Marx to analyse factory conditions and industrial relations at a distance. But then the proliferation of gothic and spectral tropes throughout *Capital* in the attempt to describe the abstractions of capital and commodity fetishism must be taken to suggest its author's recognition of the failure of 'realist' representation in certain respects or with regard to certain objects. In his 1890 'Reminiscence on Marx', Lafargue (2002) wrote that Marx 'did not publish a single work without repeatedly revising it until he had found the most appropriate form'. In these terms the resort in *Capital* to a revelatory, irrealist vocabulary that magnetises the literary form of both the gothic novel and the archaic materials of fairy tale and fabulous monsters must be taken as motivated – indeed, as consciously chosen: a vocabulary to model a particular order of reality relatively inaccessible to 'realist' representation.

If we now move back into the literary realm and consider the example of Multatuli's (Eduard Douwes Dekker's) *Max Havelaar* (1982 [1860]), we can see that the novel's biting critique of Dutch colonial policy in Java and the East Indies is made possible not only by the author's experience as a functionary in the colonial service, but by his access to documentation on the cultivation and tax collection systems of the Dutch colonial state. Relying on (and re-processing) data drawn from the state's own archives, Dekker's novel achieves something like a global awareness of the historical situation in the colonies – an awareness that exceeds the capabilities of first-person or eye-witness reportage. But again, as with *Capital*, the realist register of *Max Havelaar* is repeatedly undercut by irrealist techniques: the extraordinary split narration, frame narrative, and generically incongruous incorporation of indigenous Javanese materials such as the story of Saïjah and Adinda, for instance. We read these splits and incongruities as indicative of the text's formal registration of the compound instability of life as experienced in the periphery of the Dutch East Indian colonies and its bitter awareness that the lives of complacent luxury enjoyed by the Dutch bourgeoisie 'at home' and the colonial elite 'abroad' are precisely a product of their exploitation of peripheral populations and resources. The 'reality' of coffee merchant Droogstoppel's bombastic and mercenary world-view is deliberately undermined by the narrative construction, while an alternative 'reality', that of the abject native populace, is counter-posed through the use of residual indigenous materials. Realist content is thus conjoined to a tendency on the secondary level of form towards peripheral irrealism, particularly expressed through the literary device of unreliable narration – and here we might recall Moretti's list of 'uneasy narrators' appearing throughout semi-peripheral literatures from

India to Japan, who persistently signal the adaptation of particular imported literary devices in order to register the local experience of combined and uneven development (2004: 152–58).

The logic of peripheralisation is such that it has often not been possible for non-core societies to construct strong, centralising state apparatuses; where these existed previously, they have often been left crippled or destroyed. (Semi-)peripheral intellectuals have consequently been confronted with an underdevelopment or deficit of institutions of normative knowledge production in their own societies. In fact, to the degree that these institutions do exist in the peripheral states, they are often strongly subordinated to the interests of the core powers, so that the knowledge that emerges from them often functions to disempower local peoples. This, after all, is the thrust and effect of all colonial epistemologies – one thinks of the District Commissioner's prospective work on 'The Pacification of the Primitive Tribes of the Lower Niger' in the concluding paragraph of *Things Fall Apart*. In such instances, information given a selective veneer as 'facts' is often presented, and perceived, as antagonistic to emancipation, even at the level of its 'truthfulness'. In this light, the critique of 'Eurocentric' knowledge not only represents an insight into the power wielded by knowledge produced and imposed by 'Europeans' and 'European' agencies, but at the same time registers frustration by members of the peripheralised middle classes at being unable to develop state institutions for their own benefit, without the interference of external interests. On the other hand, local agents interested in contesting their domination must confront the peripheral state and its institutions as complicit in their domination. Whereas Marx in London could tacitly accept the validity of Blue Book data, anti-colonial and anti-capitalist agents in the peripheries often cannot be sure of the adequacy of information produced about their own societies. We think here again of Wynter's observation that all history in the plantation context is perceived by Caribbean peoples as 'a fiction written, dominated, controlled by forces external to itself' (1971: 95), so that reality itself comes to seem irreal; or of Schwarz's analogous observation that conditions in Latin America are such as almost inevitably to produce scepticism. In such conditions, the emergence of 'ideal-type' realism is foreclosed or sidetracked, and there is a resort to other (at times informal) institutions of local knowledge production. Such sources are frequently those displaced by the arrival of external agencies; associated with backcountry or agrarian lifeworlds, their substance remains comparatively weakly capitalised.

It would be a mistake to see these latter institutions as more 'authentic' than official ones, or as truly archaic. 'Tradition' here comes into existence not as the lingering forms of the past but as the coeval other of 'modernity'. It is better to understand the phenomenon *politically*: since neither the state nor the statist institutions of knowledge production are trusted, other institutions must be summoned, and these tend to be repositories of non-normative or numinous forms of folkloric knowledge, located in alternative cultural archives, often those depending on oral story-telling practices, embodied performance and the use of dialect. Culturally speaking, then, irrealist innovations, such as we find represented in the Latin American 'New Narrative' and 'Boom' novels, or in the *New Portuguese Letters* of the 'three Marias' (Barreno, Horta and Da Costa 1994 [1972]), correspond to the evolution of new forms of realism, registering not only the socio-economic experience of combined and uneven development (in general), but also the specific historical conditions of the Latin American *dispositif* or of Portugal in the final years of the dictatorship. In such instances the assumed facticity of conventional realist accounts cannot be relied upon since the institutions that produce it are either weakly present or too ideologically compromised.

In drawing attention to the fact that realism's consolidation in the core nations of the world-system in the nineteenth century is dependent on the rise of institutionalised archives and forms of knowledge production, we are not of course arguing for a normative account of realism. Quite the contrary: our interest lies in placing 'ideal-type' realism in relation to the host of different realisms that emerge from colonies and (semi-)peripheral locations, many driven by anti-colonial, nationalist, subalternist and leftist politics – among them varieties of socialist realism, the Chinese critical and social realist traditions associated with Lu Xun, Mao Dun and Ding Ling, the writing of members of the All-India Progressive Writers' Movement, the work produced in the 'fighting phase' (Fanon 1968 [1961]: 222ff) of African nationalist and liberation movements, and South American varieties of regionalist realism and *testimonio*. This is not even to explore the working-class and regional realist traditions from the peripheries of the cores. As Joseph Cleary argues,

> even though realism was devalued and pushed to the prestige-periphery of the old Europe-centred world literary system by the emergence of modernism, realism as such did not simply disappear or merely become calcified after modernism; instead, realism, an always mutating mode, underwent further major mutations after modernism and was developed along classical-traditionalist and populist or 'low-brow' as well as socialist and proletarian or subaltern trajectories. Moreover, new technologies such as radio, cinema and television stimulated new realisms in these media also, adding to the literary varieties. (2012: 267)

A central factor animating the formation of these multiple modes of realism and accounting for their surges to dominance at various periods is the presence or absence of the collective forces necessary to change a regime or challenge a particular state formation from below. The realisms that achieve the most full-fledged and dominant expression are consequently those associated with revolutions or liberation movements, with their investments in a conception of reality as apprehensible and accessible to realist representation springing directly from their political commitments. Adapting Fanon's idea of a 'fighting phase' in literary history, we might then speak of various 'fighting realisms', whose investment is not merely in mapping present realities but in the revelation of possible futures and emergent social orders. Jameson makes the point that realism should not be too narrowly defined in terms of a fixed or static processing of the available facts of a particular social order, but should be imagined in relationship to 'a history in movement and a future on the point of emergence' (2012: 479). Realism 'would thus have to do with the revelation of tendencies rather with than the portrayal of a state of affairs [...] History is in that sense like Heideggerian Being: it cannot be looked at or perceived directly or head-on; it emerges and disappears; one has to seize it at the moment of emergence' (479–80). When this moment of emergence becomes perceptible to collective society – as in the process of anti-colonial or revolutionary struggle – realist representations of the 'ideal-type' sometimes do flourish. (One example that might be given is of South African literature in the decades of the 1960s and 1970s.[27]) But in those conditions where such collective awareness is not available, or when the forms of knowledge that emerge from peripheral institutions are oriented specifically towards disempowerment, this kind of realism tends to prove inadequate, as Jameson goes on to suggest:

> This is why a historical realism of this kind falters when it attempts to deal with situations in which historical movement is not perceptible (the colonial situation, for example); and it is also left perplexed when the historical currents of a society are buried under layers of appearance of Lukacsian 'second nature' (our own society of the spectacle would appear to correspond to his dilemma). 'Essence does not always appear', to paraphrase the great Hegelian watchword'. (480)

We might examine this tendency in the Latin American context, where the dominant literary inclination from the nineteenth century into the earlier decades of the twentieth was realistic, as found representation both in the Romantic nationalist novels that emerged in tandem with the attainment of political independence, and in the autochthonous fictions of various kinds – the *novella de la tierra*, *criollista* fictions, regionalist novels dedicated to documentation of regional folkways – that flourished from 1900 into the 1930s. As Philip Swanson remarks, however, 'many of the major so-called realist novels to appear in Latin America [in the nineteenth century] [...] do not really stand comparison with the European Realism of, say, Balzac, Dickens or Galdós, or the Naturalism of, say Zola or the early Pardo Bazán' (2005: 14). The nationalist romances and allegories were invariably haunted by the kinds of incongruities that Roberto Schwarz remarked in Alencar's works, expressive of the mismatch within them between genre and local social relations; the regionalist novels that then followed in the 1920s were marked both by their ambivalence about the Eurocentrism of the received Romantic inheritance and by their desire to 'avoid the Dickensian or Galdosian model of Realism which seemed to deal mainly with urban life' (Swanson 2005: 23).

---

27 Consider the work during these decades – not always successful – of such writers as Brutus, La Guma, Gordimer, Kuzwayo, Serote and Tlali, for instance.

As Swanson makes clear, the overweighting of the Boom novel in recent histories of Latin American literature has served to create the impression of a gulf between the aesthetic experimentalism of that vaunted formation and the aesthetic of the earlier 'regionalist' novels, whose narrative ambiguities and ambivalences have not been sufficiently thought through. The portrait that has been painted of regionalist fiction as embodying a 'simplistic black-and-white social realism' is not sustainable (Swanson 2005: 28). Even when it was most dominant, moreover, the realist imperative in pre-Boom Latin American writing tended to exist alongside avant-gardist initiatives, such as are represented in Chilean writer María Luisa Bombal's gothic, posthumously narrated *The Shrouded Woman* (1938), for instance, or in Colombian José Eustasio Rivera's 1924 commodity fiction *The Vortex*, whose documentary realist attempt to expose the evils of the rubber trade is constantly undermined by narrative unreliability and the madness of its central protagonist, or the phantasmagorical stories of Uruaguayan Felisberto Hernández,[28] with their dizzying array of talking cigarettes, water-filled dolls and erotic relations with objects and furniture which capture a new era of commodity relations. All of this suggests that realism in the Latin American literary tradition was never governed by a passive objectivism, but typically manifested scepticism and ideological ambivalence, whether unconsciously, as formal and generic incongruity, or deliberately, in the incorporation of fantastic and avant-gardist methods, devices and effects.

A variant of 'ideal-type' realism flourished and achieved sub-generic dominance in the Mexican novel of the revolution in the 1920s and 1930s. Historically, the Mexican revolution was characterised not only by the mobilisation of the peasantry but also by the revolt of the middle class against the Porfiriato dictatorship and the *latifundia*. Mariano Azuela's paradigmatic novel of the revolution, *The Underdogs* (2006 [1915]), can be seen as the direct attempt to give voice to the collective forces of the period, albeit through a liberal bourgeois rather than properly radical perspective of the revolution, thus reflecting the ambivalent role of the middle classes. Even though it has often been seen as paradigmatic of the overly simplistic social realism of revolutionary novels, however, Azuela's novel in fact problematises such a reductive construction. Its realist approach is complicated by an 'uncertainty in point of view' and coupled with a 'fragmentary or episodic structural pattern' (Swanson 2005: 28), and the text is marked throughout by an attempt to incorporate indigenous and residual folk values, particularly in its rhetoric of heroic indigenous Indo-American fertility. For Swanson, therefore, whose lead we follow here, realism might have been the 'main narrative force' in Latin America in the early twentieth century, but it always appeared in an ambivalent guise that 'contained the seeds of its own transcendence' and that coexisted alongside surrealist, avant-garde and vanguardia movements, particularly in other literary genres such as poetry. All of these currents together would give

---

28 See the narratives collected in *Piano Stories* (Hernández 1993), for example.

rise to the new narratives of Asturias, Arguedas and Rulfo and the 'magical realism' of Boom novelists such as García Márquez and Fuentes, marking the transition from the emulation of received forms to the manufacture of new ones capable of capturing more adequately the experience and temper of social life in the (semi-)peripheries and of articulating more sharply the scepticism of intellectuals towards their distorted state formations and their sense that earlier revolutionary aspirations had been betrayed or incorporated.[29]

Michael Denning has proposed that magical realism, including the Mexican variety, had its roots both in left-wing writers' movements – the 'novelists' international' – and in the radical critique of capitalist society articulated in surrealism (2004: 51–72). By the 1940s and the 1950s, Mexican intellectuals' sense of the betrayal of the Revolution by the PRI, which had consolidated itself as an authoritarian state in collusion with predatory US capital interests even as it fanned a constant smokescreen of revolutionary rhetoric, had reached a peak. Given the state's co-option of radical rhetorics, the realist forms of representation previously associated with the expression of revolutionary politics could not help but be tarnished, and what had formerly seemed radical now came to seem accommodationist. The political dispensation of realism shifted towards irrealism, which moved into a position of dominance by the 1960s. The intense commodification of Latin American magical realism in the world-literary market in the ensuing decades (similar – and linked – to the commodification of the form of 'South Asian magical realism' exemplified by Salman Rushdie) has led to a stripping away of its original radical politics and the emergence of reactionary forms consonant with the tastes of metropolitan cultural elites. Texts of this latter kind demonstrate no conscious or critical registration of social unevenness but tend rather to a facile aesthetics in which globalism, hybridity and connectivity are idealised and celebrated: hence the distinction between 'faithful' and 'irreverent' modes of 'magical realism' that Chris Warnes (2009) draws in his comparative reading of South Asian, West African and Latin American magical realisms.[30] For us, this suggests a general tendency within the history of the world-literary system, where, as Jameson remarks, 'in one situation a modernist stance may be progressive (for a time), while in another it is rather the realist impulse which will be politically (and culturally) indispensable', since '[w]hat is progressive may very well harden into its opposite as the situation evolves, and the balance may well shift the other way' (2012: 483–84).

---

29 Hence the dissolution of realist conventions in Juan Rulfo's *Pedro Páramo* (1987 [1955]), for example, and the invention of a Mexican gothic irrealism couched in a fragmentary structure drawing on indigenous Amerindian mythology and orality. Rulfo's novel expresses a profound crisis of confidence in the PRI.

30 An example from another contemporary context of a magical realist text that caters to elite tastes is the swollen behemoth of Haruki Murakami's *1Q84* (2011), a domesticated cousin, we suppose, of Roberto Bolaño's properly world-systemic *2666*.

CHAPTER THREE

'Irrealism' in Tayeb Salih's *Season of Migration to the North*

There is now widespread interest in identifying the particularities of peripheral modernism, even when this is rarely named as such and even though its provenance remains unexplained. In emphasising that the internally differentiated peripheries and semi-peripheries of core capitalism extended and still extend to a larger geo-political expanse than the once-colonised regions, we assume a world-system driven to expand into the non-capitalist worlds, whether through military conquest and occupation, or gun-boat diplomacy, or the export of capital. However, we also observe the extent and degree of the coercions visited on those societies that were seized for their natural and labour resources, or invaded for both material and political reasons. Such determinants, we suggest, inflect the singular accents of literatures from these locations, engendering a consciousness of a violent capitalism that we will not expect to find in the writings of Eastern Europe or Portugal. Moreover, most of the regions once occupied and ruled by the imperialist powers continue to function as the hinterlands of capitalism's power centres, even where spectacular economic development is taking place, and are home to the majority of the world's wholly dispossessed.[1]

It is on such grounds that our reading of a novel from the peripheries departs from the assumptions of critics indifferent to the ways in which such literatures dramatise the trauma of modernity: for here the precipitate and selective introduction of capitalist productive and social modes into a non-capitalist environment produced incompatible material and existential situations, generating aesthetic forms encoding these disjunctions and constituting their stylistic peculiarities. Consider then the implication of Susan Stanford Friedman's (2006) challenge to the received conception of modernity as a 'western' invention. In attempting to reverse the systematic

---

1 See Davidson 2006a and Davis 2006.

rexclusion from the critical literature of 'the creative agencies of colonial and postcolonial subjects as producers of modernism' (428), she refers us to the 'indigenization' and 'cannibalism' of cultural traditions from the 'west' made possible by 'contact zones' (430–33). Yet while she complains about the 'curse of derivativeness' attaching to colonial and postcolonial modernisms (432), she herself situates 'Western aesthetics' (431) as the source and origin of the ('non-western') innovations she sets out to celebrate. To resolve the contradiction in her argument, she proposes the existence of 'alternative modernities' – a compensatory move that has the effect, as we have already argued above, of removing the particular inflections of social life in the contexts of colonial and postcolonial relations from the 'singular modernity' defined by Fredric Jameson as inseparable from capitalism in its global trajectory.

'De-westernising' modernism also concerns Andreas Huyssen, who questions accounts of classical modernism that overlook the modernisms of Latin America, Mexico, the Caribbean and China, and ignore the ways in which metropolitan culture has been 'translated, appropriated and creatively mimicked in colonial and post colonial countries in Asia, Africa and Latin America' (2005: 6). But because Huyssen places his emphasis on the transformative quality of the 'negotiation with the modern of the metropolis' (9), his would-be revisionary account itself situates metropolitan modernism as prior and normative, as a model that has been mimicked or replicated elsewhere (however 'creatively'). Moreover, it diverts attention from what is formally distinctive about peripheral modernism: what Jameson has termed the 'generic discontinuities' of peripheral literatures, and which involve much more than a 'transformative negotiation with the modern of the metropolis', arising as they do from situations described by Neil Larsen as 'both modern and traditional, both "ahead of" and yet "behind the times" at once, as if not one but two or multiple histories were being lived out in one and the same space' (Larsen 2001: 139–40).

Our expectation is that the writing produced in such locations is likely to be sensitive to absurdity and contradiction, disturbance and disruption, conflict and resistance, and it may well be found that the mismatches and improbable juxtapositions of the novel that we propose to consider here, *Season of Migration to the North*, have formal and structural affinities with other novels from the peripheries. This work was written in Arabic by the Sudanese writer Tayeb Salih, was originally published in Beirut in 1967 and was published in English in 1969, and our access to it is through translation. Nuances of language, allusions and much else will doubtless be lost to us as non-Arabic readers relatively unacquainted with Sudan. (We might mention immediately the repeated notations of time spans in the novel: five, seven, thirty and a thousand years, whose portent is sometimes implied but never specified.[2])

---

2 The lives of the two narrators are measured out in spans of years: the first narrator spends seven years of study in England, returning at age twenty-five; Mustafa Sa'eed's migration to the North lasts for thirty years, his imprisonment

Despite this constraint, we will venture a reading of this mysterious and secretive novel that is at the same time an overtly political book, replete with specific cultural materials and long-ranging historical resonances, and born of a consciousness of the ubiquitous ramifications of capitalism throughout the world.[3] On the assumption that the novel's cognitive and aesthetic dimensions are inseparable, we will attempt to retrieve its historically located substance and social and political registers from both 'story' and stylistics. But it seems to us that any attempt at a realist reading will be frustrated by a narrative that openly accommodates transgressions of credibility and is hospitable to the phantasmagoric.

Perhaps then we could refer to the novel as inhabiting what Michael Löwy has called 'a border territory, between reality and "irreality"' (2007: 196). A Marxist theorist and renowned interpreter of Lukács, Löwy devised the term 'critical irrealism' to describe an aesthetic 'founded on a logic of the imagination, of the marvellous, of the mystery or the dream' (194), in which what is created, accordingly, is 'an imaginary world, composed of fantastic, supernatural, nightmarish or simply *nonexistent* forms' (205). Crucially for our purposes, critical irrealism as theorised by Löwy does not, for all its investment in imagination and the imaginary, deny the existence of natural and social words independent of human perception or apprehension. This foundational homage to realism, or remembrance of it, gives critical irrealist texts the ability to articulate powerful critiques of actually existing reality, which, as Löwy writes, have variously taken the forms of 'protest, outrage, disgust, anger, anxiety, or *angst*' – as, for example, in Romanticism's opposition to capitalist-industrialist modernity, or surrealism's celebration of eroticism and obsessive love and its merciless skewering of the bourgeois social order (193–200).

Herbert Marcuse has observed the capacity of aesthetic critique to conjure up 'modes of perception, imagination, gestures' that shatter 'everyday experience', arguing that art possesses the means to estrange and subvert the quotidian by defying dominant social practices and ordinary modes of consciousness (1979: 7).[4] For Marcuse, moreover, 'the radical qualities of art,

---

    seven years and his stay in the village five years. The precise significance of the numerated years in which seven recurs is not apparent to us but would no doubt be of interest to those who attribute metaphysical or magical properties to particular numbers. Note too the repetition of the thousand years of European aggression.

3 During a conversation reported as being held in post-independence Sudan, a minor figure, Mansour, reprimands an Englishman employed by the Ministry of Finance: 'You transmitted to us the disease of your capitalist economy' (Salih 2003: 60).

4 Marcuse is here following Adorno: 'There is no content, no formal category of the literary work that does not, however transformed and however unawarely, derive from the empirical reality from which it has escaped' (1992a: 89). On Marcuse, see Robinson 1969, Jameson 1971 and Katz 1982.

that is to say, its indictment of the established reality and its invocation of the beautiful image (*schöner Schein*) of liberation are grounded precisely in the dimensions where art *transcends* its social determination and emancipates itself from the given universe of discourse and behaviour while preserving its overwhelming presence' (6). This idea that literature can constitute 'a subterranean rebellion against the social order' (20) by revealing 'tabooed and repressed dimensions of reality' (19) may provide an insight into *Season of Migration to the North*'s startling and problematic critique of imperialism, which, we will suggest, proceeds through its establishment of an analogy between the insult and violence inflicted on subordinated peoples, on the one hand, and a degrading and death-driven heterosexual eroticism, on the other.

From the very beginning, conventional narration in the novel is inhibited by formalities that draw on traditional Arabic modes. One is the hieratic popular oral delivery of the *hakawati*, a public teller of tales in the Arab world ('It was, gentlemen, after a long absence [...] that I returned to my people' [Salih 2003: 1] is a an address that echoes the traditional opening 'You will recall, gentlemen'). The other is mimicry of a sophisticated literary technique, *mu-arada* (or *mucdradah*), which adheres to strict dialogical rules of proposition and counter-proposal.[5] This last is used to hold in tension and position as irreconcilable the differing stances of the narrator (named as Meheimeed in the Arabic original, but nameless in the English translation) and Mustafa Sa'eed – such as attachment to and alienation from the traditional, attraction and resistance to modernity, and the pleasures and pains of place and displacement.

The artifice of the whole is enhanced by a narrative in which there is a discrepancy between the chronology of events and the order in which these are related: reference to future events is prematurely made, and there are recollections of moments that precede their telling. This is further enhanced by the diegetic address in which the English-educated narrator presents a retrospect on his own experiences and his perceptions of others' lives to a select group of his peers. A closed circle, these intimates appear to be members of an elite connected to the local and rural but conversant with the distant and metropolitan – a familiarity manifest in their assumed ability to recognise allusions to both Arabic and European literary sources, without the need for any gloss. These span on the one hand the poets Abu Nuwas and

---

5 See Harlow 1985. See also Aziz 1996: '*Al-hakawati* is a Syrian term for this poet, actor, comedian, historian and storyteller. Its root is *hikayah*, a fable or story, or *haka*, to tell a story; *wati* implies expertise in a popular street-art. The hakawati is neither a troubadour, who travels from place to place, nor a *rawi*, whose recitations are more formalized and less freely interpreted. The hakawati has popular counterparts in Egypt, where he is often called *sha'ir*, or poet, and where he accompanies his tales on a *rababah*, a simple stringed instrument. In Iraq he is known as *qisa khoun*.'

el-Abbasi, a mythic figure El Kadr, and the golden age of Adad,[6] and on the other the titles of the exclusively English books on Mustafa Sa'eed's shelves in the visible but secret wing of his village house (Salih 2003: 137). Yet beyond the immediate cosmopolitan auditors is an implied larger audience, to whose partial knowledge or total ignorance no concessions are made;[7] from them the novel keeps secrets even when, as often, it feigns the transparency of an artless tale.

At the same time the novel inscribes the immediacy of history as the narrative moves between a present in post-independence Sudan in the late 1950s and Bohemian circles of the Imperial City in the 1920s and 1930s. London is the lodestar for both Mustafa Sa'eed and the narrator, who, in different decades, move from villages in the North of Sudan to the British capital (for Mustafa Sa'eed the journey north from a village to London is via the cities of Khartoum and Cairo) in pursuit of education and opportunity.[8] The respective journeys however map different directions and arrivals: Mustafa Sa'eed's migration to London is driven by elective deracination and the ostensible embrace of all that is not the South – seen by the narrator as 'the pursuit of a foreign mirage' (93). The narrator for his part has also lived in London, but he has 'lived with them [the English] superficially, neither loving nor hating them' (49); while away he is sustained by affection for tradition and community that on his return is destined to be undermined by painful dislocation. Let us consider key aspects of each of these journeys, starting with that of the narrator.

There is no discernible irony in the account of his first return to his native village after his studies in England. Delighted by the genius of his birth-place, he is aware that 'the sound of the wind passing through palm-trees is different from when it passes through fields of corn' (2); feels 'a sense of stability [...] I am continuous and integral' (5); is gratified by the organic composition of his grandfather's house, built of mud, an extension of the field on which it stands (71); and speculates that he 'must be one of those birds that exist only in one region of the world' (49).

Initially charmed by the vibrant community spirit and conviviality of his village, and reassured by its apparent equilibrium, he observes with pleasure its appropriation of modern technology. Doors fashioned from whole trees

---

6 El Kadr: the 'green man' of the Islamic tradition, a supernatural being in folklore; Abu Nuwas: a poet of the eighth century CE, influenced by Sufism and a celebrant of gay love; the age of Adad: the golden age of the Assyrians, reputed to have lasted from 33 to 1300 CE; and the poet el-Abbasi (1881–1963), born in Egypt and attracted to the nomadic life of the Bedouin of western Sudan.

7 See Allan's discussion of the 'problem of address' in *Season* (2007).

8 Anouar Majid links *Season* to Cheikh Hamidou Kane's *Ambiguous Adventure* and Ken Bugul's *The Abandoned Baobab* in this respect: in all three texts, he writes, the central protagonists are 'inserted in colonial educational systems that delink them from their traditional milieux and interpellate them into a modernity experienced as a series of multiple alienations' (Majid 2000: 79).

by the local carpenter are replaced by mass-produced ones made of iron; the donkey is supplemented by the motor vehicle; and local political initiatives, such as the building of a hospital and schools, are visibly altering an antique, but not timeless, landscape. But while the reserves and energies of a rural Islamic society in Africa are identified by the narrator, so too, and increasingly during his returns from metropolitan Khartoum, where he is employed as a teacher, are the constraints of its traditions; and having begun his story by reiterating 'I am from here', he comes to lament 'There is no room for me here' (130), his experience of the tragic coercions of custom and his acquaintance with the wider vistas known to the deracinated Mustafa Sa'eed having thrown his former happy assurance into disarray. So it is that on overhearing a bawdy conversation between the village elders, he measures his distance from their sensibilities concerning sexual relations and customary marriage norms by observing that their traditions are moribund: 'I looked at them: three old men and an old woman laughing awhile as they stood at the grave's edge' (85).

His accumulating unease at Mustafa Sa'eed's minatory influence on his own inclinations climaxes when after the death or disappearance of the man he has come to hate, he searches the visible but sealed room Mustafa Sa'eed had built onto his house in the village. Here he examines inscriptions on photographs of Mustafa Sa'eed's English lovers, recalling the stories he had been told about the frozen images, and on finding assorted papers – poems, fragments of a memoir – he hears Mustafa Sa'eed talking in his head, transcribing the words never committed to the blank 'My Life Story'. After which, he tells us, 'I left him talking […] I did not let him complete the story' (166). Seeking to dispel his rage by entering the river, he finds himself 'half-way between north and south, unable to continue, unable to return' (167), at which moment the hunger for survival prompts him to 'choose life' by screaming for help: 'there are people I want to stay with […] I have duties to discharge […] I shall live by force and cunning' (169). We will return to the possible import of this gesture to the future.

If the narrator articulates a yearning for belonging, one that is frustrated but persists, Mustafa Sa'eed by contrast emerges as a man detached from family, and his tale is one of permanent dislocation, even if late in life he sought settlement. The child of a father from the Arab north of the country, who had died when his son was in infancy, and a remote and reticent mother, a slave from the African south, Mustafa Sa'eed's genealogy internalises the scissions and entanglements of Sudan: as he later tells an infatuated English lover who is confused at his appearance: 'I'm like Othello – Arab-African' (38). This benign construction conceals the geo-political and cultural divide within Sudan, where the North – relatively affluent, culturally Islamic, with ties to the Arab world – dominates and exploits an impoverished South that is paradoxically rich in natural and mineral resources, that is ethnically African, in religion both Christian and animist as well as Muslim, and regarded by the North as without civilisation. Allusions to this internal split, together with references to the separation between a village on the Nile and urban Khartoum, register the North as privileged and the South as deprived, disadvantaged and abused, and intimate the economic differentiations within a periphery.[9]

Once in England, and despite his contrived ease with things English – its education, culture, radical politics – Mustafa Sa'eed, the rootless and precocious child who had moved northwards, from Khartoum to Cairo to London, never ceases to perceive himself as an outsider, aware that the English he speaks with such astonishing fluency 'is not my language' (29). The tormented immoralist consumed by *ressentiment* nurses a desire for revenge against his hosts, an urge to injure the imperialist nation, which is played out in his seductions of vulnerable women whom he debauches and betrays, and some of whom are subsequently driven to kill themselves. The cycle culminates in the complicitous murder of his dominant and invulnerable English wife. (We will return to speculate on the import of these and other improbable and fantastic events.) In flight from his catastrophic season abroad, he attempts settlement and family life in a village on the Nile and, after five years, disappears; whether he has drowned or been driven to flee by a kind of nomadic hunger is as unknowable as the cryptic note he leaves: 'Rationally I know what is right: my attempt at living in this village with these happy people. But mysterious things in my soul and in my blood impel me towards faraway places' (67).

In representing the exchange of opposing views on imperialism between a colonial subject (Mustafa Sa'eed) and a postcolonial subject (himself), the narrator, a product of the decolonising era, shows himself to be unperturbed by colonial modernisation: 'The fact that they came to our land, I know not why, does that mean that we should poison our present and our future? Sooner or later they will leave our country [...] The railways, ships, hospitals, factories and schools will be ours and we'll speak their language, without either a sense of guilt or a sense of gratitude' (49–50). However, Mustafa Sa'eed, a child of colonialism and an adherent of anti-imperialist nationalism, delivers an explicit critique: 'The ships at first sailed down the Nile carrying guns not bread, and the railways were originally set up to transport troops; the schools were started so as to teach us how to say "Yes" in their language' (95).[10]

As well as being a writer of analytic anti-imperialist books, Mustafa Sa'eed is the author of phrases drenching imperialism in metaphysical sickness. Hence when explaining that his seductions had awakened the urge to self-immolation

---

9 Salih's novel of course predates the formal splitting up of Sudan and the establishment of South Sudan as an independent state in 2011. Yet its attention to the rifts and discrepancies between Khartoum and the South already points to the factors that would become decisive in the decades following Sudan's formal decolonisation in 1956.

10 Remembrance of colonialism is overtly staged in comments about the schools the rulers had opened – and which the villagers had feared as 'a great evil that had come to them with the armies of occupation' (20).

in his lovers, he invokes images of imperialism as polluted: 'You, my lady, may not know, but you – like Carnarvon when he entered Tutankhamen's tomb – have been infected with a deadly disease which has come from you know not where and which will bring about your destruction' (39). The refrain of a thousand-year-old lethal disease surely alludes to Europe's long imperial history, beginning with pre-capitalist Christian raids on the riches of the Islamic world, followed by capitalism's invasion of uncapitalised spaces, and then by the 'ferocious violence' (151) of the 1914–18 war fought amongst the capitalist nations of Europe over the spoils of empire and the exercise of world-wide power. And indeed in his confessions, Mustafa Sa'eed not only conflates the pathology of this conflict with his own perverted sexual quest, but in both an actual conversation with his interlocutor and an imagined address to the English, he attributes an infectious moral corruption to imperialism, thereby inverting the colonialist dread of defilement by 'foreign' peoples and climes.

The contradictory effects of the capitalist penetration of a pre-capitalist society are patently evoked through an historically exemplary figure, a condition of combined and uneven development being incarnated in the narrator's childhood companion, Majoub. A skilled farmer, prominent in the cooperative ventures of the affluent Muslim village on the Nile, the local official of the National Democratic Socialist Party, who petitions and agitates for schools and the education of girls, for hospitals and an agricultural college (121), this same Majoub continues to intone God's forgiveness and to abide by, without endorsing, the customary marriage arrangements whereby women have no autonomy. In response to the narrator's comment that the world has changed – this following a village tragedy contingent on the subordinate position of women – he replies, 'Some things have changed – pumps instead of water-wheels, iron ploughs instead of wooden ones, sending our daughters to school, radios, cars, learning to drink whisky and beer instead of arak and millet wine – yet even so everything's as it was [...] The world will really have changed when the likes of me become ministers in the government' (100). The last sentiment articulates Majoub's consciousness of class in postcolonial Sudan and his understanding of the anti-imperialist struggle as an unfinished project.

If, as we suggest, *Season of Migration to the North* narrates the coexistence and clash of customary and emergent social and cultural practices in a traditional society in the throes of capitalist modernisation, and if its literary forms are abstracts of this substance, then we must also observe how this substance is itself estranged as it takes on literary form. Thus the representation of space exceeds the description of its physical characteristics, as the political and cultural implications are joined to intimations of the 'irreal': Sudan, 'a stone's throw from the equator' (60), marks a verifiable position on the map; and it alludes also to a place of fantasy in the imperial imagination. The Nile is a real river facilitating the transport of people and goods, and seasonally watering the crops grown on its banks. At the same time it is a mythic waterway, a 'snake god' hungry for victims (39), the torsions of its 'irrevocable journey' northwards (62, 69), across the immense expanse of a sun-scorched desert, following the route of those passages to a destination that the novel situates as both desire and destiny for the ambitious colonial elite from the South.

As with space, so too with time. The multiple temporalities extant in the combined and uneven development of a periphery are sometimes named and more often appear in metaphoric guises. Condensed in the 'season' of the title are time measured by calendar – the chronological system of the Muslim Hegira, or Hijra, marking the significant emigrations of early Islamic history[11] and the secularised almanac of the Christian Era – the recurrent natural cycles regulating the rhythm of agrarian life, and socially ordained occasions such as religious pilgrimages to the holy sites of Islam and secular journeys to foreign lands. Historiographical time is invoked in recall of the Islamic civilisation that had flowered in southern Europe from the seventh century CE, and the Crusaders' assaults on the treasure of the Eastern world – this last registering the beginning of western Europe's thousand-year project of rapacious invasion, culminating with modern imperialism. Significantly, Mustafa Sa'eed's known lifespan coincides with the colonisation of Sudan: born in 1898, when Anglo-Egyptian rule, which was effectively British domination, was imposed on Sudan after Kitchener's bloody victory over the Mahdi regime at Omdurman,[12] he disappears in 1956, the year in which Sudan, after a long struggle, succeeded in gaining an incomplete and uncertain independence.

---

11 A footnote tells us that this began in 622 CE. Edward Said refers to the voyages narrated by the novel as being converted into a 'sacralized *hegira* from the Sudanese countryside [...] into the heart of Europe' (1993: 255). There are references in the novel also to the journey taken by the narrator's grandfather to Egypt in 1306 of the Muslim calendar (1928 CE).

12 This was in revenge at the death of General Gordon at Khartoum during the Mahdi uprising of 1885, which had overthrown Anglo-Egyptian rule. Contemporary historians regard the Mahdi as an early form of anti-colonial nationalism. 'As the Knight of Empire, Sir Herbert Kitchener, made final preparations to advance, against the flow of the river, upon the town that would soon be looted and burnt to honour his victory, Mustafa Sa'eed was born in one of its dark and apprehensive alleys [...] It is around this bloody encounter and its aftermath, between an independent theocratic Sudan and an insatiable British empire, between [...] a messianic Islam and a missionary Christianity, that the entire destiny of Mustafa Sa'eed revolves' (Seikaly 1985: 136). Conscious of having inverted a subordinate Arab-African persona by taking on the role of an invader and coloniser from the South in his encounters with the Englishwomen he seduces and destroys, Mustafa Sa'eed identifies with, while excoriating, Kitchener's insolent reprimand to the defeated and shackled Mahdi rebel, Mahmoud Wad Ahmed: 'Why have you come to my country to lay waste and plunder?' It is the demented colonial logic here that chafes on Mustafa Sa'eed's sensibility. Thus his explanation: 'It was the intruder who said this to the person whose land it was, and the owner of the land bowed his head and said nothing' (94).

Such historically specific references coexist in Salih's text with accounts of voyages into the uncharted time zones of numinous experience. In the case of the narrator, these are located in a specific culturally infused landscape: travelling through the desert, he endures a hallucinatory suspension of time and dissolution of rational consciousness: 'The road is unending, and the sun merciless [...] The sun is the enemy [...] And thus it will remain for hours without moving – or so it will seem to living creatures when even the stones groan, the trees weep, and the iron cries out for help' (108–11).[13] In Mustafa Sa'eed's experience, the mystical state has historical resonance: for although, when travelling in the realm of the senses (to which we will return), he possesses or is possessed by 'rare moments' of ecstasy, which he remembers as 'outside the bounds of time' (153) and 'worth the whole of life' (61), his destructive love affair with his English wife echoes the violence of the imperialist encounter.

During a lecture at the American University of Beirut in 1980, Salih observed that 'one of the major themes of *Season* is the East/West confrontation *as essentially one of conflict*, whereas it had previously been treated in romantic terms' (quoted in Amyuni 1985: 15; our emphasis). The opposition between an imperialist centre and a distant colonial possession is made known in *Season* by way of reference and allusion to temporal events and memories; this is further underwritten by spatial metaphors – abysses, gulfs, chasms. A functional railway track 'stretching out across the desert like a rope bridge between two savage mountains, with a vast bottomless abyss between them' (Salih 2003: 54) is one of many images configuring a relationship between a subordinated population and the imperial occupier.[14] This recurs in a comment on the argument between an Englishman employed by the post-independence administration and a Sudanese university teacher about imperialism's project and legacy: 'They were not angry; they said such things to each other as they laughed, a stone's throw from the Equator, with a bottomless historical chasm separating the two of them' (69).

Such an understanding does not conform to recent discussions of *Season* in which the excesses of imperialist domination are muted in favour of

---

13 This episode in the novel might be compared with the analogous episode from 'Caves', the central, second part of E.M. Forster's *A Passage to India*. It finds a subsequent echo also in the final pages of Jamal Mahjoub's *Navigation of a Rainmaker*, in which the mortally wounded Tanner hallucinates a conversation with the prophet: '*Too late, it is all much too late. In the open tracts of the western desert the footsteps have long since ceased to echo through the unforgiving silence. The people are assembling from the shadows in numbers, arriving from all directions of necessity to find there is nothing left for charity to give. In the camps refugees huddle together and wait for fate to deliver them. In the markets the paltry gifts are priced and stacked. The grain silos lie empty; even the rats have moved out. The people are on their knees once more and the airlifts are grounded. The relief train lies broken-backed at the bottom of a windless ravine*' (1989: 169–70).
14 This idea receives further elaboration in Parry 2005, 2009

an emphasis on colonialism as an encounter effecting cultural exchange, cross-fertilisation and transformative fusion.[15] In these readings, modernity is detached from capitalism, and the focus is on the novel's figurations of the intermediate as the defining features of a new world modernism that is neither purely European nor purely indigenous. For Susan Stanford Friedman, *Season* stages mimetic cultural encounters, the intermix of the modern and traditional that constitutes 'modernism itself in its different locations' producing 'a hybrid modernity' (2006: 435, 437).[16]

This is a return to the substance of Saree Makdisi's 1992 essay, in which he argued that the novel 'shatters the very terms' of the opposition in the debate between 'traditionalism' and 'Westernism' in postcolonial Arab discourse, as it comes to occupy 'a zone between cultures' (1994: 537). Writing subsequently, Waïl S. Hassan concurs with Makdisi about 'the novel's intervention in the debates over traditionalism and modernity', but proposes that, far from 'reinventing the present', as Makdisi had argued, Salih's fiction 'reveals the bankruptcy of the present and suggests that a correct conceptualization of it lies not in the claims of Western modernity and its Arab champions, nor in those of the traditionalists, but in an often painful and difficult negotiation between old and new, north and south that erases the discursive boundaries within which each has been construed as a timeless essence' (2003: 87–88). For Hassan, *Season* deconstructs the stereotypes of colonial discourse itself, showing instead a variety of 'in between states', and indicating a 'hybridization' that undermines essentialist concepts of self and other (126).[17]

Neither reading strikes us as adequate to the consciousness of irreconcilable political conflict and cultural incommensurability that permeates Salih's novel. Rather than valorise a zone between cultures, *Season of Migration to the North* seems to us to throw into doubt whether such a zone is even *feasible* in the poisonous atmosphere of imperialism.[18] Indeed, in two meticu-

---

15 Our approach to Salih's text is also to be distinguished from earlier 'postcolonialist' readings, which had tended to centre on discussion of difference, alterity and racialised desire. See, for example, Kanneh 1998: esp. 148–52.
16 In a different but related register, Patricia Geesey is concerned with the notions of 'cultural hybridity, grafting and contamination'; these she argues 'operate on symbolic and literal levels in the text', presenting a positive message of bicultural or cultural *grafting* as an antidote to the 'germ' of cultural contagion that may be the negative by-product of European colonial endeavours (1997: 128, 139). Pursuing the problem of address, Roger Allan finds that the novel deals 'with a dislocation that results from the interstitial positioning between the Sudan and England' (2007: 11).
17 Hassan suggests that the novel pits 'several contending discourses' against one another –colonialist and Africanist, traditionalist and secularist Arabisms, Western and Arab patriarchies (2003: 82).
18 In this respect, Salih's novel might be contrasted with two other African novels, Ayi Kwei Armah's *Why Are We So Blest?* (1974) and V.Y. Mudimbe's *The Rift* (1993), which also seek to allegorise colonial relations in terms of intersubjectivity and psychosexuality.

lously described interiors, the book offers cruel parodies of transculturation: Mustapha Sa'eed's room in England, which he calls 'a den of lethal lies' (Salih 2003: 146), is furnished with an amalgam of tawdry artefacts from an undifferentiated Africa-Arabia; while attached to his village home is a simulacrum of an English-style bourgeois house built to hoard the ghoulish mementoes of his migration, its book-lined study containing 'not a single Arab book' (137).

We have attempted to address the political and historical materials infusing the novel and we now want to suggest that the fictive, illusory world of *Season* can be seen as the real world defamiliarised and transcended, while retaining its indelible imprint. Among the many distancing contrivances that intersect and undercut the novel's realist dimensions are melodramatic stories, told in exorbitant prose and conjuring into being an uncanny realm inhabited by outlandish players who may be creatures of Mustafa Sa'eed's fevered imaginings, but feature nevertheless as figures of the psychic deformation inflicted by imperialism. Mustafa Sa'eed exploits his English lovers' delirious longing for the 'tropical climes, cruel suns, purple horizons' of a crudely amalgamated Africa and Arabia (30); and they perceive him in similarly inflammatory images: 'Your tongue's as crimson as a tropic sunset [...] How marvellous your black colour is! [...] the colour of magic and mystery and obscenities [...] I want to have the smell of you in full – the smell of rotting leaves in the jungles of Africa, the smell of the mango and the pawpaw and tropical spices, the smell of rains in the deserts of Arabia' (139, 142). To designate this aspect of the novel as sensational is not a pejorative judgement but rather serves to suggest that animating the confluence of desire, violence and death in relationships under the looming shadow of imperialism cannot be contained in measured language.[19]

Mustafa Sa'eed's chronicle of seducing susceptible English women and inducing their suicides serves as a prelude to his account of the very different liaison with the dominatrix Jean Morris, in which the consensual death-driven sexual relations between the two are inflected by the vengeance sought by the subordinated, on the one hand, and the tyranny exercised by the powerful, on the other.[20] In the course of their deadly erotic games, the Englishwoman insults her lover's physical appearance and punishes him by destroying a rare Arabic manuscript and an antique Isfahan prayer rug, both symbols of his culture.[21] A relationship governed by humiliation and the infliction of physical pain reaches its climax when Mustafa Sa'eed, goaded by

---

19 See Murphy 1998, especially the chapter 'The Poetics of Hysteria: Expressionist Drama and the Melodramatic Imagination': 142–79.
20 See Abu-Haydar 1985, who refers us to Salih's close friendship with the Palestinian poet Tawfiq Sayigh, whose sadomasochistic love affair with English women is transfigured in his verse.
21 We thank Sabry Hafez for pointing this out. Interestingly, the cover photograph of a new Penguin edition of the novel displays, not these items, but the expensive Wedgewood vase which Jean Morris also smashes, juxtaposed with a fabric of indeterminate floral design.

her entreaties and impelled by his own frenzy, stabs Jean Morris, the sexually consummated death remembered by him as a rare moment of ecstasy: 'The sensation that, in an instant outside the bounds of time, I have bedded the goddess of Death and gazed out upon Hell from the aperture of her eyes [...] The taste of that night stays on in my mouth, preventing me from savouring anything else' (153).[22]

If this drama of sadomasochistic hunger[23] is enacted on a stage abundantly furnished with signs of imperialism, then we must also take account of another murderous sexual encounter that takes place in another arena: this is the one between Hosna, Mustafa Sae'ed's widow or deserted wife, and the elderly roué Wad Rayyes. Having received her father's permission to marry Hosna, in accordance with local custom but against her wishes, Wad Rayyes's lust is met with her ferocious resistance, ending in his murder and her suicide. On its own, this event could be read as a critique of the patriarchal norms prevalent in many conservative Islamic societies, and connected to the generality of degraded gender relations, North and South. However, inhibiting this gloss is the fact that the novel's linking of political oppression to the farther shores of the erotic is evidently of tremendous significance, and because an adequate interpretation of this nexus as it emerges in the novel is yet to be produced – indeed it is notable that this has in large been circumvented in the existing discussion – this could send us towards the literature on eroticism.

Georges Bataille remarked that '[s]exual pleasure has so much in common with destruction that we have named the moment of its paroxysm the "little death"', in consequence of which, 'the objects suggesting sexual activity to us are always connected to some disorder' (1994: 203). Violent death as the ultimate experience of rapture for both killer and slain is a staple of pornography, from the literary writings of de Sade and Pauline Réage/Dominique Aury, to illiterate snuff movies/videos, where the performances take place in Nowhere, whether a remote castle or a squalid room. It has also been the subject of mainstream novels such as J.G. Ballard's *Crash* (1973), Muriel Spark's *The Driver's Seat* (1974) and Ian McEwan's *The Comfort of Strangers* (1981), as well as of the art-house Japanese film *In the Realm of the Senses* (1976), in all of which the place and the time of the narratives are either transparent or intimated – indeed, in the case of *Realm of the Senses* critics have noted the connections between the central couple's terminal sadomasochism and

22 This recollected scene enacts 'the terrifying convergence of pleasure and death', a phrase used by Marcuse in his gloss on Freud's theories of the bond between the life instincts and the instincts drawn into the orbit of death, a concurrence that has entered some psychoanalytic writing on eroticism as a normative rather than a deviant variety of sexual experience (Marcuse 1969: 38).
23 In his 1980 lecture, Salih observed that when he first came under the influence of Freud's theory of man as divided between Eros and Death, he recognized this duality as present in the Arab tradition of poetry; later, in *Season of Migration to the North*, he 'tried to dramatize the polarization between the erotic and the other concept which Freud lumps together with Death' (quoted in Amyuni 1985: 15).

the rise of Japanese militarism and fascism.²⁴ In this vein, Salih's novel, which deals with pornographic matter without being pornographic, proffers an intimate link between erotic and imperialist extremity, joining the prodigious language of exorbitant desire pursued in private with imperialist aggression displayed in public, juxtaposing moments of dangerous sexual ecstasy and acts of imperial atrocity, aligning the patently political with the opacity of the psychosexual, and inflecting history with histrionics.²⁵

But *Season* does not end with this drama, and at its close the narrator, in peril of drowning, chooses life, reasserting commitments he had earlier made to the social universe. If he is contemptuous of Africa's corrupt new regimes,²⁶ its ignominious rulers described as 'smooth of face, lupine of mouth, their hands gleaming with rings of precious stones' (Salih 2003: 118), his pride and identification with the achievement and energy of the newly independent Sudanese people is palpable. On seeing the inhabitants of his home village inaugurating cooperative ventures and exercising local democracy, he protests: 'Are these the people who are called *peasants* in books?' (64; original italics) – an acknowledgment that those engaged in socialised agrarian labour, even while retaining connections to vestiges of feudal society, are in the process of developing a class consciousness. Later, when recollecting how, after a punishing journey across a desert, he had lain under a 'beautiful, compassionate' night sky, he recalls musing, 'This is the land of poetry and the possible – and my daughter is named Hope. We shall pull down and we shall build, and we shall humble the sun to our will; and somehow we shall defeat poverty' (112–13). Thus a novel written in the 1960s, when some newly independent societies were striving after some form

---

24 See for instance Turim, who refers to the film's symbolically loaded historical context (1998: 149).
25 There are perhaps affinities with Assia Djebar's *Fantasia: An Algerian Cavalcade* (1993), which disturbingly alternates impressionistic recuperations of the French invaders 'coming as lovers' to Algeria (2) with the record of their brutality – 'the silence of this majestic mourning is but the prelude to the cavalcade of screams and carnage which fill the ensuing decades' – and whose narrator is 'haunted by the agitation of the killers, by their obsessive unease' (57). 'My writing is immediately caught in the snare of the old war between two peoples. So I swing like a pendulum from images of war (a war of conquest and liberation but a war in the past) to the expression of a contradictory and ambiguous love' (216).
26 The novel juxtaposes the grandiose plans for Africa's future that result only in the construction of ostentatious buildings with popular schemes being implemented at a local level in cooperative ventures. This gap between the countryside and the modernised capital city, Khartoum, is imaged in the contrast between a dancing circle spontaneously formed by Bedouins around the narrator's crew on a journey north through the desert and the Independence Hall in Khartoum – 'an imposing edifice [...] constructed in the form of a complete circle', designed in London, using white marble imported from Italy and costing more than a million pounds (119).

of socialism, against the grain of a narrative address which offers no solace, alludes to another time and a different – crucially, a *post-imperial* – condition.

The proximity of discordant discourses and unrelated narrative registers moving between the mundane and the fantastic, the recognisable and the improbable, the legible and the oneiric, the worldly and the mystical, can perhaps be understood as stylistic forms stemming from and transcending the novel's social ground, and thus as abstracts of incommensurabilities attendant on combined and uneven development. Perhaps too the melodramas of sexual violence can be understood as analogous to the crimes committed against the people and the land by capitalism's penetration of pre-capitalist societies. These speculations call on Löwy to account for those occult aspects of the novel that would otherwise escape critical exegesis: 'Even when it takes the superficial form of a flight from reality, critical realism can contain a powerful negative critique', a word not to be understood in this context 'as relating to a rational argument, a systematic opposition or an explicit discourse', but through images of 'a different, nonexistent reality [...] another imaginary world either idealized or terrifying' (196; phrases rearranged).

CHAPTER FOUR

Oboroten Spectres: Lycanthropy, Neoliberalism and New Russia in Victor Pelevin

> In its blind unrestrainable passion, its were-wolf hunger for surplus-labour, capital oversteps not only the moral, but even the merely physical maximum bounds of the working day. It usurps the time for growth, development, and healthy maintenance of the body. (Karl Marx 1965: 24)

Recently, Stephen Shapiro has proposed a re-reading of forms of catachrestic narrative through the prism of world-systems theory in order to pinpoint how narrative devices and modes such as the gothic re-emerge at similar moments in the recurring cycles of long-wave capitalist accumulation (Shapiro 2008: 31). Similarly, anthropologist Michael Taussig has observed that cultural formations consisting of fantastic or magical reactions to 'nonfantastic' reality frequently arise in peripheral societies as a critique of their violent integration into capitalist modes of production, focusing specifically on the figuration of oil as 'devil's excrement' within countries converted to petro-regimes (Taussig 2010: 10, 18). The capitalist world-system, however, should also be understood as a *world-ecology*, in which the social transformations corresponding to different phases of capitalism are inextricable from the reorganisation of nature–society relations. Environmental historian Jason Moore argues that capitalism consists of *ecological regimes*, 'those relatively durable patterns of class structure, technological innovation and the development of productive forces [...] that have sustained and propelled successive phases of world accumulation' (Moore 2010: 392). Under the compulsion of capital's expansionary logic, ecological regimes are periodically driven to exhaustion. These cyclical, systemic occurrences correspond to upswings in gothic and supernatural tropes that register the conjuncture of fading and emergent regimes, prognosticating a revolution in nature–society relations even more pervasive and traumatic than the last. Moreover, when ecological regimes are organised around the production/extraction of single commodities, as is often the case in peripheries and former colonies, the use of catachrestic narrative devices in speculative fiction serves to mediate the intense sensations of spectrality and phantasmagoria resulting from the hyper-commodity fetishism associated with monocultural socio-ecologies.

We have argued above that the 'critical irrealist' aesthetics of texts such as Salih's *Season of Migration to the North* register the impact of combined and uneven development in the colonial periphery. However, this provokes a central typological question in respect to chronology and periodisation: whether there are different moments at which to register these disturbances, so that we could not only detect the violence of penetration under imperialism, the 'highest stage of capitalism', but also read the shock of transition from communism to neoliberal capitalism in the literatures of the former Soviet bloc, or of China, or in texts from post-communist postcolonial countries such as Angola or post-apartheid neoliberal South Africa. Another question revolves around the consciousness of critique within the texts: whether we are reading for the *political unconscious*, the way in which form is unconsciously warped and fissured, or whether we are reading for a 'critical irrealist' politics of form: the self-conscious transformation by authors of those very fissures into sources of innovation which transform the genre of realism. This would be to extend Roberto Schwarz's argument about Brazilian literature to the larger context of world literature, arguing that the 'sore spots' and 'national oddities' in literatures from the peripheries that reflect the asymmetry of the world-system are first reflected as generic discontinuities or unconscious incongruities, then transformed into conscious aesthetic experimentation which embodies negative critique of the world-historical order (Schwarz 1992: 29). A final differentiation would be between so-called 'world-system novels' such as Roberto Bolaño's *2666* (2009), a 'novel-in-parts' whose narrative structure self-consciously encapsulates the structural relations of the world-system, mapping the periphery in relation to other centres and peripheries, and those texts whose content, in stark contrast, is wholly rooted in a singular regional or national context, yet whose form nonetheless reflects their position within the world-system, and which might thus be productively compared to other texts from countries experiencing homologous relations.

In reading contemporary Russian novelist Victor Pelevin's *The Sacred Book of the Werewolf* (2008), we want to gesture towards ways in which world-literature might incorporate literary forms from semi-peripheries of the world-system where the dynamics of combined and uneven development are strikingly registered. The novel is an exemplary text that brings together several threads: the aesthetic registration of the transitions to neoliberal forms of capitalism in the post-Soviet semi-periphery of Europe; and the ways in which speculative fiction can self-consciously appropriate the phantasmic metaphorics of lycanthropy and vampirism to visualise spectral economies of oil and energy, hyper-commodity fetishism and the violent conversion into an ecological regime based on petroleum extraction. The 'resource fictions' and 'energy sources' proposed by Patricia Yaeger (2011) as a new model for reading open up productive possibilities for reading nodal points of capital comparatively across the world-ecology, articulated as networks of resource and energy extraction. Imre Szeman has called for a rethinking of capitalist modernity as oil modernity, to consider the 'history of capital not exclusively in geopolitical terms, but in terms of the forms of energy available to it at any given historical moment' (Szeman 2007: 807). In what follows, we want to explore how Victor Pelevin's novel reflecting Russia's rapid conversion into an authoritarian petro-state might be read as a semi-peripheral resource fiction registering oil shock, the violent impact of petroleum extraction and reorganisation of socio-ecological relations, not only in its content, but in its aesthetics, particularly its use of phantasmagoria and lycanthropy.

Pelevin is a popular literary sensation in Russia, the so-called 'poet of perestroika', part of the post-Soviet generation of novelists whose fiction teems with monsters, mutants, zombies, vampires, werewolves, insects and spectres. Within the field of post-Soviet literary and cultural production, a massive boom in science fiction and speculative fiction has occurred,[1] heralded by various critics as 'a renaissance of the miraculous', the 'new Gothic' and the 'new mythologism' (Lebedushkina 2010: 81). In popular fiction, the *Night Watch* series of fantasy novels by Sergei Lukyavenko (2007, subsequently transformed into blockbuster films) allegorise the fall-out of the Cold War order in a battle between the formerly socialist keepers of Light and the vampires of the Dark, who are associated with the mega-rich oligarchs of new Russia. In Dmitry Glukhovsky's blockbuster *Metro 2033* (2010), the subterranean remnants of Russian society live in the Metro following a nuclear apocalypse and do battle with mutants and supernatural forces. In literary fiction, Vladimir Sorokin's *Ice Trilogy* (2011) and *Day of the Oprichnik* (2012), Olga Slavnikovna's Russian Booker-winning *2017* (2010), Tatyana Tolstaya's *The Slynx* (2003) and Dmitry Bykov's *Living Souls* (2010) all deploy elements of dystopian, magical realist, fantastic, gothic and speculative fictions to allegorise social upheaval and transformation in the 'new Russia'. Their politics vary from the reactionary to the liberal to the post-Marxist,[2] but they all rely on spectral

---

1 According to Kevin J. O'Brien, the growth of the science fiction market across Eastern Europe and Russia corresponds to a structure of feeling produced by the dominance of market capitalism: 'the post-Soviet cycle of boom, bust and boom again feeds into the disenchantment, struggle, paranoia and fragile reserves of hope along the neo-capitalist frontier'. He cites one publisher as explaining, 'Even with all the freedom now, we are still not in control of our destinies. Big money, not government, rules everything. The leaders are distant. We are still not our own masters' (O'Brien 2006).

2 Sorokin's *Ice Trilogy* offers a conservative fantasy of Putin's Russia as regressing to a social order modelled on the medieval feudal order of Ivan the Terrible; Bykov's *Living Souls* imagines a future Russia in which the rise of fascist tendencies and competing ethnic nationalisms has provoked an absurdist civil war between racially articulated factions: the right-wing cult of the Varagians, who claim to be

and irrealist tropes and, as Olga Lebedushkina argues, their aesthetics cannot be clearly labelled according to pure ideal-types of realism or anti-realism: 'The closer one gets to the tradition the more dubious appears the boundary separating the realists from the modernists and the romantics. They all fall together into the dusky shadows of "supernatural horror in literature," as H.P. Lovecraft freely interpreted the literary Gothic' (Lebedushkina 2010: 82).

In our chapter below on Ivan Vladislavic and the neoliberal transformation in South Africa, we will note the proliferation of tropes of the spectral and supernatural within literary and cultural production and will read these as registering the imposition of neoliberalisation and the rise of corollary criminal economies in the semi-periphery. In Russia, the rapid privatisation and extreme deregulation of the economy produced an over-developed shadow economy of criminal organisations which stepped in to provide the 'insurance' and security services which the state failed to offer. In the Brezhnev and Gorbachev eras, clandestine marketisation of the Soviet literary field via internationalisation of alienated intellectuals and dissident writers such as Solzhenitszhyn had already begun, but post-1989, the breakdown of the Soviet state facilitated the final collapse of the ideological dominance of social realism that had been maintained by state censorship and the formation of private for-profit publishers made way for an outpouring of 'low-brow' and genre fiction. This proliferation was an effect of the chronological displacement and popularity of a once-banned literature, as well as a reconfiguration of the clandestine literary field into a national market, where literature's commodity status and the marketability of popular genres was suddenly emphasised. However, the accompanying flush of speculative fiction in the high-brow 'insectarium of Russian letters' (Lebedushkina 2010: 85) can also be understood directly in relation to speculation and capital, registering the fracturing of social polities in response to economic shock therapy and the violent reorganisation of the Russian petro-state.

Victor Pelevin's fiction is perhaps the most progressive of the 'post-Soviet' bodies of work in its critique of neoliberal capitalism. His six novels have been relentlessly involved with mapping the violent privatisation and neoliberalisation of the former Communist state. For Pelevin, the politics of form and genre have been urgent and ever-evolving: each of his novels tries on a different permutation of speculative fiction, offering assorted fantastic allegories of perestroika, from the time travel, future dystopia, and counterfactual history of *The Clay Machine-Gun* (1999), to the disintegrating space programme and falsified walk-on-the-moon of *Oman Ra* (1996a), to the investors

the original Aryan settlers of Russia, versus the Khazars, representing the liberals and Jews driven into exile, and the itinerant indigenes of Degunino, a magical village. Slavnikovna's *2017* similarly figures the rise of competing nationalisms and a 'regression' to a previous historical moment, when the Bolshevik revolution returns to haunt its centenary anniversary, acted out senselessly by hallucinating populations who divide into Red and White guards, yet without political purpose.

who metamorphose between humans and blood-seeking mosquitoes in *The Life of Insects* (1996b), to the hallucinations of Che Guevara which appear to a drug-addicted ad-man awash in the free market in *Generation П* (English title *Babylon*, 2001), to the cyberspace labyrinth of simulacra in *The Helmet of Horror* (2006a), to the vampirism of *Empire V* (2006b), where humans serve as milch cows to superhuman vampires in 'the Fourth Rome of globalism'.[3] Although nearly all his novels playfully incorporate and parody elements of genre fiction, Pelevin's work has been positioned in the market as literary fiction, characterised by dazzling allusion, intertextuality and a kaleidoscopic fusing of sociological observation with ontological speculation and Buddhist philosophy. He is most frequently labelled a postmodernist author, and his novels fluently name-drop Francophone theorists from Saussure to Foucault, as well as meta-fictionally acknowledging a debt to postmodernist aesthetics, as in the pseudo-preface to *Werewolf*, allegedly written by a team of doctrinaire 'experts' including philologists, an FSB head and a TV presenter, which proclaims,

> This text is not, of course, deserving of any serious literary or critical analysis. Nonetheless, we would like to note that it presents such a dense interweaving of borrowings, imitations, rehashing and allusions (not to mention the poor style and the author's [quite] exceptional puerility), that its authenticity or genuineness do not pose any question for any serious literary specialist: it is interesting purely as a symptom of the profound spiritual decline through which our society is currently passing. (2008: ix)

This nationalist propaganda of Mother Russia's 'spiritual decline' is clearly to be taken as parody, and yet the novel, like all of Pelevin's work, is most certainly concerned with the violence of social transformation and the erosion of cultural values. To read his fiction as primarily concerned with a poststructuralist staging of the indeterminacy of language and history or with the decentring of the meta-narratives of nation and selfhood is to miss the material conditions that structure the playful absurdity of his metafictional tricks and hyperactive paronomasia. In a 2002 interview with Leo Kropywiansky, Pelevin reflects on the influence of Mikhail Bulgakov on his own style:

> The evil magic of any totalitarian regime is based on its presumed capability

---

3 Russian vampire mythology is distinctive from Western European conceptions (such as Bram Stoker's) in that their vampires not only drink blood, but eat bodies. As Sara Buzadhi (2011) observes, there is no local tradition of the zombie as a mindless cannibal in Russia, unlike in Euro-America, where cannibal zombies often figure anxieties revolving around the potential revolution of the underclasses, around economic crisis or around crises of food production and consumption. Russian vampires take on this cannibalistic function, yet they are conscious, rather than controlled (like *utomatons*) from without. The flesh-eating of the vampires in Pelevin's *Empire V* corresponds to this local tradition and figures a political critique of a class elite that consciously cannibalises lower classes and peripheral regions.

to embrace and explain all the phenomena, their entire totality, because explanation is control [...] So if there's a book that takes you out of this totality of things explained and understood, it liberates you because it breaks the continuity of explanation and thus dispels the charms [...] *The Master and Margarita* didn't even bother to be anti-Soviet, yet reading this book would make you free instantly. It didn't liberate you from some particular old ideas, but rather from the hypnotism of the entire order of things. (Kropywiansky 2002)

Pelevin's own novels invent a similarly absurdist, spectral aesthetic that subverts conventional realist prose in order to break the hypnotism of the dominant social order and make visible the hallucinations of perestroika and the petro-state. The play between internal and external appearances, between ideology and the Real, is an obsession of all his fictions, one which derives from his own Buddhist metaphysics but which also expresses a specific cultural logic: not precisely that of postmodernism as the logic of late capitalism in the world-system's core states, but rather the phantasmagoria of the imperfect, unevenly developed transition into neoliberal capital in Europe's semi-periphery from the 1990s to the 2000s. In an earlier interview with Sally Laird, he had similarly conceptualised 'real' literature as possessing the ability to make the 'unreal' real, as well as the reverse (Laird 1999: 186). His novels are saturated by irrealism, but in every instance, the insectoids, vampires, werewolves and other metamorphs that people his fiction correspond to real social formations and agents: advertisers, investors, mafiya, KGB men, mega-rich 'New Russian' billionaires. Their supernatural capabilities satirise social transformations and are often cast in a welter of ambivalence, making it difficult to tell whether they are real or figments of the protagonist's hallucinatory consciousness and unreliable narrations. The preoccupation with the nature of reality – or rather, its seeming irreality – that haunts his protagonists does not stem from the inherent instability of language or emerge merely from the paradoxes of consciousness and epistemology that are so obsessively explored. Rather, it is an expression of the schism between the ideological mystification of social relations and the reality of a structurally uneven world-system cleaved by the international division of labour. As such, his fiction could be characterised as critically irrealist in the sense that Michael Löwy has defined it: wilfully expressing the contradictions of a social order and critiquing it, while reactivating the tradition of oneiric, surreal and critical irrealist fictions from Gogol, Dostoevsky, Kafka and Bulgakov onwards.

Future work on Pelevin will need to explore how the irrealist elements of his aesthetics are refined and progressively developed across the span of his novels. The novels can be read as periodising the different political formations and phases of economic neoliberalisation under the post-Soviet regimes from Gorbachev to Yeltsin to Putin. In an interview, Pelevin describes the 'P' in *Generation П* as signifying simultaneously Pepsi, Putin and the Russian obscenity 'pizdets', translating loosely as 'fucked-up', but above all referring to the free market generation: 'It's Generation Pizdets, which means a generation that faces catastrophe. And now, you know, some of our newspapers think that this is Generation Putin' (Pelevin 2000). At the same time, the zen philosophical concerns of the earlier books, such as *Clay Machine Gun*, which are immaturely and diffusely worked-out (to the extent that in the *Werewolf* preface he satirises his own 'pseudo-oriental pop-metaphysics' [2008: ix]) are increasingly sharpened and yoked to a more prominent materialist socio-economic critique, which delves beneath surface politics to the economic relations underpinning the social totality. However, we will focus here on one of his most recent novels and the way in which it specifically develops the metaphorics of lycanthropy to encapsulate the latest stage of Russia's uneven development into a petro-regime.

In *Capital*, Marx famously characterised finance capital's overreach beyond the physical maximum bounds of the working day as motivated by 'blind unrestrainable passion, its were-wolf hunger for surplus-labour'. The more familiar metaphor for capital deployed by Marx is vampirism, and indeed, as we have noted above, Pelevin already deployed vampirism as a complex allegory in a previous novel, *Empire V*. But lycanthropy has its own peculiar significance for registering a particular phase of the ecological revolution of nature–social relations represented by the petro-economy. Werewolf folklore frequently originates in traumatic transformations of local ecologies by imperialism or modernisation. In Ireland, as geographer Kieran Hickey has traced, werewolf legends and myths greatly increased in the Planter era in the 1600s, registering the mass deforestation of Ireland that was enacted in the conversion to plantation mono-agriculture. The destruction of the wolves' oak forest habitats drove them out of the woods into human habitation, where they were systematically exterminated to extinction by professional hunters, altering the eco-system so that humans, not wolves, became the dominant predator. At the same time, imperialist rhetoric used werewolves as an ethnic discourse to vilify the native Irish and naturalise them as 'sub-human', pointing to the significance of the wolf in pre-capitalist Irish culture, registered in geographical names for 'wolf ridges' and surnames of chiefs meaning 'wolf-head' or 'son-of-the-land' (Hickey 2011).

Stefan Donecker identifies a similar process in the peripheral territory of Livonia on the eastern shores of the Baltic Sea in the sixteenth and seventeenth centuries. Here, in the 'utmost periphery of early modern Europe', roughly corresponding to modern Estonia and Latvia, the declining Teutonic Order struggled to maintain feudal control of the territory, against the colonial invasion of the Muscovite army, and the region became a site of bitter contest for supremacy between Russia, Sweden and Poland (Donecker 2009: 63). Military reports of the contesting armies and of the German feudal aristocrats similarly reported the prevalence of werewolves and shape-shifters across the region, and provoked a host of measures to suppress perceived indigenous resistance, including legal measures such as lycanthropy trials, and commissioned bounties for wolf-hunting. For Donecker, these werewolf myths were generated by the need for would-be imperialists to justify the continuing exploitation of indigenous peoples through serfdom (under the German order) and their subsequent conquest and incorporation into the Muscovite quasi-colonial regime: 'A land where humans regularly lost their humanity and turned into beasts was in dire need of conquest, civilization and education. Werewolves had become a discursive concept that confirmed the German nobility's rule over the indigenous peasants and justified the "civilized" countries' ambitions for hegemony and conquests in the Baltic region' (70). In this case, as in Ireland, the werewolf myth could be seen as signifying more than the political naturalisation of myths of ethnicity between *cultural* frontiers; rather, in both instances they are directly tied to the economy and ecology of peripheral territories as they are forcibly incorporated; indeed, as Donecker notes, not merely was the monstrous an inherent aspect of the Baltic frontier, but shape-changing was a phenomenon primarily associated with 'peripheral regions' across the northern, eastern and western peripheries of early modern Europe: '"Sorcerers used to be less numerous than they are today," states the notorious French witch-hunter Pierre De Lancre. "They dwelt at remote places; in the mountains, in deserts, or in the Northern Lands, such as Norway, Denmark, Sweden, Götaland, Ireland, and Livonia"' (Donecker 2009: 69). The liminal transformations between man and beast suggest the interruption of previous relations to the land and the environment, a reorganisation of nature–social relations, in which the socio-ecological 'archaic' comes into tension with 'modern' capitalist formations.

In the post-Soviet gothic, the magnetic affinities of previous encodings of periphery–core relations through phantasmagoria such as Gogol's vampires and witches, Pushkin's *vurdalak* and Bulgakov's dog-man Sharik are reactivated, registering the present inauguration of an analogous moment to prior systemic cycles. 'Phantasmagoria', Theodor Adorno argues, 'comes into being when, under the constraints of its own limitations, modernity's latest products come close to the archaic' (Adorno 2005: 84). Instead of the forcible conversion to plantation regimes, the moment registered here is the stage of primitive accumulation which marks the transition to neoliberal capitalism, characterised by asset-stripping, mass privatisation and the conversion to a petro-regime, alongside a dizzyingly rapid subordination to the logic of the commodity form, a moment marked by spectrality, abstraction, dematerialisation of the body and disembedding of identity, and an all-pervasive illusion of 'the absolute reality of the unreal' (Adorno 2005: 84). Olga Lebedushkina detects the cyclical nature of the gothic in Russian literature, the strange 'return' of Gogol's horrors and miracles at three different moments, but is unable to account for the world-systemic relations that might produce such spiral contiguities:

> There is in this Christmassy early-century atmosphere something elusively similar to the days of the first Gogol centennial, when – through the efforts of Merezhovskii, Bely, and Rozanvb – the 'father of the naturalist school'

> [...] began to morph into a mystic and a medium. The next year [2009] is Gogol's, too [...] The century before last, the last century, and the current century coexist [...] in terms of horrors and miracles. (2010: 83)

Later, she attempts to explain these resurgences as a product of the interruption of previous genre development by the enforced aesthetic preferences of the Soviet state, which meant that the first flush of magical realism expressed in the political satires of Mikhail Bulgakov's *The Heart of a Dog* (1999) and *The Master and Margarita* (2007) was suppressed, despite acquiring a whole secret underground life as banned manuscripts secretly circulated amongst writers and readers:

> From the mid-nineteenth century on, Russian literature has been far distant, both chronologically and culturally, from those manifestations of the European novel in the late seventeenth to the nineteenth centuries that are commonly termed 'Gothic' [...] Maybe another explanation for the current surge of interest in miracles and horrors is that they have indeed been so far distant – that we are today gathering together what had been left ungathered in both the nineteenth and twentieth centuries [...] In the twentieth, entire genre systems were outlawed and suffered a lengthy displacement by socialist realism (and not only socialist). Now the dam has broken [...] Has it come to pass, then – the renaissance of the 'miraculous' and the 'literature of supernatural horror' that was held up for more than a century and a half? (Lebedushkina 2010: 99)

The genealogy of Russian gothic may be distinctive from other European literatures in these particular 'displacements' where historical circumstances interrupted the development of genres. And yet its 'return' might be understood as more than the return of a politically repressed literary form, or even as more than the Freudian return of the political and psychic traumas of the Soviet 'catastrophe', to which Alexander Etkind attributes the 'haunting' of contemporary Russian literature (Lipovetsky and Etkind 2010: 6). Rather, the supernaturalism and reworking of myths and folklore in post-Soviet literature constitute a mining of materials produced at previous moments of socio-ecological revolution in order to represent the present. Writing in 1925, Leon Trotsky observed that 'artistic creation is always a complicated turning inside out of old forms, under the influence of new stimuli that originate outside of art' (2005: 150). For Trotsky, because human imagination is 'economical' and makes use of the '"secondhand" wardrobe of the past', literary themes and devices can migrate through time and across space, 'from people to people, from class to class, and even from author to author', since 'a new class does not begin to create all of culture from the beginning, but enters into possession of the past, assorts it, touches it up, rearranges it, and builds on it further' (149). Thus, the phenomenon which John Givens observes in contemporary post-Soviet neo-gothic, by which each writer 'seeks to cope with the recent past by exploring more ancient history or by returning to old literary forms' (2010: 3), might be understood in Trotsky's terms as a process of assimilation and turning inside out of earlier forms necessary to the construction of a new imaginary through which to represent the contemporary moment of the emergent capitalist class. This reactivation of residual forms is not arbitrary, but seems to draw on texts and tales congruent at similar points in long waves of boom-bust cycles and eco-revolutions, even if these points occur in different temporalities.

Postmodernist readings of Pelevin and his contemporaries mischaracterise their genre hybrids as 'flat' pastiches of different generic conventions whose primary aim is deconstructive abstraction and a celebration of the cultural logic of late capital. Rather, these writings should be taken as the revelation of the sense of unreality produced by rapid subordination to the commodity form couched in a reworking of previous irrealist aesthetic modes to produce a critique of socio-economic conditions. As Lebedushkina comments, 'The principal tendencies of contemporary literature in this country can hardly be described in terms of "realism," "modernism" or "postmodernism."' (2010: 99). However, if the folklore produced in response to sixteenth-century transformations functioned more on the level of the political unconscious as an expression of social anxieties, here the aesthetic adaptation of folklore and catachresis to encapsulate unevenness is conscious and deliberate.

In Russian fairy tales such as 'The Firebird', the grey wolf was traditionally a mediator of class and ecological relations between forest dwellers (both peasants and non-humans) and the royal aristocracy. The wolf was most aligned to power struggles for the kingdom, helping return usurped or betrayed princes to their 'rightful' throne. Capable of reanimating the dead and transforming itself into other beings, the wolf was a liminal figure whose appearance in plots catalysed static situations to move forward and enabled the restoration of feudal relations. In Pelevin, the werewolf is similarly aligned with governance and power, but this time associated with the capitalist state rather than the feudal monarchy, representing the FSB, the state security forces which succeeded the KGB and whose support stabilises Putin's authoritarian regime. However, they also mediate social-ecological relations between the environment and the capitalist state, howling at the earth in order to dredge up oil for the Yukos corporation. The Russian word used for the werewolves in the novel is оборотень or *oboronten*, which translates as shape-shifter, rather than *verwolf*, the word used in Pelevin's earlier short story 'A Werewolf Problem in Central Russia' (1998). In Russian folklore, *oboronten* refers to people, usually sorcerers, who can turn themselves into animals or take on other forms, before reverting to their original appearance. Unlike the *verwolf*, whose horrific transformation from man to beast is involuntary, the *oboronten* elect to change into grotesque forms in order to slake unholy appetites or accomplish acts of evil will. Metaphorically, an *oboronten* can also signify a person whose true nature is hidden. In contemporary Russia, the phrase 'werewolves in epaulets' signifies policemen who on the surface represent the law, but who are secretly engaged in criminal deals with the mafiya (Oushakine 2010: 380): in newspaper and media discourse, these werewolves in shoulder-straps have become lightning rods for the condemnation of corruption. In their protean, thrilling transformations, *oboronten* represent the unmitigated rapacity of neoliberal capital and the phantasmagorical reality of oil modernity. Because *oboronten* always return to their original form, they are also metaphors of the hollowness of Putin's nationalist reforms, the stagnation of the dominant social order, in which the political ideology of the state may shift, but the concentration of wealth remains in the hands of political elites, many of them ex-Party.

The Sacred Book of the Werewolf is narrated in the first person by A Hu Lui, a 2,000-year-old fox spirit. When pronounced aloud, her name sounds like an obscenity in Russian, but it derives from the Chinese expression 'fox spirit', or *huli jing*, which can also signify a promiscuous woman or adulteress. In Chinese culture, the trickster fox spirit serves as a mediator of class and gender relations during times of social crisis: during periods of large-scale economic transformation or capitalist modernisation, anxieties about the rupture of social fabrics are displaced onto the 'treacherous' or adulterous figure of the *huli jing*, who is blamed for haunting domestic spaces and catalysing the breakdown of family relations and fortunes. In the novel, A Hu Lui makes her living as a high-class escort to investment bankers, whom she stalks at the generically named National Hotel. However, she does not sell sex, only its illusion. Able to manipulate the perceptions of her clients through the power of her magic tail, she masquerades as a 14-year-old nymphet and hypnotises her clients into onanistic simulations of their own fantasies, rather than having physical intercourse with them. One day, she is startled to encounter other were-creatures, a cadre of werewolves working for the FSB, formerly known as the KGB, and in a reworking of the Little Red Riding Hood tale, she falls in love with Sasha Grey Wolf.

With its supernatural wolves and foxes, the novel borrows heavily from speculative fiction, yet it is more a political and philosophical satire in the mode of *Master and Margarita* than a fantasy novel, self-consciously literary, packed with puns and playful allusions to Nabokov's *Lolita*, Bulgakov's *The Heart of a Dog*, Dostoevsky, Pushkin and Blok, mingled with Russian fairy tales, Nordic sagas, Chinese fox mythology and Buddhist teaching, suffused throughout by a racy, lupine humour. It is werewolf literature as the modern reinvention of the man-and-beast moral fable, grafted onto a sly reworking of the sex worker's diary, set in a country known for its exploitation and export of women sex workers. Throughout the novel, the fusion of lycanthropy and vampirism in the figure of A Hu Lui, with her professional extraction and expenditure of sexual energy, creates space for meditation on the illusions of commodity fetishism, the commodification of labour and the contradictions of the oil economy.

For A Hu Lui, the 'unofficial' dollars she is paid in offer 'a glimpse of the intimate linkages in [her] Homeland's economic mechanism' (Pelevin 2008: 63), and 'the fundamental contradiction of the modern age is the contradiction between money and blood' (84). In a Freudian twist, she reads her clients' fetishes as scatological manifestations of the logic of finance capital: 'Sex is the favorite sport of portfolio investors. There's a simple psychoanalytical explanation for this – just try comparing the prison slang term "shoving shit" with the expression "investing money"' (23). She conceives of sexual exchanges in language mirroring the oil economy with its logic of unlimited extraction: 'Entering into the act of love a human being becomes a channel for this energy and is transformed from a sealed vessel to a pipe that is connected for a few seconds to the bottomless source of the life force' (23). A Hu Lui's draining of her partner's life-force in intercourse is correlated with the resource extraction performed by pipe-lines that suck out the earth's hidden marrow: it is an ecological image of the metabolic rift which extracts resources without returning, but it also suggests the privatisation and reformulation of bodily dispositions and sexualities under the cultural logic of neoliberal capital. A few pages later, strengthening this correlation, A Hu Lui explicitly compares her sex work to the privatisation auctions of state assets, with the crucial distinction that she herself recognises the need to limit her consumption and not drain her clients dry, and is tormented throughout the novel by pangs of guilt: 'The difference here is exactly the same as that between an armed robbery and a privatization auction. Formally speaking in the latter case there is no crime for the spirits to punish. But there's still no way you can trick your own conscience, so it's best just to leave it out of things' (24). Just as the novel's plot and metaphorics are permeated by the language of oil, A Hu Lui sees the whole of Russian society as permeated by the spectre of the oil economy and its perpetual stage of primitive accumulation, as she sardonically explains in a letter to her sister fox in Thailand:

> The elite here is divided into branches, which are called 'the oligarchy' (derived from the words 'oil' and 'gargle') and the 'apparat' (from the phrase 'upper rat'). The oligarchy is the business community which grovels to the authorities, who can close down any business at any moment, since business here is inseparable from theft. And the 'upper rat' consists of the authorities, who feed on the kickbacks from business. [...] The reforms that you have heard about are by no means new. They have been going on here constantly for as long as I can remember. What they essentially come down to is the choice, from all the possible versions of the future, of the one that is the most disgusting. Every time the reforms begin with the declaration that a fish rots from the head, then the reforms eat up the healthy body, and the rotten head swims on. (85)

This is the post-communist landscape as described by Georgi Derluguian, dominated by 'commercialized politicians, their allied oligarchic capitalists, or enterprising gangsters and warlords', where 'private businesses based on former state property [...] typically behaved like gangs' and 'actual gangs [...] behaved like businesses' (Derluguian 2005: 304–05). The neoliberalisation of the country in the 1990s was characterised by the rapid privatisation of Russia's massive energy resources and the creation of an oligarchy from the remnants of the *nomenklatura*, a handful of super-rich elites whose security and scandalous accumulation of wealth was protected through their alliance with ascendant Mafiosi and warlords and the remnants of the secret police. Meanwhile, the rest of the country was subjected to deindustrialisation and rapid immiseration, plunged below the poverty line, stripped of social benefits and deprived of basic resources, stable wages and employment. In the initial phase of primitive accumulation by dispossession, capital haemorrhaged out of the country as national assets were purchased at subsidised rock-bottom Soviet prices and then sold off at world-market prices, generating vast profits for the former *nomenklatura*, who promptly deposited their money in off-shore accounts. Both the 'shock' of this mass evacuation and the unreality of the immaterial circulation of capital are captured in A Hu Lui's description of the boom: 'In Moscow they are building skyscrapers, eating sushi by the ton and bringing billion-dollar court cases. But this boom doesn't have much to do with the economy. It's just that the money from all over Russia flows into Moscow and moistens life here for a bit before it departs for off-shore hyperspace' (Pelevin 2008: 84). When Putin came to power, he renationalised some of the privatised resources, only to create an 'oilopoly' through the formation of state-dominated mass corporations like Gazprom, the third-largest in the world (Goldman 2008: 2). Gazprom controls all of the natural gas and oil pipelines in Europe, and subsequently has the ability to cut off energy resources for political reasons, as in 2006, when it reduced the flow to the Western Ukraine. In 2006, Russia became the world's largest producer of petroleum, beyond even Saudi Arabia (Goldman 2008: 3). For A Hu Lui, the grotesquely uneven development of the modern Russian petro-state, with its parasitic bureaucracy of former Party apparatchiks entangled with the criminal shadow economy and the oligarchy of financial elites, can be summarised in the image of an 'oil pipeline with a fat rat hanging over it, giving itself a royal autocephalic uroborus. It sometimes seems to me that the only goal of Russian life is to drag this rat across the snowy waters trying to make some geopolitical sense of all this and inspire the minor nations with it' (Pelevin 2008: 86).

Imre Szeman argues that oil capital 'seems to represent a stage that neither capital nor its opponents can think beyond'. Despite the 'looming demise of the petrochemical economy', capital remains blindly 'dependent on continuous expansion, which enables not only profit taking but investment in the reproduction of capital that is a necessary condition for its continuation on into the future' (Szeman 2007: 807). The imminent disaster of resource exhaustion haunts the novel as it attempts to expose the hallucination that is oil modernity and break the link of the uroborus. The horror of unsustainability lurking beneath the illusion of infinite consumer plenitude is encapsulated in a letter from E Hu Lui, another fox sister in England, who describes the anamorphic 'black hole in reality' (139) that explodes the logic of commodity fetishism and renders the world of consumption meaningless: 'The joy of shopping cannot conceal the unbearable awareness that our entire world is one huge ski shop standing in the middle of the Sahara Desert. You don't just have to buy the skis, you have to buy the imitation snow as well' (139–40). This seemingly surreal reference to the Sahara functions on multiple levels. The absurdity of skis in a desert gestures to the 'illusion of the absolute reality of the unreal' produced by the logic of the commodity form, in which exchange-value is divorced from use-value and presented as the only value-form. Yet, such phenomena are not merely phantasmagorical, but literal: in the desert city of Dubai, sports complexes offer real ski slopes, whose maintenance entails an obscene expenditure of water and energy resources and the production of hydrological rifts. As such, the image ineluctably recalls the acceleration of desertification that is the product of anthropogenic global warming: petro-modernity's blind dependence on oil and its unrelenting drive to expansion.

E Hu Lui's letter goes on to illuminate Russia's semi-peripheral relation to the capitalist world-system: 'Your world will soon be like ours (at least, for those who are kept on to service the extraction and export of oil), but as yet it still has twilight zones where a salutary ambivalence is the rule' (140). This is Russia as the semi-periphery mediating the extraction and processing of raw resources, characterised by incongruity and unevenness: it is, as described later by another fox, 'no more than a raw-material appendage of the developed countries' (80). When E Hu Lui visits A Hu Lui in Russia, she brings in tow a British aristocrat seeking investment opportunities, a representative of the vanguard of shock doctrine capitalists and foreign investors who descended on Russia to buy up assets in the 1990s. As such, Pelevin persistently situates the main narrative of the text in relation to different zones of the world-system, opposing capitalist core states in Western Europe, the United States and Japan to peripheries in Asia, from which even more impoverished labourers and sex workers come to work in its emerging markets, and the emerging new core of China, itself pioneering a version of authoritarian capitalism.

When A Hu Lui misguidedly falls in love with Alexander the Grey, the seductive werewolf general in the FSB charged with managing the Siberian oil fields, she travels with him to Nefteperegonievsck, a town with a 'phantasmagorical appearance' mingling the archaic and the modern:

> The buildings in it reminded me of cottages for the middle class outside Moscow. There was only one difference – the cottages were raised above the ground in an absurd fashion, on stilts that were like the hut's chicken legs in the fairy tale. That was the precise association evoked by the combination of the piles hammered into the permafrost and the red crests of the tiled roofs, and it was impossible to free myself of it: the houses became rows of chickens with their hindquarters raised high to display the black opening of the doors [...] In between the 'eurohuts' I could see figures of street traders selling [reindeer meat] from pieces of oilcloth spread out directly on the snow beside their Buran snowmobiles [...] I was very impressed by the Calvin Klein boutique, located in one of the cottages on

> piles. Its very presence in this place was impressive – it was probably the most northerly outpost of lesser Calvinism in the world [...] I couldn't help noticing a large children's playground [...] that reminded me of an ancient hunters' camping ground preserved among the snow. (209)

Nefteperegonievsck is a shanty town thrown up by the Yukos Oil Company, in which the archaic mercantilism and subsistence economy of the reindeer hunters exist alongside the rapid invasion of the industrial technologies and commodities brought by the petro-economy. Those Baba-Yaga huts standing beside western chain stores and hi-tech vehicles recall once more that evocative passage which has previously been cited throughout this volume in which Jameson modifies Trotsky's words, to comment on 'handicrafts alongside the great cartels, peasant fields with the Krupp factories or the Ford plant in the distance' (Jameson 1995: 307): it encapsulates the surreal experience of combined and uneven development, though in a different phase – here the penetration of the Siberian hinterlands and peripheries of Russia and their uneven incorporation in the post-Soviet neoliberal market, primarily through the extraction economy of the petroleum industry.

Alexander believes that the construction of oil pipe-lines will bring to life the fable of the money tree, with petroleum acting as the magic exchange-value which produces the 'sacred $100 a barrel' (Pelevin 2008: 200): '*Calculating men will haul a slaking apparatus in to the crown of fire and force the Tree's black trunk to grow into a cold steel pipe stretching right across the Country of Fools to the port terminal, to various Chinas and Japans—so far that soon the Tree will be unable to recall its own roots*' (208; italics original). In the attempt to extract more oil from a Siberian field already mined to exhaustion, he acts out the Russian fairy tale 'The Apple Tree', a variant of the Cinderella tale, in which the orphaned Little Khavroshka is helped by a brindle cow instead of a fairy godmother. Her stepmother slaughters the cow, but Khavroshka buries its bones and an apple tree springs forth with golden leaves and apples. Placing a cow's skull on the oil rig, Alexander transforms himself into a wolf and howls a litany whose cynicism is calculated to make the skull weep black leaves. In the wolf's monologue, Pelevin slyly draws a structural homology between the eco-regime of petrolic extraction in neoliberal Russia, whose ghostly profits circulate in off-shore banking havens, registered here in a satirical gothic or fantastic mode, and the mono-commodity eco-regimes of banana and fruit plantations in the Latin American periphery in the early twentieth century, as registered famously in García Márquez's 'magical realist' depiction of the United Fruit company in *One Hundred Years of Solitude*:

> How many times that brindle cow has been slaughtered. And how many times it had returned, either as a magic apple tree or an entire cherry orchard. Only where had all the apples gone? You couldn't find them anywhere. Except maybe by calling the office of United Fruit ... But no, that was nonsense. 'United Fruit' was last century, but now any call you

made would get lost in the wires on its way to some company in Gibraltar, that belonged to a firm from the Falkland Islands that was managed by a lawyer in Amsterdam in the interest of a trust with an unnamed beneficiary owner. (1970: 219)

The wolf begs 'nature' for more even as he wearily concedes the immorality of unregulated consumption in the face of environmental disaster and human degradation: 'And do you know how we feel swallowing sashimi that smells of oil and pretending not to notice the final ice-floes melting under our feet? Pretending this is the destination towards which the people have striven for a thousand years, ending with us?' (Pelevin 2008: 219). Despite his awareness of the absurdity of neoliberal myths of 'the end of history', Alexander is obsessed with the Nordic apocalypse of Ragnarok, dreaming that he will become the Nietzschean *über*-wolf, Fenrir, and swallow the sun. His apocalyptic will to power satirises the fascist tendencies of the paternalism, ritualised nationalism, and cult of the ruler associated with Putin's authoritarian petro-state, even as it predicts the disastrous eco-futurity associated with such a limitless desire for domination of nature.

By contrast, A Hu Lui forswears narratives of apocalypse and creative destruction, asserting that the 'super-werewolf' is not an individual but a Buddhist state of enlightenment. She realises that in 'creating the world' with the hypnotic resonance of their magic tails, foxes are blinded by 'relict radiation' (318), mistaking their own perception of reality for the world itself. To enter the nirvanic Rainbow Stream, they must direct 'love' into their own tails, thus interrupting the generation of the illusion of reality. Her rejection of reality as a projection is not merely a consequence of abstract linguistic indeterminacy or fallible perception, but directly symptomatic of imaginary social relations in modern Russia, where, according to A Hu Lui, the word 'real' has four basic uses, all describing financial transactions or commodity relations. Its most common form as an 'adjective with the meaning "having a dollar equivalent"' makes '"real" a synonym for the word "metaphysical", since nowadays the dollar is an occult, mystical unit based entirely on the belief that tomorrow will be like today' (229). At the beginning of the novel, A Hu Lui proudly informs us that she is mentioned 'in one of the greatest works of world literature [...] *Anecdotes of Spirits and Immortals*, written by Gan Bao' (5), but immediately goes on to describe her work as a prostitute. Just as she constantly draws our attention to the commodification of her body, the text announces its own status as a commodity in the world republic of letters. Overseeing the eclectic pastiche of decorating styles and paintings at the National Hotel, A Hu Lui observes that '[the pictures] all share the most important artistic attribute of all – they're for sale. As soon as you remember that, the remarkable stylistic unity of the interior becomes clear [...] you realise there is no such thing as abstract art at all, it's all very concrete' (14–15). It is an observation that applies equally to the novel itself.

Elsewhere, A Hu Lui sharply rebuts her 'rightwing liberal' client's reading of Nabokov's *Lolita* as celebrating hedonism:

> Nabokov isn't speaking for himself when he describes the forbidden charms of a nymphet at such length. He speaks for himself when he describes in meager terms, in the very merest hint, the impressive financial resources that allow Humbert to freewheel America with Lolita. A writer's true heart speaks out very furtively [...] For me Dolores Haze was a symbol of the soul, eternally young and pure, and Humbert Humbert was the metaphorical chairman of this world's board of directors. (51)

A Hu Lui's appearance is itself modelled on a Lolita-esque nymphet, establishing another structural homology between contemporary Russia and previous petro-regimes, and performing a critique of the objectification of humans within commodity relations. *Lolita* can be read as another petro-fiction registering the earlier flush of oil intoxication in 1950s America, after the infrastructure of roads laid down in the New Deal era enabled the country to be thoroughly integrated into an oil economy: it is, as A Hu Lui suggests, an incarnation of automotive culture, in which Humbert's seductive, pornographically unreliable narration and the extraordinary flexibility and profligacy of his use of language invite the reader to critique the material capital and natural resource extraction that makes his extraordinary mobility possible. Pelevin's own novel uses A Hu Lui's unreliable narration and reflections on reading to speculate on the role of dialectical hermeneutics in the revelation of ideology and mystification.

A Hu Lui's own mode of thinking is represented as peculiarly dialectical and processual: 'The mind follows several different paths at the same time, keeping an eye open to see which will lead to the light of truth first' (37). She is prone to designate these multiple levels of dialogue in numbered lists of four items, but the appearance of hierarchy is misleading, since the various positions develop simultaneously in her consciousness. As she seeks to understand the antinomies of her social order, the reader is forced into a mode of dialectical interpretation, deepened by the additional difficulty of A Hu Lui's own unreliability as a narrator, since she is prone to regurgitate and reformulate ideas she has heard before. For instance, when she first hears the 'right-wing liberal' Pavel Ivanonich berate detective novels in which 'the people who write them start explaining how we ought to arrange things in Russia', comparing them to 'some underage prostitute who's been given a lift by a long-distance truck driver so she can give him a blowjob suddenly stops work, looks up and starts giving him instructions about how to flush the carburettor in a frost', she furiously rebukes him with a reply whose humour acknowledges the vulgarity of the novel as a commodity but defends its propensity to illuminate: 'Maybe she's serviced so many truckers that she's picked up all the subtle points and now she really can teach him to flush his carburettor' (48). Pelevin seems to be slyly defending his own particular use of speculative genre fiction.

But later, arguing with Alexander, A Hu Lui finds herself, to her horror, defending a notion of literature as 'high' art whose aesthetic value is measured by its difficulty and the effort it demands from its reader. She trashes the detective novel he is reading, *Werewolves in Shoulder Straps*, as 'literary junk food' driven by crass market values – the author killing the characters for 'money' – using the same metaphor of the trucker picking up illiterate prostitutes for blow jobs, only to retract it later in the novel. The role of the reader oscillates in her unreliable perception, but for Pelevin, it is the reader who ultimately infuses the text with meaning, since it is the reader who is required to interpret the multiple positions offered by the narration and to acknowledge the extent to which the novel as a commodity form is always already embedded in ideology and consecrated as market object, even as it attempts to demystify or expose those same ideologies. In its estrangement effect and 'sense of wonder', speculative fiction bears a structural relation to the anti-realist avant-garde. In employing catachrestic modes of the gothic or the supernatural, Pelevin's speculative fiction repudiates the illusory representation of reality that is ideology. A politics of genre emerges from the layered narration of the novel, which stages a critique of fantasy and genre fiction in its conservative mode and distinguishes between *negative hallucination* that mystifies and *speculation* that leads to revelation.

After she is abandoned by Alexander, A Hu Lui writes the sacred book of the werewolf – the novel we are reading – as a guide to enlightenment and then enters the 'Rainbow Stream', disappearing in a flash of ball lightning. Reviewers have noted that in the second third of the book, the plot, dialogue and tone of narration become more leaden, as A Hu Lui debates the nature of perception with Alexander. James Urquhart (2008), for instance, argues that the 'brisk chaos' and 'mischievous entertainment' which 'crashes the voracious vitality of the werewolf into the carapace of a spiritually beleaguered Russia' gives way to Buddhist meditations which 'weigh down the perky satire of his plotting', usurping the previous core strength of Pelevin's writing, 'its unruly, suggestive energy'. Indeed, the novel is most ebulliently erotic when satirising a society consuming itself: its negative critique of capitalist Russia is imbued with the intoxication of petro-modernity. By contrast, it is unable to make libidinal A Hu Lui's concluding release, because it cannot formulate a futurity beyond oil capital, only offer a vision of the nirvanic cessation of desire that could be mistaken for quietism, but whose emptiness is better understood as the formal counterpoint to the void underlying capitalism and to the ecological exhaustion of the intensifying metabolic rift. It strips away the hallucination but can reveal nothing beyond the hollowness of ideology – the nightmare of totalitarian Communism succeeded by the hallucinations of free market capitalism. As A Hu Lui reflects, 'everything in Russian life had shifted around so much that is was hard to reach any final conclusion' (Pelevin 2008: 210). Crystal Bartolovich (2010) has recently spoken of oil as the Adornian preponderant object that says 'no', that can only protest its own exhaustion. This novel too offers oil's recalcitrant negative, but cannot move beyond ideological and ecological exhaustion to any vision of individual or collective agency.

Howling in agony as they inject themselves with ketamine and attempt to squeeze more tears from the cow's cracked skull, the werewolves encapsulate the torment of oil shock, and the repressed fear of peak oil and ecological exhaustion that undergirds petro-modernity. By contrast, the fox spirit, with her ancient moral traditions and 'social instincts acquired in other times [...] in a culture that was very dissimilar' (52), is the figure of the 2,000-year-old residual past swept away by the lightning convulsions of capitalist Russia, a past whose Chinese and Asian cultural traditions are repressed and denied within contemporary nationalist narratives.[4]

She can no longer persist in neoliberal Russia and must leave the narrative; yet the book she writes remains in our hands, spectre from the past and key to understanding the present social order. Indeed, she writes the book precisely as a refutation of facile encomia to 'globalisation' as bringing a rising tide of prosperity and equality to countries inaugurated into the 'global village', specifically identifying herself as writing against Martin Wolf's *Why Globalisation Works* (323), in order that the reader might 'learn from it how to liberate yourself from the icy gloom in which the oligarchy and the public prosecutors, the liberals and conservatives [...] werewolves in shoulder-straps and portfolio investors wail and gnash their teeth' (321). Paradoxically, it is the antinomy of A Hui Lui's absence – her simultaneous disappearance from the narrative and presence through the form of the narration – that offers a faint revenant of a future 'which is not the most disgusting' emerging from the 'twilight zones of ambivalence' in the semi-periphery of the world-system.

---

4 A Hu Lui frequently recalls her Chinese origins, proudly citing Alexander Blok's famous pronouncement on the Scythians, 'yes, we are Asiatics', in reference to her own identification as a Russian (vii, 52).

CHAPTER FIVE

The European Literary Periphery

Bratislava, 1989

Not much is explained about the woman who strips naked in public in Peter Pist'anek's Slovakian novel *Rivers of Babylon*. 'A nervous breakdown' is offered as a possible reason for her disrobing, which occurs in front of the Hotel Ambassador on a busy street in central Bratislava, on a sunny August morning in 1989 (2007: 17). Impervious to the consternation of passers-by, and to a gypsy who robs her, she is eventually taken away in a police car, in one of the few civic gestures made by representatives of a rapidly vanishing state.

Initially, the woman's anguished gesture is focalised through the public's reaction to an apparently random 'extraordinary situation' that 'has brought them together, just as a calamity to be overcome brings people together' (17). But as quickly as the collective expressions of sympathy, outrage and anxiety appear do they subside and disintegrate. The vaporisation of empathy or even adequate response in *Rivers of Babylon* indexes the transition from an exhausted communist system to what Peter Petro and Donald Rayfield, in their introduction to the novel in English translation, call 'another world, of rampant robber barons' capitalism' (Pist'anek 2007: 5). But public atomisation and exhaustion are consistent features not only of *Rivers of Babylon* but also of the fiction of post-communist 'transition' in general. As the neoliberal 'shock doctrine' rapidly privatises space (urban or otherwise) entirely, alien civic and cultural environments are formed, leaving individuals dangerously exposed in their fungibility and portability, cut off and disconnected from one another: 'an individualistic society of transients', in David Harvey's evocative summary of the contemporary – putatively 'postmodern' – capitalist lifeworld at large (1989: 288).

115

Of course, the representation of urban space as both baleful and liberatory is a familiar feature of all literary modernisms. But Bratislava's shift to free-market capitalism impresses a particularly *contemporary* stamp on this representation. Pist'anek's narrative has uncertainty coded into its very structure. The received modernist narrative modes seem inappropriate for the unbounded world of the post-communist 'transition'. While many characters 'lose the plot' like the stripped woman, others emerge to rig the system criminally – and often brutally – in their favour. Among the spectators at the strip scene are several characters central to the novel's satiric perspective on the new economy born out of the Czechoslovak 'Velvet Revolution'. Crucially, rather than entirely disappear, elements of the previous communist order persist and even flourish in the new configuration. The 'black' market, for example, blossoms, deepens and booms. The sole purpose of the Mafia-style managers running the Hotel Ambassador in the novel is to seize its assets and make quick money by buying and selling all manner of newly available goods and newly commodified materials: from hotel rooms and 'western' currency to city parking spaces and local women for sex tourists. Viewed from this angle, the stripping woman becomes a representative figure, not only of a general breakdown of social relations or stubborn defiance, but also of newly capitalised labour capabilities – through a savage irony, the woman's breakdown is also readable as a pornographic performance for the benefit of those running the hotel and the 'new' Slovakia beyond it.

The structure and plot of Pist'anek's novel challenge its readers to reflect on the credibility of events as they unfold. The central plot line itself – the incredible rise of the novel's anti-hero Rácz from peasant to political oligarch – is designed to give readers several pauses for thought. Rácz's initial 'leap' – straight from the pages of Trotsky's formulation of the law of uneven and combined development – from rural field to urban boiler room is presented, in a circumspect movement between present and future imperfect tense, as simultaneously plausible and unbelievable. Temporal challenges punctuate the narrative, indexing anxious attempts on the part of the new plutocrats to break decisively with and supersede the past. The chapters move forward in staccato fashion, with unbalanced leaps and bounds, mirroring the outlandish yet startling 'progress' possible for some, such as Rácz and his various hangers-on, in this new world of temporal unsteadiness and altered social relations.

Pist'anek's is a novel of combined and uneven development, presented in what might best be described as a kind of modernist picaresque satire that attempts to capture what the novel itself describes as 'unthinkable just two or three months ago' (2007: 203). Rácz's power grows, in these hyper-accelerating circumstances, through the capital he comes to command by virtue of his control of the flow of energy and currency around the hotel. He takes charge of its heating system – a pointed parody of the post-communist order's energy oligarchs and their dramatically expanded new power in domestic and international energy markets that have disturbed the settled determination of European cultural and political flows, and established the semi-peripheral nature of the former Soviet countries, most notably Russia.[1]

In the novel, the freshly floodlit buildings of the Rácz Corporation come to dominate the newly privatised city of Bratislava. Rácz's command of space and illegal foreign currency exchange pave the way for his move into politics. Penetrating to the very political and financial heart of the new Slovakia – at the time of the novel's writing still ten years away from its full-blown 'Tatra Tiger' phase – Rácz's rapacious clientelism offers an ironic portrait of the drastically unbalanced features of the newly 'modernised' economy, in which short-term accumulation and the desperate urge to own property are presented blankly as the routine, if plainly fetishistic, obsessions of any nascent bourgeoisie. By the close of the novel, the kinds of absurd contradiction endemic to capitalist modernity are apparent: 'in these unsettled times debts are the best and safest investment' (236). The novel concludes as the Slovak neoliberal bubble, underwritten by the representatives of the new state, enters its phase of unbridled expansion: it offers a final vision of the city as a bleak horizon, 'empty, dark and overcast […] the river muddy, black' (256).

Those who sound the rallying cry of 'modernisation' most often present it not merely as an irresistible tide raising all boats, but also as an unambiguously progressive social force. But it has not typically been portrayed thus in the literary and cultural work to have emerged from the peripheries and semi-peripheries of Europe: in the work of many writers and artists from these locations, the

---

1 See Simon 2009, who argues that in the aftermath of the enforced – 'shock' – restructuring of their economies after 1989, the post-Soviet societies – and Russia above all – have not managed to integrate themselves into the core of the world-system but have instead retained (and expanded) multiple aspects of their own long histories of semi-peripherality. Simon refers us, in the Russian case, to the over-reliance on extractive industries – most notably oil and gas – and to the 'passive revolution' in terms of which the devolution of power to a neo-*nomenklatura* of media, state and oligarchical business elites has prevented the emergence of a strong liberal bourgeoisie. The result has been a series of privatisations the general populace has not shared in, a massive increase in wealth *and* poverty – in other words, in *inequality* – generally unknown in the Soviet era, the spread of organised crime, and fluctuating extremes of inflation. 'Since the collapse of the USSR', Simon notes, 'Russia has become a semi-peripheral state, albeit an atypical one, because the "passive revolution" has entailed the retention and recombination of significant components of the Soviet system at the same time as reintegration into the world-economy primarily through the medium of energy and raw material exports […] Changing Russia's industrial structure and addressing other potential obstacles to capitalism required re-subjecting Russia to combined and uneven development […] [T]he result of these cross-cutting influences from the Soviet past, on the one hand, and integration into the capitalist world-economy on the other, was a social formation based on different relations of production in different sectors of the economy generating contradictory pressures which combined with those created by being pulled between core and periphery' (126–30).

rhetoric of 'modernisation' has been cast as 'affirmative culture' in the precise, Marcusean, sense – that is to say, as ideology, pure and simple. The true face of modernity represented in these works is the face of capitalism, in which the profit and prosperity of a few are made possible through the exploitation of most. 'Modernisation' is phrased, in these terms, as a powerfully seductive millennial dream, the shimmering illusory (and compensatory) projection of an alter-world in which equality and wealth are offered and afforded. Like so many other novels of the European peripheries and semi-peripheries, *Rivers of Babylon* treats the rush for 'modernisation' and 'westernisation' with sardonic reserve. We are presented with 'western' Europeans who are involved in sex tourism or shady deals with local 'entrepreneurs' and covetous politicians. Rácz's overwrought 'peasant' aspirations to be 'European' need to be set against the wishful dream, pervasive across the zones of post-communism, to be seen as 'western'. Slavenka Drakulic speaks of the 'longing' of many from 'the old communist Eastern Europe' to be taken to belong to *western* Europe – or more particularly, 'to a preconceived idea of Western Europe': 'In fact, there can never be enough signs to indicate and emphasise that this is not the old, communist, poor, primitive, Oriental, backward Eastern Europe any longer. Can't you see that we belong to the West too, except that we have been exiled from it for half a century?' (1999: 10). As a peripheral modernist novel, *Rivers of Babylon*, via Rácz's recalcitrant 'country ways', affords a critique of that instantaneity where the leaps and accelerations of capitalist 'development' leave large and unbridgeable gaps between the new business elites and the masses in the urban peripheries and rural hinterlands. As Rácz looks forward to his indebted 'success', for example, the narrator immediately recalls the unknown fate of 'two solitary prostitutes' sold into sex tourism somewhere between Slovakia and Austria (Pist'anek 2007: 257). This, it is emphasised, is now a commonplace disappearance – the girls are described as 'two drops in the ocean', caught in the unregulated space between west and east. Rácz's visit back to his village, of which he is now contemptuous, also provides an unsubtle reminder of the people left behind but not totally out of sight in the Tatra's vision of the new 'west/east'. He is unable to erase this background from his conscience and consciousness.

A Singular, Uneven Europe

To the question, 'what does Europe mean to the Eastern European imagination?' Drakulic answers:

> It is certainly not a question of geography, for in those terms we are already in it and need make no effort to reach it. It is something distant, something to be attained, to be deserved. It is also something expensive and fine: good clothes, the certain look and smell of its people. Europe is plenitude: food, cars, light, everything – a kind of festival of colours, diversity, opulence,

beauty. It offers choice: from shampoo to political parties. It represents freedom of expression. It is a promised land, a new Utopia, a lollipop. And through television, that Europe is right there, in your apartment, often in colours much too bright to be real. (1999: 12)

Drakulic encounters this dream of 'Europe' as 'plenitude' in her travels around the former 'Eastern bloc' countries in the years of the post-communist transition, although it often assumes nightmarish forms. What is at issue here has less to do with the difficulties of 'transition', we think – chaotic and unregulated as that process was and remains – than with the volatility and crisis-ridden quality of capitalism itself: what Drakulic encounters is a particular sounding of a general contemporary theme. The 'Europe' that looms in the fervid imaginations of long-suffering 'eastern' Europeans is obviously a fantasy projection. It does not exist, certainly not in the east of the actual continent, but not in its western reaches either. Indeed, we can identify this 'Europe' most exactly as the halo of capitalism. For Drakulic, writing at more or less the same time as Pist'anek, the tragic irony is that no lessons seem to have been learned from the disastrous modernisation policies of the long years of Soviet overlordship. In Romania, for example,

> The communist crash course in urbanisation did not help the newcomers to change their habits. [Under communism] people were forced to jump from a village into a city, to make the giant leap from feudalism to communism, without the time or education to develop a civic society and all its values and habits [...] This historical mistake has to be corrected now but I am afraid that it will take time [...] People need time to change habits and to understand and implement new ideas and values [...] If we are to undergo yet another crash course, this time in democracy, the result will be more or less the same. (36–37)

The capitalist order that imposes itself behind the veil of the ideological dreamscape of post-wall 'New Europe' is emphatically different from the Keynesian social democracy that stabilised western European states in the 'boom' years of the Cold War. In 'Eastern Europe' the post-communist transition to capitalism has been profoundly *destabilising*, not simply because it has involved the tearing down of the discredited communist structures, but because it has compounded and exacerbated the distorted patterns of development that marked the communist era. The dehumanising violence and brutality of the old dispensation has been matched and even intensified by the new, ferociously unbound, neoliberal dispensation, bent on imposing 'market democracy' through economic shock therapy. As Neil Lazarus has written,

> in the post-Soviet contexts, the full implications of the fact that liberation *from* 'actually existing' socialism has been liberation *into* the world-system of 'actually existing' capitalism are now having to be confronted. For this latter is a world-system, already and in principle deeply uneven, and now undergoing profound contraction and structural crisis besides. Forever

> invoking the shibboleth of 'globalisation' and chanting that 'there is no alternative', its elites are currently doing everything they can to strip away what meagre social provisions and benefits still remain from those it had proved possible to win – in the 'east' and the 'south', significantly, as much as in the 'west' – in the 'golden age' of the post-1945 boom. (2012: 121)

A comparative reading of a selected number of texts such as we offer here, from the European peripheries and semi-peripheries, will, we think, help to demonstrate that the realities of combined and uneven development – so often conceived as characterising the *non-European* world – are in fact constitutive of *European* modernism also, *and remain so* in the contemporary moment. That it is necessary to call this body of literature *modernist* is one of our central claims in this book, and potentially, we believe, of considerable consequence for those interested in the comparative analysis of literary form in the global arena. Eschewing the normative periodisation of modernism, we insist on its temporal and geographical elasticity. A widening of modernism's parameters – geographic, temporal and technical – allows us to understand better its perennial attachment to processes of modernisation everywhere, that is, to repeat, throughout the world *including* Europe. 'Peripheral modernism' is then emphatically not to be thought of as an exclusively 'non-European' development. On the contrary, to the degree that capitalist modernity exemplifies the logic of combined and uneven development in its inner tendency, the link between modernisation and modernism – and hence the emergence of 'peripheral modernisms' – seems to us unforgoable.

We should note that the proposal to expand the historical parameters of modernism has been heard before in modernist studies. Some thirty years ago, Marshall Berman reminded us that 'going back', beyond the dates usually understood to mark the inception of modernism,

> can be a way to go forward [...] [R]emembering the modernisms of the nineteenth century can give us the vision and courage to create the modernisms of the twenty-first. This act of remembering can help us bring modernism back to its roots, so that it can nourish and renew itself, to confront the adventures and dangers that lie ahead. To appropriate the modernities of yesterday can be at once a critique of the modernities of today and an act of faith in the modernities – and in the modern men and women – of tomorrow and the day after tomorrow. (1983: 36)

Following Jameson's more recent re-emphasising of the singularity of modernity, we might also argue the inverse: that the modernisms of the *present* can also help revise, expand and reformulate our understanding of the modernisms of the *past*. Pist'anek's novel, for example, contains a precise echo of a scene of urban distress in a novel written 130 years before his, one that Berman reads as part of a wider literary movement dealing with forms of uneven development in the periphery of Europe in the nineteenth century. The scene takes place in mid-1860s St Petersburg – an archetype of the modernising city of the peripheral 'eastern' Europe, founded on the

Tsarist urge to implant, and (literally) concretise the terms and infrastructure of the 'west'. The city is seen, throughout this literature, struggling in the grip of the shock phase of this long and difficult process of modernisation. In the packed, claustrophobic streets around the Nevsky Prospect, another impassive woman has a sudden public meltdown. She decides to drown herself in front of a horrified crowd by jumping from the Voznessensky Bridge into a canal. Like the woman in *Rivers of Babylon*, she seems impervious to everything around her. Standing in the middle of this bridge is a 'dreadfully weak' Rodya Raskolnikov:

> He longed to sit or lie down somewhere in the street. Bending over the water, he gazed mechanically at the last pink flush of the sunset, at the row of houses growing darker in the gathering twilight, at one attic window on the left bank, flashing as though on fire in the last rays of the setting sun, at the darkening water of the canal, and the water seemed to catch his attention [...] Suddenly he started, saved again perhaps from swooning by an uncanny and hideous sight. He became aware of someone standing on the right side of him; he looked and saw a tall woman with a kerchief on her head, with a long, yellow, wasted face and red sunken eyes. She was looking straight at him, but obviously she saw nothing and recognised no one. Suddenly she leaned her right hand on the parapet, lifted her right leg over the railing, then her left and threw herself into the canal. The filthy water parted and swallowed up its victim for a moment, but an instant later the drowning woman floated to the surface, moving slowly with the current, her head and legs in the water, her skirt inflated like a balloon over her back. (Dostoyevsky 1972: Chapter 6, Part Two, 194–95)

As several commentators have noted, Raskolnikov's various sojourns on bridges clearly express his internalisation of the dichotomies, polarities and contradictions of Russian social conditions. The most obvious of these contradictions is that between 'Russian' (or 'Slavic') tradition and 'western' modernity – a structuring opposition in all of Dostoevsky's work and, indeed, throughout modern Russian literature. Raskolnikov is simultaneously Russian *and* modern, 'Slavic' *and* 'European', progressive *and* orthodox, criminal *and* anti-hero. The fracture, instability and volatility of his socio-historical constitution speak to the paradoxes intrinsic to the experience of modernity in Russia. But our point is that the intolerable social pressures indexed by Dostoyevsky are not limited to him or to the literature of Russia. Raskolnikov's trauma finds its echo in the lives of characters sketched in cities across Europe – from St Petersburg to Berlin, Madrid to Paris, as well as Aberdeen, Tirana, Oslo, Reykjavík, Sofia, Palermo, Lisbon and Warsaw. Dostoevsky's proto-modernism, in which a bizarre or absurd reality is presented as simultaneously ordinary and unexceptional, has been spoken of as a kind of 'fantastic realism': a corollary of the physical absurdity of the unregulated slums that sprouted around the imposing boulevards built under Tsar Peter's despotic rule, this defamiliarising 'realism' might be interpreted as an attempt to record the 'unreal reality' brought about by the unevenness of capitalist modernisation. In Döblin and Baudelaire, Zola and Hamsun too, we see that the grandiose redevelopment projects that opened up new sightlines for a modernising bourgeoisie also confront the members of this class with the ineradicable presence of the newly visible poor and dispossessed, who occupy the same city, but appear (at least from the standpoint of the bourgeois observers) as if from an alien place and another (earlier) time. As we saw in Chapter Two, above, Lukács diagnosed the situation of Raskolnikov's disorientation as one in which the anti-hero 'came from a far-off, unknown, almost legendary Russia to speak for the entire civilized West' (1962: 146). For Lukács, Dostoevsky was 'the first and greatest poet of the modern capitalist metropolis [...] drawing the mental deformations that are brought about as a social necessity by life in a modern city' (153). This deft placement finds an echo in one of the most famous studies of the Russian novelist, by Bakhtin, who wrote not merely that '[t]he polyphonic novel could [...] have been realized only in the capitalist era', but, even more specifically, that

> The most favorable soil for it was moreover precisely in Russia, where capitalism set in almost catastrophically, and where it came upon an untouched multitude of diverse worlds and social groups which had not been weakened in their individual isolation, as in the West, by the gradual encroachment of capitalism. Here in Russia the contradictory nature of evolving social life, not fitting within the framework of a confident and calmly meditative monologic consciousness, was bound to appear particularly abrupt. (2003: 19–20)[2]

Despite his well-known antipathy to modernist form in general, Lukács insisted on grasping Dostoevsky's writing as an index of the deformations of peripheral capitalism, though it is only with Berman that it proved possible to extend this conception and to refine into the argument that writing of this kind might best be analysed under the rubric of the 'modernism of underdevelopment'.

Dostoevsky gave his own experience of modernity a new, feverish register that would prove paradigmatic for such other writers of the European periphery as the Norwegian Knut Hamsun, the Spaniard Pio Baroja and the Scot James Kelman. Berman noted that 'the anguish of backwardness and underdevelopment' found in Dostoyevsky is archetypal for writing from the European periphery as well as writing from the 'emerging twentieth-century Third World' (1983: 175). But he also drew our attention to the fact that development in the 'Third World' context is marked – where development in the context of peripheral Europe is not, or at least not to the same degree

---

2 While we endorse Bakhtin's general reading, we would put some pressure on his identification of 'the exceptionally acute contradictions of early Russian capitalism' (35), which seems to us to be the product of an overly schematic opposition between 'Russia' and 'the west'.

– by the determined efforts on the part of the imperialist 'First World' powers to retard or neutralise any progressive possibilities within the process of modernisation. For Berman, the dialectic between containment and liberation opens up

> a larger polarity in the world history of modernism. At the one pole we can see the modernism of advanced nations, building directly on the material of economic and political modernization and drawing vision and energy from a modernized reality – Marx's factories and railways, Baudelaire's boulevards – even when it challenges that reality in radical ways. At an opposite pole we find a modernism that arises from backwardness and underdevelopment. This modernism first arose in Russia [...] in our own era with the spread of modernization – but generally, as in old Russia, a truncated and warped modernization – it has spread throughout the Third World. The modernism of underdevelopment is forced to build on fantasies and dreams of modernity, to nourish itself on an intimacy and struggle with mirages and ghosts. In order to be true to the life from which it springs, it is forced to be shrill, uncouth and inchoate. It turns in on itself, and tortures itself for its inability to singlehandedly make history [...] [T]he bizarre reality from which this modernism grows, and the unbearable pressures under which it moves and lives – social and political pressures as well as spiritual ones – infuse it with a desperate incandescence that Western modernism, so much more at home in its world, can rarely hope to match. (1983: 233)

There is much we can take from Berman's illuminating differentiation between modernisms in the world-literary system, but we would also want to propose some amendments to his analysis. One such amendment, in particular, might be mooted immediately. For, notwithstanding his argument that the 'modernism of underdevelopment' arises first in nineteenth-century Russia, Berman tends increasingly to situate this modernism as a 'non-western' phenomenon, to be distinguished more or less categorically from the 'western' variant that, on his reading, is 'so much more at home in its world'. The problem here is that, just like Susan Bassnett and Rey Chow, whose work we have discussed in Chapter One, Berman tends to speak of 'western modernism' without reference to the language of core, periphery and semi-periphery, paying no attention to what, on our reading, are the crucial and constitutive developmental gaps and unevennesses *within* the 'west' – as between Berlin and Copenhagen, say (a relationship between two capital cities), or between the Home Counties and Wearside (a relationship between two unevenly developed regions within the same country). The very idea of the 'European literary periphery' is decisive in this context, it seems to us, since it automatically directs us to the insight that 'core', 'periphery' and 'semi-periphery' are *multi-scalar* and *relational* rather than *geographical* or *geopolitical* concepts. 'Peripherality', in these terms, is not to be thought of as a 'condition' marked by lack of development, or by mere geographical remoteness from a given 'core' or 'centre'. Rather, it names the modality of a specific *inclusion* within a system: a given formation is 'peripheral', that is to say, not because it is 'outside' or 'on the edges' of a system, but, on the contrary, because it has been incorporated within that system precisely as 'peripheral' – hence the descriptor 'underdeveloped', as distinct from 'undeveloped', upon which the dependency theorists used to insist. It is helpful to recall Neil Smith's argument that (semi-)peripherality is produced and conditioned by a *peripheralising system* (Smith 1990). Many of the texts that we read as peripheral modernist *do* stem from countries and regions on the continental fringes of Europe – but not necessarily from the eastern or southern fringes. Texts from Scandinavia, Iceland and the UK can also be read as (semi-)'peripheral' in their formal registrations, their thematic preoccupations, their positioning within an institutionally complex world-literary system.

Comparativism and Postcolonial Europe

We have already welcomed Lucia Boldrini's reframing of the question of 'European' writing in the afterglow of the postcolonial unthinking of Eurocentrism. Yet in Boldrini's own account, it is *cultural* imperialism that seems to provide the dominant analytical category. Our own approach is more closely addressed than is hers to the specifically *capitalist* dimensions of European modernity. Over the past two decades or so, identifiable if controversial off-shoots or appropriations of postcolonial studies have emerged and developed in various sites across Europe. Ireland is in some ways the original model here, notable for its oft-cited exceptionality as a bona fide Euro-postcolonial qualifier.[3] But we have also seen the emergence of Gaelic, Baltic and Balkan postcolonialisms, of 'postcolonial' London, Lisbon and Paris, and of a British devolutionary literature formed in many ways under the influence of academic postcolonial literature and criticism.[4]

There is some social scientific scholarship that attempts to code peripheral European regions as colonies of the more powerful core states surrounding

---

3 See Kiberd for an interesting discussion of contemporary Irish culture as vacillating between the definition of itself as 'postcolonial' and as 'European': 'the Irish experience is at once post-colonial and post-imperial [...] The real challenge today is to find a truly contrapuntal narrative which projects both aspects of the national experience and captures the complexity of being at once postcolonial and European, an experience which is not in fact unique now that the European Union has received applications for membership from the recently-liberated nations of Eastern Europe' (1997: 97).
4 See the discussion of these ideas in Coombs 2011; Gould 2013; Hargreaves and McKinney 1997; Kelertas 2006; McLeod 2004; and Sandru 2012; and the articles by Cervinkova, Cornis-Pope, Gosk; Lazarus; Pavlyshyn; Popescu, Tlostanova, and Velickovic in the special issue of *Journal of Postcolonial Writing* (2012), edited by Dorota Kolodziejczyk and Cristina Sandru.

them.⁵ This tendency is especially marked where the focus falls on Russia's relations with satellite states in the Soviet system.⁶ However, most analysis of 'postcolonial' Europe has been culturalist and identitarian in outlook and has emerged within the broader fields of literary and cultural studies. We can immediately note the clear mismatch between the avowed anti- and post-nationalist temper of postcolonial studies in its consolidated ('western'!) aspect and the foundationalism of the nationalism that underlies the 'post-colonising' gesture in much of the new ('eastern') 'post-communist' scholarship. But mostly what we want to suggest here is that a vocabulary and conceptualisation derived from world-systems theory are more appropriate to discussion of 'expanded' Europe than a vocabulary and conceptualisation derived from postcolonial studies. It is possible to pay due attention to specific questions of coloniality within an analysis of core, semi-periphery and periphery, we believe; it is not really possible to address peripheralisation as an historic process with the toolkit bequeathed by postcolonial studies or colonial discourse theory. The general point has been well made recently by Anna Klobucka:

> While many of the historically occurring cultural and political phenomena of the European periphery parallel those manifest in the cultures and societies of former European colonies, the paradigms of colonial and postcolonial development offer an analytic tool that is only partially adequate (and, on occasion, patently inadequate) to describing their 'semiperipheral' specificity. For one thing, the historical (as well as metaphorical) colonizer/colonized divide cuts across the varied spectrum of cultures and societies located on the margins of the Northwestern European core. (1997: 125–26)

Just as elsewhere in the world, so too in the European hinterlands the problematics of modernisation, modernity and modernism are ultimately world-systemic rather than national or regional. Central to our considerations in this book, indeed, is the question of how to compare (semi-)peripheral modernisms across national, regional and global scales.

Any contemporary sociological reading of world literature, or of the world-literary system, will have to deal with the large shadow cast by Pascale Casanova's model of a relatively autonomous international literary space. Casanova's Bourdieusian method measures international networks of resistance to national forms of 'domination' by tracking the counter-measures writers deploy in bypassing purely domestic frames of reference and consecration. Her mapping of the 'internationalism' of the literature deriving from 'small nations' seeks to connect writers and writing – often, it must be conceded, canonical 'modernist' writers and writing – with literary formations inside and outside the Parisian literary meridian (2004:

---

5 See Aldcroft 2006, for example.
6 See the relevant discussions in Etkind 2011; Etkind, Finnin et al. 2012; Ghodsee 2011; and Outhwaite and Ray 2005.

esp. 247–53). Casanova's critics have tended to focus on the first section of *The World Republic of Letters* and to ignore the comparative readings that she offers in the second half of that text. But in these later chapters, her initially rather rigid formulation of the distinctness of economic from cultural forms of globalisation relaxes and wanes somewhat, and she offers us a model of peripheral writing across continents, times and spaces, connected by homologous situations of historical 'backwardness'. For instance, in tracing the lineage of 'the Faulknerian revolution' in several writers from various (semi-)peripheral zones – among them Juan Benet, Rachid Boudjedra, Gabriel García Márquez and Mario Vargas Llosa – she comes close to our understanding of what a (semi-)peripheral modernism can demonstrate in its registration of combined and uneven development.

Casanova's thoughts can be usefully extended in order to correct a trend in recent debates about the extension of modernism, in terms of which aesthetic sensibilities are seen to radiate from ('western') Europe and North America to other, 'underdeveloped', parts of the world. This perspective, of course, leaves out the question of the uneven development of modernism *within* Europe, whether 'old' or 'new', 'east' or 'west'. We refer here both to an unremarked *provincial* modernism and to the specific formations – thus far unconnected and under-compared – of European *rural* modernism, neither of which have been given much attention in standard conceptions of European literary modernism.[7] With the academic institutionalisation of postcolonial and world-literary studies, indeed, the attention given to non-European literatures has resulted, as Theo D'haen has argued, in 'an ever growing marginalization, or perhaps we should say "peripheralization," of Europe's minor literatures' (2012: 153). D'haen sounds a necessary protest here against the competitive pseudo-universalism of today's global literary marketplace, which celebrates developments in the dominant languages and literatures while neglecting or disregarding altogether those in the 'minor' languages and literatures.[8] But the problem might also be seen as presenting an opportunity for us to engage anew with the questions of how best to think systematically about literary comparativism on a world scale.

D'haen is right to point out that 'Europe's minor literatures' are not merely 'minoritised' but actively 'peripheralised' by current institutional structures: the translation deficit in the Anglo-American sphere; the centripetal tendencies of pan-European agencies; the continuing allure of 'core' European

---

7 Still following Casanova, we might think here of Juan Benet, of Faroese, Icelandic and Scottish modernist work, of Hamsun's country novels, Lampedusa's *The Leopard* and indeed the work of such other Sicilian writers as Giovanni Carmelo Verga, Leonardo Sciascia and even Salvatore Quasimodo, whose receipt of the Nobel Prize for Literature in 1959 does not seem to have been sufficient to afford him 'international' consecration.
8 The phrase 'global literary marketplace' is Brouillette's, of course: see Brouillette 2007.

texts across educational syllabi; and the relative international weakness of regional and critical sub-fields in the 'small' European literatures dominated by the 'larger' literatures surrounding them. But if we put various (semi-) peripheral European works – set in different places and written at different times – into conversation with one another and read them together without ignoring what we might call their non-simultaneous simultaneity, we begin to discern the ways in which they typically register the 'local' and 'global' aspects of modernity as at one and the same time traumatic, destructive, stimulating and profoundly transformative. This seems to us to be crucial to the comparative reading of modernism in texts from such disparate (semi-) peripheral countries as Spain, Hungary, Scotland, Ireland, Norway, Portugal, Poland, Wales, Iceland, Slovakia, Italy, Serbia, Albania and Russia, as well as from relatively peripheralised locations in the core societies of England, France and Germany. To place such writing in relation to a heterogeneously conceived capitalist modernity is to read against the grain of the generally understood 'time' and 'place' of modernism. What we are trying to do is to develop a model or interpretive frame capable of holding together not only such texts as Dostoevsky's *Crime and Punishment* (St Petersburg, 1867), Knut Hamsun's *Hunger* (Oslo/Kristiania, 1890), Pio Baroja's *The Quest* (Madrid, 1903), Deszö Kosztolányi's *Skylark* (Serbia/Hungary, 1925) and Lewis Grassic Gibbon's *Sunset Song* (Scotland, 1932) – whose chronological placement as 'modernist' is relatively uncontroversial – but also such other, more recent, but in our view analogous, texts, which equally figure the *worlding* of capitalist modernity: Halldór Laxness's *The Atom Station* (Reykjavik, 1948), for instance, Ahmet Hamdi Tanpinar's *A Mind at Peace* (Istanbul, 1949), Lampedusa's *The Leopard* (Sicily, 1958), George Mackay Brown's *Greenvoe* (Orkney Islands, 1972), James Kelman's *The Busconductor Hines* (Glasgow, 1984), Ornela Vorpsi's *The Country Where No-One Ever Dies* (Tirana, 2004), Irvine Welsh's *Trainspotting* (Edinburgh, 1993), Pist'anek's *Rivers of Babylon* (Bratislava, 1991) and Andrzej Stasiuk's *9* (Warsaw, 1999).

Madrid, 1904

Mary Lee Bretz (2001) offers a compelling explanation for the exclusion of Spanish modernism (and indeed Latin American and Hispanic American modernism with close ties to Spanish *modernismo*) from established narratives of European (and global) modernism, by noting a consensus in the field of modernist studies that 'Europe' begins (or ends) at the Pyrenees. This consensual perspective exoticises Spanish culture and society, xenophobically equating it with a pre-modern Africa or a backward Latin America.[9]

---

9 This despite the fact that Latin America has a very good case for having instigated the very concept of 'modernism'. Perry Anderson has written that 'Contrary to conventional expectation, [modernism was] [...] born in a distant periphery

Combined and Uneven Development

It also speaks, as Susan Larson and Eva Woods point out, to a misguided understanding of Spanish modernity as somehow always lagging behind other ('core') European states. Larson and Woods counter this misconception by arguing that 'even the most hegemonic of modernities draws on the peripheral or the marginal. The specificity of Spain's modernity does not mean that it lies outside of a larger European modernity' (2005: 5). Certainly the earlier industrialisation of 'core' European countries left Spain on the wrong side of what Sidney Pollard has called 'the great divide in Europe', where 'the economy of the servile lands of eighteenth- and nineteenth-century Europe resembled that of the underdeveloped countries of the second half of the twentieth' (1998: 81). Larson and Woods try to problematise the tendency to assume that what happened in Spain did not really form part of modern European history by pointing both to the *equivalencies* that existed between Spanish and other European colonial modernisms and to Spanish neglect of its own 'internal and colonial others' (2005: 5). Read from a world-systemic perspective, however, Spain's evident 'backwardness' can easily be grasped as typical of capitalist modernisation in the semi-peripheries. As Aldcroft observes, somewhat crudely, the form of development that we call 'western' or 'European' was in fact quite unevenly distributed, even in Europe itself: before 1914, he writes, '[t]rue industrial development was often highly concentrated spatially [in Europe], sometimes forming islands of capitalism in a sea of primitivism, while the level of efficiency fell well short of Western standards' (2006: 9). As a country notably pockmarked by these internal 'islands', Spain was not *outside* 'European' modernity; nor was its 'development' belated. Just the reverse: in Spain, as Larson and Woods point out, 'the imposition of modernity led to a brutal, chaotic industrial

---

rather than at the centre of the cultural system of the time: [it comes] [...] not from Europe or the United States, but from Hispanic America. We owe the coinage of "modernism" as an aesthetic movement to a Nicaraguan poet, writing in a Guatemalan journal, of a literary encounter in Peru. Rubén Darío's initiation in 1890 of a self-conscious current that took the name of *modernismo* drew on successive French schools – romantic, Parnassian, symbolist – for a "declaration of cultural independence" from Spain that set in motion an emancipation from the past of Spanish letters themselves, in the cohort of the 1890s. Where in English the notion of "modernism" scarcely entered general usage before mid-century, in Spanish it was canonical a generation earlier. Here the backward pioneered the terms of metropolitan advance – much as in the nineteenth century "liberalism" was an invention of the Spanish rising against French occupation in the epoch of Napoleon, an exotic expression from Cádiz at home only much later in the drawing-rooms of Paris or London' (1998: 3). See also Santiáñez 2005: 479–80. Alex Longhurst argues that Spanish modernism, fitting neatly with the 'pushing back' of the temporal coordinates of modernism famously proposed by Malcolm Bradbury, in many ways preceded – and formed prototypes for – the great stylistic developments of post-World War I 'European' modernism, perhaps because 'the historical process that took the novel from Realism to Modernism was rather more condensed in Spain than it was in England or France' (1999: 2–3).

development and an accelerated rhythm of life, exacerbated by mass media images that seemed to legitimate modernity's empty promise of a new world' (2005: 6).

This discussion proves an apposite context for a reading of Pio Baroja's peripheral modernist fiction, in particular his novel *The Quest*, the first in his Madrilenian trilogy, *The Struggle for Life* (1922–24). In order to make sense of Baroja's work, we need to make a few more preliminary remarks regarding the cultural and historical situation of Spain in relation to the European literary and politico-economic systems at the time of his writing.

According to Bretz, the critical neglect of Spanish modernism can be correlated with the widespread perception that Spain failed to 'undergo modernization' in the 'core' European sense of the term in the *fin de siècle* (2001: 27). Observers have not, of course, denied the evidence of economic, technical and industrial development and massive social restructuring during the 'high' period of Spanish modernism (from 1890 to 1930), but they have judged these to constitute 'irregular encounters with modernization' (Larson and Woods 2005: 8). The specific pattern of Spain's modernisation – of a piece with capitalist development within the matrix of global modernity – has been misconstrued as incomplete or arrested.

Bretz draws attention to a series of contradictions in late nineteenth-century Spain: new developments (promising a transformation in existing social relations) being met with conservative opposition; pockets of society in which transformation had in fact occurred existing alongside feudalistic and archaic structures; and so on. In Spain, as elsewhere in Europe (including in sectors within 'core' Europe), there was evidence of changing and rapidly evolving cultural attitudes around the issues of 'race', self and nationhood, with changing class relations as the soil in which all these new attitudes took root and grew. This unevenness proved fertile ground for the emergence of modernist ideas:

> New perceptions of time and memory affect both the vision of nation and individual subject. In the context of Spanish social development, relations among the bourgeoisie, aristocracy, and lower classes, both urban and rural, also require reassessment. The interaction of city and country and of individual subjects and rapidly changing surroundings, in spaces ranging from the subatomic to the galactic, figures prominently [...] [A] destabilised world sees an increase in irony and ambiguity that transforms traditional interactions of author, narrator, and reader, as well as inherited visions of art and the world. (2001: 23)

These social developments found a transcoded literary representation in the uneven (or even unstable) modernism of restlessly experimental Spanish writers such as Baroja, José Martínez Ruiz ('Azorín') and Ramón María del Valle-Inclán, whose careers, consistent in their inconsistency, were marked by audacious risk-taking and refusal of orthodoxy. Santiáñez notes that their resistance to normative realist-mimetic forms should be read principally as 'a form of opposition and resistance to the irrational forms of modernity' that were taking root throughout the region (2005: 486). Other critics, however, see *The Quest* (and indeed the trilogy overall) as belonging to Baroja's 'realist/naturalist' phase, while conceding that the persistent intrusion of an ironic, doubting tone works against its realist credentials (Longhurst 1999: 28–29; Denning 2004: 55). This view often attempts to read the uncertainty and irony of the novel as a subjective exploration of existentialist concerns typical of the time. But we see these elements rather as registering a general anxiety about modern life in Baroja's Madrid, which in turn forces an interrogation of the world-system as ultimate political horizon. There is in Baroja what we might call a 'realist modernism' that ceaselessly traverses the transitional ground between realism, naturalism and more experimental forms of writing, reflexively assessing the efficacy of the encounters of these different modes with changing historical conditions.

Cast in the shadow of the post-1898 decline of Spanish economic power and the loss of its colonial holdings, Baroja's *The Struggle for Life* trilogy details the extremes of Madrid's backwardness (in comparison to other Spanish and European regions), experienced (and largely focalised) through the consciousness of Manuel – a young rural migrant whose arduous existence in the city is contained in a fragmented, wandering narrative. Madrid (and Castile generally) was, at the time of Baroja's writing, much less socially and economically developed than industrialised regions of the Basque country and Catalonia.[10] The famed 1898 literary generation hailed mostly from 'peripheral' areas of Spain: moving to Madrid to seek careers as writers, they found a city lurching between past and present, innovation and retrenchment, and spasmodically seized by 'progressive' and 'reactionary' ideologies.

Contingency and uncertainty are consistent features of the trilogy, discernible in the first novel of the sequence, *The Quest*, in a twitchy plot, non-linear structure and persistent anxiety over mimetic stability. The narrator begins by confessing his uncertainty regarding the time, as three clocks each strike a different hour. Such 'chronometric disorder' (Baroja 1922: 3) – a marker of modernity's acutely transformative effect – is exacerbated by the setting: a half-way boarding house, its inhabitants unsure of their next meal and fretting over their futures at a time when it is very difficult to find work. This anxious, unreliable narrator appears throughout Baroja's work, displaying a penchant for self-consciousness that can be hinged not only to emergent modernist discussions about the perceptive qualities of the artist in fragmentary and incomprehensible times, but also to the broader, altering and alienating, historical and spatial context.

---

10 This is not to present these latter territories as exemplars of comprehensive modernisation. Recalcitrant agrarianism pervaded the entire country: throughout the nineteenth century in the Basque country, for example, re-ruralisation programmes continued to announce themselves as the alternative and antidote – admittedly feudalist – to industrialised modernity.

Consider the opening of the first chapter of the book's second part:

> The inhabitant of Madrid who at times finds himself by accident in the poor quarters near the Manzanares river, is surprised at the spectacle of poverty and sordidness, of sadness and neglect presented by the environs of Madrid with their wretched Rondas, laden with dust in the summer and in winter wallowing in mire. The capital is a city of contrasts; it presents brilliant light in close proximity to deep gloom; refined life, almost European, in the centre; in the suburbs, African existence, like that of an Arab village. Some years ago, not many, in the vicinity of the Ronda de Sevilla and of el Campillo de Gil Imón, there stood a house of suspicious aspect and of not very favourable repute, to judge by popular rumour [...] In this and other paragraphs of the same style I had placed some hope, for they imparted to my novel a certain phantasmagoric and mysterious atmosphere; but my friends have convinced me I ought to suppress these passages, arguing that they would be quite in place in a Parisian novel, but not in one dealing with Madrid, – not at all. They add, moreover, that here nobody goes astray, not even if one wishes to. Neither are there here any observers, nor houses of suspicious aspect, nor anything else. In resignation, then, I have excised these paragraphs, through which I hoped some day to be elected to the Spanish Academy; and so I continue my tale in more pedestrian language. (1922: 53–54)

Despite the apparent rejection of 'Parisian' realism that the meta-fictional interruption enacts here, we should recognise a typically Barojan irony in the faint lament for a Balzacian or Dickensian observational style, shaded – and contradicted – by the acknowledgment of such a style's impossibility and unsuitability for the times.

There are several issues that this passage throws up in relation to the critical assessment of the 'peripheral' forms of Spanish modernism, understood in Richard Sheppard's words as 'a heterogeneous range of responses to a global process of modernization' (quoted in Bretz 2001: 29). Contradictions and overlaps are manifest not only in the passage's stark depiction of urban spatial and material unevenness, but also in its attention to foreign material and cultural presences. This kind of 'transnationalism' is central to Castilian as well as Catalan modernism, and is identifiable in other Barojan novels also, which work to displace assumptions about 'European' cultural forms through their considered focus on the African connection with Spain.[11] The juxtaposition between a 'refined *almost* European' life (our emphasis) and the 'African/

---

11 Bretz draws attention to Baroja's 'criticism of European imperialism and the imposition of European institutions in Africa', noting that 'the future Spain will link up not with Europe but with Africa [...] Spain may spread a vision that contrasts with the European model.' This she sees as typical of a more general attitude in Spanish modernism: 'The defense of African and Asian civilizations as equal or superior to European culture occurs throughout Spanish modernist writing in connection with the rejection of racial theories and imperialism' (2001: 138–39).

Arab' existence on the edges of the city is pitched and tossed, spun in paradox and irony, confirming but also satirising a Eurocentric metropolitan outlook from a position attentive to conditions on the (semi-)peripheries.

Such a 'juxtaposed combination' is typical of the radical tendencies of the 1898 literary generation, who sought to challenge both the exclusivist visions of Spain as non-European *and* the significant internal attempts to promote xenophobic forms of cultural uniformity. The so-called 'native' culture of Spain, from Catholicism to bull-fighting, appears as outmoded and in decline throughout the novel. On the other hand, an obsession with regeneration courses throughout the work, often framed conflictually and bathetically, and carefully contextualised in the general eclipse of historical colonial prestige by the lurch to industrial culture and the configuration of new class relations. Bretz argues that 'peculiar historical conditions [...] mark Spanish national development as the first post-imperial European nation' (2001: 18), suggesting that the exclusion of Spanish from 'European' modernism is compound and in a sense double-determined: 'The persistent 'othering' of Spain has impeded the inclusion of the Spanish modernist exploration within studies of European and global modernism and remnants of an imperial, xenophobic Spanish ideology have similarly obstructed the mapping from within of connections between the Spanish culture of the period and the rest of Europe and the world' (19). The argument that the Spanish conditions are 'peculiar' might be challenged through reference to the recent insistence in European postcolonial studies, mentioned above, that the coloniser/colonised or European/other divide is applicable to other European regions and nations as well. Again, however, we would prefer to argue that such conditions, far from being 'peculiar', are in fact typical of (semi-)peripheral development, and thus homologous with developments within and without Europe at various times throughout the nineteenth and twentieth centuries.

What is clear from the long passage cited above is the novel's conscious search for a more effective, *modern* form intending to 'jolt the bourgeois reader into new habits of seeing and understanding' (Bretz 2001: 46). The reflexive elaboration of a 'pedestrian' language – one elaborated on the hoof, as it were – in order to best present the story of the brutal, dissipated and unsettled life of the rural *and* urban dispossessed as they negotiate a disorganised and chaotic metropolitan capitalism, is generally characteristic of *noventayochismo* ('1890ism'). It appeals to the uncertain, anti-Restorationist landscape of the post-1898 Spanish imperial culture. Equally, it constitutes an unevenly developed literary form, where modernism and naturalism meet, engage, coalesce and contradict, often within the same text. Bretz calls this form 'syncretic': it 'purposely promot[es] [...] the coexistence of opposites' (52–53); it is discernible across Castilian modernism in general. But, as Michael Denning argues in *Culture in the Age of Three Worlds*, it is also discernible as a global form, where, in the shape of what we are calling peripheral modernism, it attempts to register and transcode the problematics of combined and uneven development.

Particularly in her intuitive reading of temporal discontinuity, Bretz effectively sketches the cultural coordinates that compel the Barojan text's preoccupation with, and aesthetic rejoinder to, the experience of rapid change. But she is less expansive on the sociological determinants of the 'increasing emphasis on chance over causality, temporal jumps over succession' that she identifies (2001: 246). The Madrid of Baroja's novel was experiencing the effects of failed local and national attempts to speed up a belated industrialisation process that had experienced fits and false starts throughout the nineteenth century. A sustained wave of imposed modernisation – from infrastructure to culture – was attempted throughout the reign of Alfonso XIII, but the drive to impose capitalist social relations throughout the society experienced significant resistance from firmly entrenched and recalcitrant feudal elements.[12] Industrialism was thus highly uneven throughout the country. The labour opportunities in the novel demonstrate this, with Manuel confronted by semi-proletarianised work – he drifts from artisanal baking to irregular cobbling work to recycling the waste goods of the city. A picture of routinised labour is cast up near the close in the image of a wasted 'worker' family – from which the protagonists recoil in revulsion.

Baroja's sceptical narrator baulks at 'phantasmagoric' modes of expression, yet the novel details people living Goya-esque existences in caves on the outskirts of a peninsular European capital. Within the city a significant number of people live in slums and among the scraps of refuse dumps, chewing on leftovers and bones. But throughout the novel significant technological development is also always apparent, often in the kind of hallucinatory and hellish descriptions reminiscent of Baroja's acknowledged influences – Dostoevsky and Dickens. The Dostoevskian motif of the bridge as a site between different structures of experience is apparent in a scene near the beginning, where we find Manuel on a bridge over a river in the provincial town of Almazán (itself a suggestively located place, situated halfway between the capital and the 'advanced' regions of the Basque country and Catalonia). The town, initially viewed through 'the gloom of a dimly starlit night', appears 'fantastic and mysterious', yet Manuel's gaze is diverted between the 'pale electric lights' of the main plaza and the belfry of a church (1922: 20). The river is divided into islets, shining 'like mercury', and such figurative distinctions and overlaps between modern and traditional perspective, between nature and artifice, and between the old world and the fantastic new one become increasingly apparent as Manuel heads towards the city on a train:

> a thousand recollections thronged his imagination: the events of the night before at his uncle's mingled in his mind with fleeting impressions of Madrid, already half-forgotten. One by one the sensations of distinct epochs intertwined themselves in his memory, without rhyme or reason and among them, in the phantasmagoria of near and distant images that

---

12 See the introductory commentary in Sampedro Vizcaya and Doubleday 2008.

rolled past his inner vision, there stood out clearly those sombre towers glimpsed by night in Alamazán by the light of the moon. (22)

The fleeting yet impressive signs and appearances of modernity are common throughout Baroja, as is the kind of wandering narrative and erratic characterisation seen in *The Quest* (see Bretz 2001: 243). The 'distinct' epochs Manuel holds in his consciousness are manifest in a narrative register that lurches between the contingent modernist, the phantasmagoric and the classical bourgeois realist. The juxtapositioning of these styles clearly indexes the simultaneity of the modern and the archaic throughout Madrid.[13] The expansion of the electricity grid, for example, the vanguard industry of modernisation, allows the expansion of the rail network that carries Manuel from the rural provinces into the heart of the halogen-lit city, where he is immediately cast into a marginal slum lit by candles. An arc-lamped city centre is ringed by 'shanties', consisting of 'African huts built upon a framework of rough sticks and cane' (71). In rendering Manuel's drifting, violent, contingent experience of this 'half-modern' city, *The Quest* mixes identifiable modes of excessive naturalism with a kind of abrupt, unstructured episodic narrative we can only see as a form of fantastic modernism seeking to capture these new exigencies of modernity appearing throughout the country in shocks, fits and starts. Bretz sees this unevenness also registered in a later Baroja novel, *La dama errante* (1908), which explores the intrusion of modernity into rural life:

> an accelerated modern temporality enters into contact with traditional rhythms [...] Characters comment on the intersection of these distinct experiences of temporality. After observing a rustic celebration in a country hermitage and the toothless, hairy, rural participants, María and a more educated farmer remark that they feel they are living in the Bronze Age.

---

13 Arguments and conversations about 'the future of Spain and the reasons for national backwardness' (42) take place at all levels of Madrilenian society as represented in the novel. The notion of 'regeneration' is a theme in the text, and a topic of some debate. Manuel takes a job as a cobbler, forced to regenerate old shoes rather than make new ones – the lack of demand indicating the general lack of prosperity. He also ends the text as a worker in a recycling business, literally living among the detritus and waste of a modern capitalist metropolis – the throwaway culture of ephemeral modernity, whose 'dark depression attracted [him] somehow or other, with its rubbish heaps, its gloomy hovels, its comical dismantled merry-go-round, its swings, and its ground that held so many surprises, for a rough, ordinary pot burgeoned from its depths as easily as a lady's elegant perfume phial; the rubber bulb of a prosaic syringe grew side by side with the satin, scented sheet of a love letter' (258–59). For some, 'regeneration' is clearly suggestive of a rehabilitation of traditional monarchical and colonial interests, a restoration of Spanish 'prestige'. For others, it can only come with modernisation – of political institutions, social deprivation and economic infrastructure. Both sides seem to imply that becoming more 'European' is essential to their separate objectives.

María finds it hard to believe that trains, telegraph lines, and electric lights exist nearby. In this mix of temporal rhythms, many different stories and modes of narrating are possible. (2001: 244)

The identification here of the simultaneity of the non-simultaneous and the unification of difference speaks precisely to the logistics of combined and uneven development: it links Baroja's jagged novels to a whole range of other (semi-)peripheral European texts that chronicle and document the experience of modernity in similar ways.

Reykjavik, 1948

Iceland does not matter very much, when one looks at the total picture [...] we have been rather an insignificant nation. (Laxness 2004: 171)

The context of (semi-)peripherality immediately characterises Halldór Laxness's *The Atom Station*, a novel written partly in response to the author's disgust at the 'selling' of Icelandic sovereignty to US political and economic interests at the close of World War II. As the commanding NATO power at the start of the Cold War, the US sought to build an air base at Keflavik for strategic military purposes. This proposal encountered a considerable popular Icelandic resistance movement (Laxness, a Nobel Laureate, was a prominent member), and remains an enduring point of controversy in modern Icelandic history. In many respects, the model of 'postcolonial Europe' is especially applicable to this key moment, in which, ironically, after having at long last gained full independence from Danish dominion only a few years previously, in 1944, a hitherto 'marginal' nation on the Euro-global stage was rapidly yoked to the larger imperatives of the world-system. Fears relating to the loss of hard-won cultural sovereignty pervade many of Laxness's novels, along with expressed anxiety over the political corruption of a comprador elite engaged in clandestine deals to facilitate American economic, political, military and cultural supremacy in Iceland.

The period of the composition of *The Atom Station* had seen spectacular accelerated modernisation in Iceland, hitherto a predominantly rural nation. Here again we have a novel registering – at the levels of form and content – how jaggedly unsyncretic this process was – and adopting a distinctly modernist literary framework to express the attendant disquiet. However, it is more than just a foreign political presence on Iceland that Laxness's novel is concerned with – it is the very process of capitalist modernity's embedding within a whole lifeworld, from youth sub-cultures to welfare organisations, political parties to commodity habits, art practices to banking and agricultural methods. The threat to traditional ways of life is perceived as at the same time local, continental and international, as all levels of society become infected by the 'world bacterium' of transnational capitalism. It is the entire reshaping of Iceland's social and natural ecologies – its peaceful valleys and marginal towns and cities – into the epicentre of the atomic threat and the site of operation of transnational corporations and stock markets that Laxness takes as his subject matter.

The novel's opening records this disjunctive modernity in microcosm. Ugla, a young woman from the rural north, has come to Reykjavík to learn to play the organ for her traditional church, and finds employment as 'the new maid' (2004: 1) for the family of a politician heavily involved in 'selling the country' to the Americans. The very first line in the novel – 'Am I to bring in the soup?' – emphasises a wary servitude born of the new class relations experienced by rural migrants in Iceland in this period. The lady of the house disdains Ugla's struggle to learn to use the new electric floor polisher – a commodity that signals the increased presence of technology in a novel which is also about the sinister threat of that technology in the form of the nuclear bomb. By the third page, Ugla – like most of the protagonists of peripheral modernism – confesses to the cognitive dissonance that the accelerated time-space compressions of modern urban life generate: she is 'left alone in this new world which in a single day had made my previous life a dim memory – I am tempted to say a story in an old book' (7). She struggles to comprehend the ownership of so many things in her master's house:

> There were three reception rooms, forming an L-shape, crammed full of treasures. Three thousand lovely objects seemed to have made their way there of their own accord, without any effort, as livestock make for an unfenced meadow in the growing season. Here there was not one chair so cheap that it could be bartered for our autumn milch cow; and all our sheep would not fetch nearly enough to seat this whole family at once. I am sure that the carpet in the big drawing room cost more than our farm. (7)

Ugla's language clearly indicates her rural background. But rather than letting these indicators of a past or outmoded life fade, the novel persists with them. It wants to investigate whether these 'backward' elements of Icelandic life and culture are seamlessly reprocessed into art and myth for the modern urban citizens, or whether they prove to be stubbornly resistant to the forces of modernity.

Ugla's responses begin to be overtly politicised. 'Why do those who labour never own anything? Or was I a Communist to ask such a question?' (7), she asks, an inquisitive perspective deliberately manipulated by Laxness for maximum political and documentary effect. Such interrogative naivety will prove an excellent mode of characterisation and subtle satire in a novel interested in the shock of the new. The reach and power of the new transnational companies are everywhere evident. On a visit home to her remote valley church, Ugla meets – he materialises as if out of thin air – a former associate, who has secured a job with 'The Northern Trading Company', selling 'Cars, bulldozers, tractors, mixing machines, vacuum cleaners, floor polishers: everything which whirls, everything which makes a noise; modern times' (145).

By the novel's close, Ugla has become urbane enough to perceive that what the 'free market' promises is not to be trusted, and that the 'protection' that the US offers to Iceland is fundamentally self-interested. In his other novels, Laxness often mocks the idea of the Icelandic smallholder peasant as being a peripheral figure in a peripheral world. Instead, he characteristically emphasises just how connected they are to the world-system, even if not on conditions of their own choosing. The most notable example is found in *Independent People* (2008 [1934]), where there is a sudden flush of prosperity among the sheep farmers of northern Iceland, caused by the boom in wool prices brought by the hitherto 'remote' Great War. In *The Atom Station*, the world-market is synchronous with negotiations over the military base, and manifests itself in unexpected spaces in surreal moments, such as in the discovery in a remote valley in the north of a crate of Portuguese sardines (shipped from America) belonging to the newly present 'Northern Trading Company'. This is offered as a sure sign of the commodity logic of the world-market, which ships sardines to a country so well stocked with fish reserves that 'even the dogs walk out and vomit at the mere mention of salmon' (2004: 150).

Why though, did Laxness choose a particularly *modernist* form for this novel, rather than the naturalism or social realism of his previous novels? Why opt for a surrealist plot line, full of (seemingly) implausible and oblique events, packed together somewhat disjunctively with a series of short, allegorically oriented vignette 'chapters' for *The Atom Station*? The answer has to be two-fold. It has to do, first, with the manner in which the novel's surreal and mythic modernism manages to register the disjunctive character of Iceland's historical transformation. As elsewhere, this appears seemingly fantastic and unreal but utterly consistent with the kinds of reactions to modernity we have seen in other (semi-)peripheral works, European and non-European alike. The reader is forced to engage with the disorientating experience of being wrenched from relatively stable world-views, forced to become suspicious at the events of the plot, bizarre, secretive and unseen as these are often presented as being. The second reason has to do with Laxness's interest in presenting the *modern* significance of 'native form', exemplified in his insistence on the relevance of the saga and other folkloric forms to the everyday lives of modern Icelanders. The novel is punctuated with saga elements such as the 'kenning' of character names – all of which bespeak Laxness's attempt to chart the in-mixing of global with regional, national and local cultural forms.

For David Damrosch, this kind of penetration of regional culture by forms of globalisation is nothing new, but a consistent feature of Icelandic history from at least medieval times:

> As a writer from a peripheral region of Europe, Snorri [Sturluson, writer of the *Prose Edda* (c. 1240)] was well aware that his traditions were in danger of being overwritten by the global traditions that entered Iceland in Christianity's wake. As a result, a concern over cultural memory pervades

the *Prose Edda* [...] It is a rare country that develops its own script and its own literature in fundamental independence from other societies; ancient Egypt and Shiang China are more the exception than the rule. Most literatures – from Latin and French and from Hebrew to Icelandic – have been formed with broad systems grounded in the power of cultural traditions to cross the boundaries of time, space, and language. Arising within a transcultural context, a local or national literature must negotiate a double bind: the new influences that can help shape a people's traditions also bring them the threat of the local culture's absorption into a broader milieu. (2007: 141–42)

We take the point. But what then needs to be noted about modern forms of trans- and inter-culturation are their speed and scale, on the one side, and the specific modalities through which dominant forms are imposed and 'absorbed', on the other. These dimensions are all registered in the anxious, 'double-bound' form of Laxness's novel. The fact that Laxness (and subsequent writers from the Scandinavian 'fringe', such as the Orcadian writer George Mackay Brown and the school of 'Faroese modernists') seeks to resist the lure of an 'international modernist' stylistics with a 'combined' modernist saga form of his own is a good example of peripheral modernism's 'worldly' response to the penetration of modernity. By the close of Laxness's novel, both saga and collective cultural memory have become politically modern(ist) art. Ugla, resigned to her urban future, nervously awaits the next stage of its entrance into the world-system: 'The conflict is between two fundamentals [...] The battlefield covers all lands, all seas, all skies; and particularly our innermost consciousness. The whole world is one atom station' (2004: 163).

Glasgow, 1984

It may seem counterintuitive, or even perverse, for us to propose now that our analysis of the literature of the European (semi-)periphery should also include discussion of the work produced by a contemporary writer based in one of the most developed and powerful states of the modern world-system – the UK. Yet the work of the Scottish writer James Kelman is replete with features that we can immediately recognise as transcodings of the lifeworld of the (semi-) periphery: experience, built environment, lived space, and so on. As David Harvey and Neil Smith (among others) have compellingly demonstrated, the definitive spatial lexicon of urban peripheral zones – edges, ghettoes, slums, projects, gap sites, dilapidated zones, sink estates (or, in Glaswegian parlance, *outer-city schemes*), wastelands, nowheres, no-go areas – does not imply a world beyond or excluded from capitalist 'modernisation' or 'development'; on the contrary, zones of this kind are the very face of such modernisation and development in peripheral (that is to say, peripheralised) locations.[14] Such

---

14 See, for instance, Harvey 1985, 1989, 2001 and 2009; Smith 1990 and 1996.

spaces exist even, or in some respects especially, in the most developed states, often produced by the machinations of corporatised capital, and subject to the volatility endemic to its operating contradictions. These spaces constitute the prevalent zones of Kelman's fiction from the late 1970s onwards, whose particular brilliance – and the root of whose 'supreme universality' – lies, as James Meek has recently written in reviewing *Kieron Smith, Boy* (2008), in their uncompromising and radical formal *modernism*.[15] In examining the powerlessness caused by a consistent process of displacement and marginalisation characteristic of the post-1960s Clydeside modernisation plans as well as the more recent neoliberal revolution and its devastating deindustrialisation programme, Kelman charts the atomisation of social experience in contemporary Britain. As his work has developed it has provided with increasing clarity the resources to survey and assess the creation of a British/Scottish periphery in the context of the Thatcherite neoliberal revolution that began in 1979.

Kelman's second novel, *The Busconductor Hines* (1984), details Rab Hines's mental breakdown as he is threatened with unemployment and homelessness as the neoliberal modernisation commences in earnest. Hines is an archetypical victim of the transformation sweeping across his region: he loses his job in a time of rampant privatisation of the 'public' transport service. The final phase of deindustrialisation of the west of Scotland is rapid, and Hines and

15 'Removing all those capitalised nouns from the narrative of a young boy's life is an effective blow against a nostalgist reading of *Kieron Smith*; and nostalgist literature can all too easily turn to sentimentality and marketing. It's not without its cost. It's a step away from pure realism, and the lack of conventional time-pulses does make the book more difficult to read: at least until awareness of Kelman's skill in making Kieron's changing voice and perception mark time begins to kick in. But the reward is not simply the psychologically subversive one of making the readers question the acceptance of acquired labels. It is to give *Kieron Smith* a supreme universality, making it both a lasting work and one broad enough to be appreciated by any one of the billions of people who have shared its hero's experience in the last sixty years. In Mumbai, in Shanghai, in Alexandria, poor boys have grown up in industrial cities by great rivers, in cramped flats, fought in gangs, been beaten by parents and punished by teachers, found other castes or ethnicities to despise, climbed drainpipes and escaped into books, been moved to new estates [...] There's a reluctance to accept Kelman for what he is, a perfectionist and a radical Modernist writer of exceptional brilliance, and this reluctance is not just bourgeois superciliousness [...] The real reason Kelman, despite his stature and reputation, remains something of a literary outsider is not, I suspect, so much that great, radical Modernist writers aren't supposed to come from working-class Glasgow, as that great, radical Modernist writers are supposed to be dead. Dead, and wrapped up in a Penguin Classic: that's when it's safe to regret that their work was underappreciated or misunderstood (or how little they were paid) in their lifetimes. You can write what you like about Beckett or Kafka and know they're not going to come round and tell you you're talking nonsense, or confound your expectations with a new work. Kelman is still alive, still writing great books, climbing' (Meek 2008: 7–8).

his fellow workers struggle to seek some form of collective representation at the very moment in which union power is being decimated. Hines's world of tenement apartments is also disintegrating, literally being cleared and demolished in front of his eyes as part of the history of demolition and renewal of the Glaswegian urban landscape that is coterminous with the UK government's privatisation of council housing and social provision. As collective forms of life shrink and retreat, Kelman's prose shuttles between sober modes of documentary naturalism and intense bursts of subjectivist modernist narration, often rendered in the working-class dialect of his main characters. This modernist consciousness is conveyed through a narratological procession of esoteric thoughts and visions combined with linguistic denotations of sensory overload and psychic disturbance. Temporal shifts are also apparent throughout, down to the granular level of the tense phrasing in many sentences.

Like many of Kelman's characters, Hines constantly covers his ears and blocks his eyes in his struggles for objective clarity. There is a point in the narrative at which his increasingly detached perspective threatens to collapse into what might be read as a redundant inarticulacy. However, the breakdown of his linguistic ability is better read as a psychosomatic registration, on one disintegrating body, of the effect of generalised top-down social violence. As time and space are compressed in the novel, setting, narrative expression and organisation are altered to draw attention to the ways in which shifts in the regional economy are affecting local conditions of production and development, shattering the stability of social relations and challenging cemented class solidarities. The reader is deliberately confronted with the limitations of Hines's cognitive competence, his inability to put his own abruptly transformed and diminished life into larger objective perspective or relief.[16]

Modernist narrative techniques, of course, are superbly suited to perform such instability. *The Busconductor Hines*'s narrative style is hinged to the traumatic, disorderly experience of (environ)mental collapse: his perspective is progressively fractured as the wrecking ball approaches the tenements. Realist or naturalist description and external dialogue are replaced by an

---

16 This is a consistent feature of Kelman's Kafka-like approach to subjunctive forms of plot development, which is best exemplified by his Booker Prize-winning novel *How Late It Was, How Late*, set in the early 1990s, roughly ten years after *Hines*, during a subsequent gentrifying phase of major capital investment in Glasgow, by now a radically deindustrialised city but one which had had the masque of 'European Capital of Culture' imposed on it by the European Union in 1990. The novel features a recently blinded unemployed man as he tries (quite literally) to find his way in a city that seems to have no room to accommodate him any longer. Sammy's gradual cognitive mapping of his experience at the hands of a PFI State welfare shrinkage (in health, social benefits, unemployment checks) is rendered in painstaking monologue, forcing the reader to grapple with the difficulties of living in a weakened, marginalised condition in the neoliberalising metropole.

atrophied, often hallucinatory internal monologue (though deployment of the self-referring 'You' serves to fuse together disintegrating mental and material landscapes). The overall effect is a growing textual disorder as the novel progresses, and this is symptomatic of the approaching material disintegration and social and economic capitulation.

Hines feels unable (and perhaps unwilling) to make the leap from being a bus conductor to enrolling in 'the school of driving' demanded by the newly privatised 'public' economy. Similarly, he cannot contemplate owning his own house in the aggressively expanded owner-mortgage economy. The threat of the loss of physical shelter and of long-term social security generates a form of representative instability that indexes Hines's own struggles to comprehend a reordered world. The narrative response becomes charged with heightened irony, as the protagonist's attempts to get what is happening to him into perspective become more and more unavailing. Consider this excerpt, where an attempt to comprehend the spatial geometry of the tenement's layout is conveyed in a tentative prose that ironically reveals the over-simplified ideals of the brutalist architectural rationale:

> This rectangle is formed by the backsides of the buildings – in fact it's maybe even a square. A square: 4 sides of equal length and each 2 lines being angled onto each other at 90°. Okay now: this backcourt a square and for each unit of dwellers up each tenement close there exists the 1/3 midden being equal to 2 dustbins. For every three closes you have the 1 midden containing 6 dustbins. But then you've got the prowlers coming round when every cunt's asleep. They go exchanging holey dustbins for nice new yins. Holey dustbins: the bottom only portionally there so the rubbish remains on the ground when said dustbins are being uplifted. What a bastard [...] having to rush out to the midden motor and get your shovel and back again to swipe it all away before the animals get a whiff and come out to get into it [...] And they are not to be having anywhere to live. They keep trying to stay one jump ahead of the demolition men. You get the building knocked down and then the equipment gets transferred round the corner, and so on down the line, getting nearer and nearer to this very window. And all the time the poor auld animals go running for cover, scrambling along beneath the floorboards and up and down the stair they go dropping between walls, in behind all those layers and layers of fucking wallpaper dating back to Christ knows when. (Kelman 2007: 79–80)

The 'But' that begins the fourth sentence here interrupts any idealist configuration of communal inhabitation by emphasising the anti-social elements and informal, unequal and unfair modes of exchange. The normative idealism associated with the square form – the classically functional space of public meetings and openness – does not relate to the reality of cramped living in difficult urban environments. These are conditions that the state cannot regulate, and that the turn to privatised modes of ownership only exacerbates.

This reflection occurs in the midst of Hines's experience of the sharp end of Glaswegian modernity. The demolition occurs as part of Glasgow's large-scale renewal plan, one increasingly deformed by the iron hand of the 'demolition men' of the London government. The tonal shift between regular sentence structure and a more scattered, unhinged commentary hints at the way in which the functionality of modernist idealism and 'communal' spatial organisation has given way to a social world unsupported by public infrastructural ecologies. The combination of council ownership, 'old' landlordism and private ownership has led to a physical and social disaggregation and disorganisation that Kelman's literary modernism must somehow seek to register. Conjunctions pile up, tenses become jumbled, narrative progression becomes difficult to piece together. Linear chronology is lost as the classical modernist dream of 'straight lines' begins to fade. Spatial modernism thus meets its peripheral literary apotheosis in Kelman's 1980s shock-Glasgow. 'What next?' is the unstated question at the end of the long passage cited above, challenging in both lexis and syntax. The narrative loses its thread as the transition is experienced, and operates increasingly on the principles of contingency, anecdote and momentariness.

The mechanism shaping the novel's orthographic composition also becomes apparent as the inexorable momentum of demolition is caught in a disjunctive, crumbling narrative constructed of blocks of text, separated by dots of suspension, as if to emulate the larger disintegration of social life and public infrastructure that Hines is caught up in. The empty spaces between sections on the page throw conventional narrative progression into some disarray, and the reader is confronted by a form of spatial and chronological flux, forced to consider the holes – the gaps – that emerge in the world represented.

In *The Busconductor Hines*, as in several other contemporary Scottish novels, privatisation has become a predominant feature of public life. The situation is then compounded by the fact that Hines's class is split into increasingly smaller, self-serving units, forced to change their living spaces and habits and to compete against one another – for jobs, housing and other forms of social security. All of these novels document the glaring contradictions and oppositions between space and time – the experience of psychological confusion and spatial displacement, of being lost in familiar territory or finding oneself located suddenly in new and unfamiliar surroundings. Hence the ubiquity of fragmented plot lines, meandering narratives, random and restless focalisation, the concern with memory and memorialisation that disrupts the progression of story, and the use of contingency and surprise events, of spatial deformation and of anecdote and compression.

CHAPTER SIX

Ivan Vladislavic: Traversing the Uneven City

> Johannesburg seems to have no genre of its own.
> (Nadine Gordimer 1976 [1958])

Consider three moments in the life of one city:

- A 38-year old man is arrested in a shopping mall after he tries to sell a pair of blue eyes;
- A man is minding his own business in a bank, trying to withdraw some cash from an automatic teller machine, when his hands burst into flames;
- A giant, ramshackle spacecraft appears above the city. Its filthy and sick passengers – 'aliens' – are interred in prison camps, where illegal medical experiments are conducted on their dying bodies.

The city, of course, is Johannesburg and only one of these moments is non-fictional, but it may not be immediately obvious which one this is. Taking the first incident as a point of departure in their analysis of 'postcolonial' South Africa (the report of the arrest of a man for attempting to sell human body parts in a shopping mall was carried by the leading Johannesburg daily newspaper, *The Star*, in 1996), Jean and John L. Comaroff detect 'symptoms of an occult economy waxing behind the civil surfaces of the "new" South Africa' (1999: 283). This occult economy is characterised in their view by its fusion of cultural elements with long indigenous histories (such as witchcraft) with other cultural elements registering the particular velocities of contemporary 'globalisation'. The fusion produces what they call 'millennial capitalism', one of whose distinguishing features is a pervasive double consciousness:

On the one hand is a perception, authenticated by glimpses of a vast wealth that passes through most postcolonial societies and into the hands of a few of their citizens [...] to capital amassed by the ever more rapid, often immaterial flow of value across time and space [...] On the other hand is the dawning sense of chill desperation attendant on being left out of the promise of prosperity, of the telos of liberation. (283–84)

The Comaroffs are careful to point out that 'millennial capitalism' is a global, and not just a (postcolonial) South African, affair. The recent proliferation of vampires, zombies and witchcraft[1] is surely evocative of a cultural logic of tragic historical contradictions generated by the sheer speed of systematic extraction, abstraction and alienation authored by capitalism in its contemporary, 'globalised' phase. And the attention the Comaroffs pay to the structural logic of the 'occult economy' that lies beneath the façade of the 'new South Africa' – the conflict between a radically uneven distribution and development of wealth and space and a political and ideological language of liberation and equality – is surely generally applicable to the global postcolonial condition as such.

Yet, Johannesburg's position as the 'pre-eminent global city' of Africa, the paradigmatic 'Afropolis', crystallises certain trends within what we are calling the aesthetics of uneven development. The two other moments in the life of the city alluded to at the beginning of this discussion – the arrival of alien refugees in a junk spacecraft and the unaccountable pyrotechnics of an ordinary citizen – are also, to our eyes at least, strikingly successful 'local' cultural expressions of the contradictory logic of globalised capitalist modernity. The former appears in *District 9* (2009), the South African director Neill Blomkamp's debut feature film, which went on, despite its modest budget and lack of international stars, to become a multi-award-winning and Oscar-nominated hit. The other moment appears in a short story published by Ivan Vladislavic in a collection called *Missing Persons* (1989).

The film and the story seem, at first sight, to occupy quite different registers. While *District 9* blends the idioms of space opera, 1980s 'hard core' sci-fi, steam punk and the 'first-person' shooter style of video games like *Halo*, Vladislavic's short story, written over 20 years ago, seems to be an example of what commentators have liked to speak of as African 'anti-' or 'magic' realism.[2] But what seems striking to us is precisely the fact that, spanning two decades of historical transformations and turbulence in South

1 Represented *in* the globally teleportable cultural media of popular television serials, cinema and fiction (*True Blood*, *Twilight*, etc.); and representative *of* the conflicts between the legislative arms of modern state systems and cultic practices and belief systems (ranging from scientology and 'end times' groups in South Africa as well as the United States, to witch hunts in India, South Africa and Latin America).
2 See the discussion of the critical reception of Vladislavic's fiction in Helgesson 2004.

Africa, the film and the short story so decisively *exceed* the sum of the generic and formal parts that they employ. Just as the tags of space opera, steam punk and 'first-person shooter' gaming codes are utterly insufficient as classificatory devices as far as Blomkamp's film is concerned, African 'anti-' or 'magic' realism only partially capture the specificity and complexity of Ivan Vladislavic's work. In both cases, what has been achieved is the aura (in the Benjaminian sense) of a *particular* historical space (Johannesburg) and time (the era of 'late' or 'millennial' capitalism) that nevertheless allows us to witness and reflect upon a *general* and *global* structure of feeling formed over the long duration of modernity's unfolding. Read alongside the incidents of occult, witchcraft and trade in human organs in contemporary South Africa, it points to the historical compulsion under which cultural modes operate in conditions of uneven development – the compulsion to fuse disparate idioms, languages, genres and forms in order to meditate upon ordinary lives captured by the dark magic of history. And since it is the city space of Johannesburg itself that is both the site and the key of these cultural expressions, they draw us to an evaluation of the relationship between the material space of the city, historical time and cultural representation. And so we turn to post-apartheid Johannesburg and one of its most interesting chroniclers, Ivan Vladislavic.

Vladislavic's works have rightly been seen as innovative and stimulating interrogations of the material and lived conditions of contemporary South Africa. Stefan Helgesson, for example, has pointed out that by thematising 'language itself as the very material of understanding and being', Vladislavic's writing 'confronts [...] what is not often acknowledged in South African literary debates, namely the exceptionally high visibility of commercialism and consumerism in South Africa, as well as the role of private capital in the proliferation of various media technologies' (2004: 777, 785). An important (but not the only) site for these corporatised consumption patterns is, obviously, the city, and in the South African context, urban configurations like Johannesburg, Cape Town and Durban assume a paradigmatic importance. Vladislavic has himself talked about the correspondences between the experience of being in the city and the style and form that his own writing takes:

> Just spending a day in the city is to be pushed, literally hour by hour, between exhilaration that you live in such an exciting, dynamic place where there's so much potential, and complete despair that things haven't changed, or that there are so many basic problems. Perhaps the existence of these extremes helps to explain the appeal of the story, as opposed to the novel: it does give you extraordinary freedom to move between points of view, between moods, between perspectives, that is more difficult to achieve in the novel. (Vladislavic 2000: 280)

If, at one level, a formulation such as this might seem to position Vladislavic very generally in relation to the dialectics of urban modernity as explored in canonical writings from Walter Benjamin to Marshall Berman, what we need to take on board in particular is the additional registration in his work of the deeply consequential (and disturbing) incompatibility between the built fabric of South African cities – Johannesburg especially – and the aspirational politics of the 'new' South Africa. The question is whether a city like Johannesburg can ever be 'decolonised', that is, liberated from the divisions of labour and living that its constructed material form, its design and layout, its roads and communications networks, continue to encode and institutionalise, even after their specifically apartheid-era reasons for being ('separate development') have been consigned to the dustbin of history. The point has been well made by James Graham, whose article 'Ivan Vladislavic and the Possible City' is incisively directed to the fully *dialectical* quality of the writer's representation of Johannesburg. 'I suggest that the term "possible city" offers a concise conceptual description of the way in which the city and its social imaginary interact in Vladislavic's writing on Johannesburg', Graham notes (2008: 334). '[R]ather than forging a straightforward connection between Vladislavic's work and – to take one prominent example – Nuttall and Mbembe's call for the city to be read as an aesthetic project in process rather than a crisis-ridden "space of division", I argue that [Vladislavic's] […] self-conscious technique […] renders this distinction ironic'. For Graham, as for us, Vladislavic's portrait of Johannesburg pivots on contradiction: the 'dynamism and multiplicity of the city space' are real enough; but their social potentiality is desperately compromised by the limits set by the dead weight of the past: 'while it is necessary to recognize the new ways in which people are making use of the "old" city, the memory of that city, with its separations and inequalities encoded within its very fabric, still has a significant bearing on the present' (Graham 2008: 335). Much of Vladislavic's writing, as Graham demonstrates, is an exploration of these paradoxes and contradictions embedded in the everyday life of post-apartheid South Africa.

We want to take up here precisely these suggestions that Vladislavic's thematic and formal concerns are to be read as expressions of historical-material contradictions and paradoxes. Our specific interest lies in uneven development and the aesthetics that this historical condition demands. Of course, from one angle uneven development in post-apartheid South Africa is merely a local instance of a global trend underscored by the neoliberal 'supply-side' economic orthodoxy and the political victories of the 'Washington consensus' inaugurated during the Thatcher–Reagan years. However, as Martin Murray warns, any analyses of the South African condition must also pay attention to certain peculiarities of its 'racially inscribed capitalism', among which might be listed 'the legacies of labour coercion and economic concentration, undue dependence upon overseas investment, skilled labour shortage amidst layers of "casualised" work and widespread unemployment, and weak internal markets' (1994: 3).[3] For Murray, writing just after South Africa's first post-apartheid general elections in 1994,

3 For additional commentary on the political economy of South Africa in the

> What is taking place in South Africa is not a simple linear progression from the rigid, constricted apartheid social system [...] to a race-blind post-apartheid meritocracy, but rather a complex and multifaceted transitional process involving an almost imperceptible re-alignment in the structural underpinnings that sustain capital accumulation and [...] a sea-change in surface appearance on the terrain of politics. (3–4)

Thus, while the post-apartheid ANC-led South African government remained *politically* committed to the rhetoric of wealth redistribution and social equity, the signal for its *economic* alignment to the global neoliberal orthodoxy came from no less a figure than Nelson Mandela, who used a speech in the UN to invite foreign investment in order to rejuvenate the finance and service sectors of the country's economy:

> Since Mandela's United Nation's speech, the US Congress cleared the way for South Africa to begin receiving IMF loans, lifted most of the remaining federal restrictions on doing business in South Africa, and urged the quick removal of state and local sanctions [...] With more than six hundred listed stocks, the Johannesburg Stock Exchange boasted a market capitalization of $215 billion. The JSE was the largest emerging market in the world. (Murray 1994: 25)

As a result, what became known in post-apartheid South Africa as GEAR (Growth, Equality and Redistribution strategy) displayed all the features of

> an orthodox neoliberal package – tight fiscal austerity, monetary discipline, wage restraints, reducing corporate taxes, trade liberalization [that would] lure private investments (both domestic and foreign), unleash rapid growth, tighten labour markets, and drive up wages. In presenting GEAR as a *fait accompli*, ANC Finance Minister Trevor Manuel made clear that it was non-negotiable. (Hart 2002: 18)[4]

---

post-apartheid years, see, *inter alia*, Barchiesi 2011; Bond 2000, 2004, 2006; Desai 2002; Marais 1998, 2011; Saul 2005.

4 For an alternative, insider's view of the implementation of GEAR, see Feinstein 2009: 59–62. As a member of the South African government's Finance and Public Accounts Committees, Feinstein was one of the architects of GEAR and defends it in the global context – 'as a small, open economy South Africa had little choice but to engage with the global economy largely on its terms' (59) – and on the grounds of wishing to avoid what he calls the 'macroeconomic populism' that had led to stagflation in many Latin American countries. Yet, Feinstein also notes the contradictions and conflicts generated by GEAR. For example, the ANC's own rhetorical commitment to social justice and equality was at least partially translated into economic policies of providing partial protection and stability to the labour market. This clashed with GEAR's demand for 'flexibility' and has generated a series of disabling and contradictory practices. Moreover, according to Feinstein, the 'historic language of revolution was utilized to make palatable an ostensible neoliberal approach to the economy. So the idea of a significant role for the private sector was presented as "the National Democratic Revolution

A few striking results of this post-apartheid economic compromise in South Africa are immediately discernible. First, there is the rapidly and *unevenly* widening gap in the distribution of wealth. The per capita income of white South Africans was almost nine times higher than that of their non-white counterparts in 1996; and while the share of non-white income rose from 29.9% to 35.7% between 1991 and 1996, almost all of this increase was experienced by the top 10% of non-white households, with the poorest 40% having to endure a 21% fall in their household incomes (Hart 2002: 20). This was not much of an improvement from the situation on the eve of the historic first election in 1994, when 5% of the population, almost exclusively white, owned 88% of the wealth, while 84% of the population lived below the so-called 'minimum living level' of R700 per month for a family of five (Murray 1994: 28). But the key difference in the post-apartheid era is the new access to wealth being enjoyed by a small non-white elite class – an access corresponding to their access to political power.

Second, this unevenness at the level of economics is coded into the fabric of built space in South Africa. The rigidly structured and 'racially' planned cities of the apartheid era are being transformed into mega-urban configurations with uneven population densities and built structures. The Pretoria, Witwatersrand and Vereeniging (PWV) region, with Johannesburg at its centre, contains more than a quarter of the entire population of the country itself, with well over a million people daily entering the Johannesburg Central Business district; but while 'townships' like Soweto and Alexandra have between 250 and 300 people living per square kilometre, the population density for the rest of Johannesburg varies between 30 and 60 per square kilometre (Murray 1994: 44–45). The spatial configurations of these 'townships' also often defy the classical models of urban growth. As Mzwanele Mayekiso, the president of the Alexandra Civic Organization, has noted:

> You always remember your first sight of Alexandra township, it is so striking. Visitors to Johannesburg's nearest black ghetto expect to see many high-rise buildings [...] Instead, you are immediately surprised as you enter 'Alex', dodging cows, goats, chickens, and mangy dogs that no owners would claim [...] shack huts of plywood, cardboard and zinc roofing stretch before your eyes like muddy sea, occasionally punctured by old 1920s era brick houses. (Mayekiso 1994: 8)

The interstitial character of the townships, 'neither rural nor urban', as Gillian Hart puts it (2002: 5), might point to a peculiarity of contemporary 'global' capitalism – 'rural industrialisation' or the dispersal of industries into non-urban areas in a reversal of the classical model of accumulation by dispossession. Yet, since the global industries that put their roots down in

---

and the state presiding over it coexist with private capital..."' (62). This is a good example of paradoxes and contradictions percolating across political, economic and cultural levels that characterise 'globalisation'.

these spaces do so because of the ready availability of non-skilled, casualised labour there (as Hart's own study of small- and medium-scale Taiwanese industries in South African townships shows), it is by no means clear that this process is a departure from, rather than a signal contemporary feature of, the historical accumulation of capital. This 'mixed' and uneven spatial nature of contemporary South Africa, incidentally, is also readily visible in the architectural styles of the urban space. Here we see the seemingly bewildering juxtaposition of the 'indigenous'/'vernacular', the 'folk'/early Dutch, the 'empire', the 'apartheid modernist' and the 'township metropolis' styles, each corresponding to a particular layer of historical habitation and mode of production – the San and the Khoikhoi peoples (pastoral), the Dutch (early colonial capitalist), the British (imperial capitalist), apartheid capitalist, and so on (Murray, Shepherd and Hall 2007: 2–7). One of the aims of writers like Vladislavic, we argue, is to embody this spatial unevenness *formally* even as their work *thematically* assists a reflection on the process of its historical formation.

Thirdly and finally, the political-economic and spatial unevenness of South Africa is extended to what may be called the individual and collective modes of human existence. It has been understood for some time now that in South Africa, the radically unequal distribution of wealth has led, despite the formal end of apartheid, to increasingly balkanised patterns of settlement along ethnic and 'racial' lines. While 'white' South Africans in Johannesburg cluster in areas like Northcliff, Roodepoort and Sandton, 'black' South Africans dominate in Soweto, Diepkloof and Midrand, while 'coloured' and 'Asian' South Africans are distributed across Northcliff, Inner City and Orange Farm (Tomlinson et al. 2003: 11). On the other hand, the increasing 'casualisation' of the labour market means that this ethnic and racially balkanised pattern of habitation is disrupted by the constant flow of economic migrants forever looking to gain a toehold in the interstitial niches of the cityscape. This dialectic between stasis and mobility of the post-apartheid urban South African human body, in its individual and collective, ideological and material, dimensions, has recently attracted much attention from theorists committed to the notions of 'Afromodernism' and 'Afropolis'.

Paradigmatic here is Achille Mbembe and Sarah Nuttall's work on 'global' African cities. Mbembe and Nuttall fully acknowledge that what they call 'African modernity' was shaped, '*as elsewhere* [our italics] in the global south [...] in the crucible of colonialism and by the labor of race', and that this process resulted in a peculiar compression of space and time – 'A trajectory that in the West took ages to unfold and to mature was here compressed into under a century. The speed and the velocity with which the city has experienced modernity has been dizzying' (Nuttall and Mbembe 2008: 18). Yet, since they at the same time wish to argue for an essential difference between 'African' and 'global' modernities and between 'Afropolis' and other cities of the 'global south', they quickly move to discount the possibility of reading the African urban mass as a continuation, albeit with specific 'local' idioms, of the uneven unfolding of global capitalism. Taking Johannesburg as the prime example of the 'Afropolis', Nuttall and Mbembe complain that

> Most studies of Johannesburg have interpreted the city as nothing but the spatial embodiment of unequal economic relations and coercive and segregationist policies [...] Modernity has been perceived as nothing more than the development of the capitalist mode of production and the process by which capitalism as a socioeconomic formation in turn transformed social relations and consciousness of black urban dwellers. (2008: 11)

Yet, curiously, the 'something else' of 'Afropolitan modernity' that Mbembe and Nuttall detect in the everyday life of cities such as Johannesburg turns out to be precisely the product of contemporary global capitalism – the presence of migrant workers flitting from one insecure job to another in the casualised and 'informal' economy that is a feature of all the global cities of our time: 'The figure of the black migrant worker, a temporary sojourner in the city, also marks one of the limits of the classical theories of the metropolis [...] [B]eneath the visible landscape and the surface of the metropolis, its objects and social relations, are concealed or embedded other orders of visibility, other scripts that are not reducible to the built form' (22). Their focus on the embodied 'scripts' of these mobile human beings then provides the template for Mbembe and Nuttall's reading of the 'informal' and 'transnational' economy of Afropolity, its 'geography of fortifications and enclosures', its proliferation of aesthetic labours, its monetary instabilities. In the 'Afropolis', they write, '[t]he built form is not, or no longer, the product of a careful planning or engineering of the urban space [...] the main infrastructural unit or building block is the human body' (7). AbdouMaliq Simone, similarly, identifies the social interactions of the African migratory body as a new infrastructure that marks the unique dynamism of the new African cities:

> But in these ruins, something else besides decay might be happening [...] African cities are characterized by incessantly flexible, mobile, and provisional intersections of residents that operate without clearly delineated notions of how the city is to be inhabited and used. These intersections [...] have depended on the ability of residents to engage complex combinations of objects, spaces, peoples and practices. (Simone 2008: 68–69)

We agree with these urban theorists to the degree that they see in the lives and experiences of the contemporary inhabitants of African cities the logics of 'flexible accumulation' and 'informal economy' that are the hallmarks of contemporary global capitalism. We also, up to a point, concede the reasonableness of architect Rem Koolhaas's assertion that many of the 'organizational models of dispersal and discontinuity, federalism and flexibility' that are amongst the most touted mantras of contemporary capitalism have been perfected in the African cities, such that 'Lagos is not catching up with us. Rather, we may be catching up with Lagos' (quoted in Nuttall and Mbembe 2008: 4). For it is certainly true that the contemporary version of the 'creative destruction' of global capitalism is releasing certain dynamic human possibilities and kinds of energetic labour, including aesthetic labour. However, we decisively differ from Nuttall and Mbembe, and other likeminded urban theorists, where the paeans that they offer to the 'mobility' and 'flexibility' of contemporary African (or in some versions 'global southern') human existence are concerned. Against the suggestion, frequently encountered today, that this casualised and migratory mode of human existence signals a unique African form of modernity, we insist that it instead signals the unfolding of a singular global modernity, however uneven over time and space, and that the lived experiences of the inhabitants of African cities find precise counterparts in the lived experiences of the inhabitants not only of cities elsewhere in the 'global south' but also in certain spaces within cities across the 'global north'. Against the suggestion that the 'provisional intersections' of these migratory lives must be celebrated for their adaptability and creative energy, we insist that these latter are achieved occasionally and then despite, and not because of, the systematic dehumanisation and immiseration of migrants and other disenfranchised people under the regime of a predatory transnational capitalism that seeks to erode whatever national and local securities might have been collectively and historically bargained for over previous eras. We argue, moreover, that it is precisely in the *resistance* to the *enforced* and *involuntary* conditions of migration and 'flexible existence' (including to their euphemised presentation by social elites, including intellectuals) that the creativity and dynamism of contemporary modernity's human subjects are best seen. That is, such subjects often fully realise themselves in acts of *rooting* and *habitation*, rather than through acts of *uprooting* and *travel*. With these agreements and disagreements in mind, let us now turn to Ivan Vladislavic's Johannesburg.

Johannesburg's historical emergence in 1886 was characterised by its constant escape from, rather than submission to, the strictures of planned urban growth. The city's location on the world's largest gold deposit meant that it 'grew too rapidly to allow for the coherent urban planning represented by the standardized form of the grid' (Kruger 2006: 143). For some observers, it is this incoherent urban form that has remained the signature of Johannesburg, despite the strict planning regime of the apartheid years, attracting critical terms such as 'edge city' for the purposes of description: 'Calling Johannesburg an edge city captures in the first instance its uneasy collocation of unevenly linked and possibly incompatible urban, sub-urban, and ex-urban forms as well as the urbanity or its lack that may derive from these forms' (Kruger 2006: 142). It is thus the coexistence of apparently incongruous material forms and the modes of living to which they give rise and to which they correspond that is said to give the city its distinction. With its combination of the high-tech world of stock markets and fluid finance capitalism alongside a low-tech and informal trade sector, Johannesburg is said to provide an alternative model to the developmentalist paradigm that is conventionally applied to read most of the cities of the 'global north'.

This reading of Johannesburg as a city of edges, unplanned extensions, leakages and boundary transgressions requires us to read the era of apartheid planning and segregation as an always-failing racist fantasy. The economic requirements of the 'free-market' restructuring that was inaugurated as early as the 1970s contradicted the political philosophy of segregation that sought to keep South African urban areas predominantly or even exclusively 'white'. More and more impoverished and 'casualised' rural South Africans found their ways around the draconian 'pass laws' to infiltrate Johannesburg and other cities (Murray 1994: 41–46). This 'molecular process of gradual decay that eroded formalized segregation from the inside', achieved at an almost unimaginably tragic human cost, illicitly turned officially sanctioned areas of exclusive 'white' ownership steadily 'grey' (42–43). Thus, what was conceived of as 'the model apartheid city', which relied on both spatial engineering and violent state-sponsored repressive measures such as forced evictions, never succeeded in wholly wiping out the existence of either the memory of past 'mixed' communities or the living vitality of present ones (Czeglédy 2003: 24).

Yet, once segregation or apartheid is properly understood not just as a 'racial' policy, but as one produced by an unholy nexus of race and class politics, it is not possible to consign it to the dustbin of history. As we have seen above, one of the signal features of post-apartheid Johannesburg is the increasing balkanisation of its residential patterns along ethnic lines. Even areas such as Johannesburg's Central Business District (CBD), characterised by the large flow, and not stasis, of human population, are experiencing a pattern of ethnic/racial homogenisation corresponding to the disparate commands of wealth. Whereas in the 1960s, 'white' South Africans working in the CBD outnumbered 'non-whites' at a ratio of 7:1, by the turn of the millennium, this ratio had nearly been reversed (Tomlinson and Larsen 2003: 46). Urban planners and researchers have also documented the combination of 'horizontal' (spatial) and 'vertical' (social) segregation in re-ghettoising former townships, and contrary to the slogan of a 'rainbow nation', 'The white population has been reacting to the in-migration of the black population with white flight. Johannesburg is disintegrating into residential islands with different degrees of security, different images, and dominated by individual ethnic groups' (Jürgens, Gnad and Bähr 2003: 68). These new forms of segregation have triggered violent struggles over access to the basic amenities of urban life, with the highest levels of violent crime being experienced in 'black'-dominated areas. One particularly vicious form this has assumed is that of systematic sexual violence against women, with 'black' South African women suffering 70% of the total recorded incidents of rape in the city and only 42% of the women being familiar to their attackers, a trend significantly at odds with such attacks elsewhere in the world and pointing to the randomised nature of these crimes (Palmary, Rauch and Simpson 2003: 102–08).

In the light of this hardening of borders along class and ethnic lines in post-apartheid Johannesburg, a celebratory critical focus on the creative chaos of the 'informal' economy, unplanned growth, edges, 'desire lines' and leakages seems premature at best, and perhaps even deliberately obfuscating. The new developments must rather be situated within an analytical framework in which they exist in reciprocal relationship with a host of newly empowered segregationist elements. Instead of talking of a city of multiple edges, we might instead talk of a 'city in fragments'. Here is Martin Murray's description:

> The 'garrison city', the 'dual city,' or the 'carceral city', where the urban zone is partitioned into what Saskia Sassen has called an 'urban glamour zone' [...] and an 'urban danger zone' – the interstitial places of confinement, with their broken-down infrastructure, few social amenities, and restricted opportunities for escape, where vast legions of service workers and the casually employed compete with the unemployed, the unemployable, and the marginalized [...] for survival. (Murray 2008: 145)

In addition to the dizzying scrambling of space and time, and the constant, exhausting search for social, economic and political 'entitlements', this city also reveals its core rhythms via certain contrapuntal keys – the tension between memory and forgetting coded into its 'monumentality', the tension between licit and illicit modes of habitation coded into its surfaces and depths, and tension between movement and stasis coded into the bodies of peripatetic human subjects.

Johannesburg's museums, monuments, shopping malls and casinos have all been read as sites of the dissolution and re-fabrication of certain kinds of memory. Lindsay Bremner, writing about the city's apartheid museum, has noticed how it has become the site of extensive nation (re)building: 'Museum space is a synecdoche for this process of new memory work, where antagonistic, competing, conflicting, non-compatible histories are brought together and rewritten. These are not only sites of memorialisation, but also instruments for the invention of a new political identity, the post-apartheid nation' (Bremner 2007: 85). The museums and monuments of Johannesburg and South Africa accrue all the contradictions inherent in this process. Lynn Meskell, for example, has shown how the double compulsion of remembering the multi-layered past of southern Africa and the injunction to 'forget and move forward' means that South African monuments speak of a double temporality (2007: 167–71).[5] These contradictions within a fractured and fracturing sense of historical time are also embedded in the structures of those other monuments of contemporary Johannesburg – the shopping mall and the casino. Comparing the pastiche architecture of the opulent casino

---

5 On the disturbance created by the very presence of the monument or statues in the contemporary consciousness, see Fredric Jameson: 'The statue often seems to stigmatize its moment of the past with a greened and bespattered boredom and stifling dustiness that unremarked glories do not have to contend with [...] The commemorative statue, in representational or allegorical form, is so foreign to the contemporary aesthetic that it may well be the style of the art rather than the content of the memorial that drives this dreariness and death of the past so strongly home' (1999: 72).

Montecasino and the decayed and degraded form of Huguenot Hotel, now converted into a gigantic brothel, Martin Murray sees a Gramscian war of position between the aspiring middle classes, the 'casualised' working classes and the migrants arriving in the city (2008: 147). The fantasy of consumption and access that is an integral part of the 'upward mobility' of Johannesburg's middle classes is now fabricated in the architectural discourse of the casino resort, which offers a 'collage of themed destinations which borrow from other places and other times' – the mythical representation of a Tuscan village, for example. Although visually separated from the degraded façade of a brothel like Huguenot Hotel, the two are dialectically linked through the patterns of hyper-consumption that govern and structure their existence – 'they are integrally connected, and the production of one presupposes the production of the other' (Murray 2008: 153).

The manifold contradictions within the vertical façades of memory and historical time in Johannesburg are extended to the city's multiple depths. A city founded on the gold mines, Johannesburg is riddled with holes, shafts, sunken pathways and shallow graves. These abrupt descents into what Nick Shepherd and Christian Ernsten call the 'underneath world' of the city reveals its grounding reality – 'the pulse of the mines becomes the pulse of history itself. Colonialism, apartheid, the wars of dispossession [...] all responding to the imperatives and opportunities of the world below' (2007: 215). For Nuttall and Mbembe, the boreholes and the drilling footages that lie under Johannesburg's CBD are nothing less than

> A testimony to the way in which, in the production of this South Hemispheric modernity, the world of race and systematized human degradation became a part of the calculus of capital and dispossession, technology, labor and the unequal distribution of wealth [...] this dialectic between the underground, the surface and the edge is, more than any other features, the main characteristic of the African modern of which Johannesburg is the epitome. (2008: 16–17)

Looking beyond the formulae of 'Afropolis' and 'Afro-modernity' here, about which we have already registered our reservations, we suggest that this portrait of a city with a hollow core on which a vertical modernity is raised positively calls out for interpretation on the model suggested by Siegfried Kracauer in 'The Mass Ornament': 'The surface-level expressions [...] by virtue of their unconscious nature, provide unmediated access to the fundamental substances of the state of things. Conversely, knowledge of this state of things depends on the interpretation of these surface-level expressions (Kracauer 1995: 75). What is required is a reading of the political unconscious of the surfaces and façades of urban forms.

The peripatetic existences of the migrant figures that traverse these vertical and horizontal lines of the city, as we have seen, are component elements of the forms of 'belonging and becoming' constructed in Johannesburg. Migration within the radically fragmented city is by and large not a matter of volition or a gesture of creativity, but a sign of permanent crisis. As Graeme Gotz and AbdouMaliq Simone find in their study of inner-city Johannesburg, migration 'represents a veritable vacuum of belonging, where almost no one presently living there can claim an overarching sense of origin in this place or a real wish to stay [...] The inner city therefore represents a process of "running away". Black South Africans are escaping the implosive sociality of township life [...] Foreign Africans are running away from the impossibility of being at home' (2003: 129–31). Thus the city is also crisscrossed by these lines of enforced flight – 'desire lines' that indicate unfulfilled demands and yearnings: 'the space between the planned and the providential, the engineered and the "lived", and between the official projects of capture and containment and the popular energies which subvert, bypass, supersede and evade them' (Murray, Shepherd and Hall 2007: 1). It is possible to argue that at least some of these 'desire lines' express a paradoxical call for belonging, not becoming, for stasis and not movement – and that the dialectic between inhabitation and migration is what forms the embodied urban subject of contemporary South Africa.

The Johannesburg of 'casualised' zombie economy and globally networked liquid finance; of new forms of segregation, edges and depths; of lines of flight, desire and struggle in between fractured and interstitial spaces; of the mobile, uprooted, peripatetic bodies as well as those who resist such forms of mobility; of monuments, malls and their forms of memory; of violence – these have been Ivan Vladislavic's subject from the very beginning of his literary career. We have already seen his stated preference for the short story (with its mobile points of view, shifts in mood, switches in focalisation, and relative autonomy from plot and linear narratives) as the appropriate representative form for the extreme reality of the city. In the two early short story collections *Missing Persons* (1989) and *Propaganda by Monuments and Other Stories* (1996), nearly all these cultural indices of uneven development are present and fully formed.

The sheer weight of monumentalised memory and the difficulties of negotiating with it appear in a story like 'We Came to the Monument', which is built around two narrative strands. The first is that of an unnamed protagonist who has returned to a ruined and devastated city with her tribe and found shelter within the precincts of a gigantic monument, the details of which recall the historic Voortrekker Monument outside Pretoria. The other is that of the monument itself as it gazes down at the returning tribe. The story catches the anxiety and terrific uncertainty of the final days of apartheid, and imagines that the war that seemed historically unavoidable between the liberation movement and the apartheid government has actually occurred, devastating the country. As a result of a curious elliptical swing of history, this post-apocalyptic scene then replays the original myth of Afrikaner nationalism – the 'Great Trek' that signalled the Boer challenge to British imperial monopoly of southern Africa. But what the tribes trek back to is not tribal hinterlands which they can then colonise and 'develop', but the very scene of their expulsion, where they themselves are colonised by the monument's injunction to memorialise the myth of the original trek: 'My father stopped in the doorway and the rest of us crowded around, peering into the gloom. He pointed, and I saw that a narrow beam of sunlight, marbled by dust motes, fell from a crack in the ceiling onto a dead, unintelligible face. My grandfather fell on his knees, and began to wail in the old language' (Vladislavic 1989: 74). Here, the architectural logic of the Voortrekker Monument, which is designed to let a shaft of sunlight fall on an inscription taken from the Afrikaans anthem 'Die Stem' ['The Voice'] – and which was later used as the national anthem of apartheid South Africa – is converted to the dead, unintelligible weight of the past. But nonetheless, this past maintains its malign hold on the population. After taking shelter in the monument, the human narrator discovers a museum where relics of an idealised rural Boer existence are captured in life-size models of farmhouses, and loses herself amidst the 'rough fabric of their clothes, their cold hands' (77). The story ends with her facing a panel depicting one of the establishing myths of Afrikaner nationalism – the signing of an 'honourable' treaty between the 'founding fathers' and the indigenous Africans. The final view of the 'enemy' – 'He sits awkwardly on the edge of his chair. He looks like a man who has never sat on a chair before. He holds a quill in his left hand […] behind him, his people kneel' (79) – demonstrates the durability of the monumentalised colonial past and the difficulties of breaking free from the grip of certain kinds of memory when they are coded into the built fabric of everyday life.[6]

Vladislavic's scepticism about the power of political 'transition', with its injunction to 'start anew', is also captured in a later story like 'Courage', published after South Africa's historic first post-apartheid election in 1994. Here, a white South African sculptor has been dispatched by the new government to one of the former tribal 'homelands' to find a human subject for a statue that would symbolise the courage of the new nation. The artist's

---

6 See the discussion of 'the possibilities and impossibilities for rehabilitating a monument with an explicit history as a foundational icon of the apartheid state' in Coombes 2003: 19–53. As Coombes notes, 'the Voortrekker Monument is of critical significance for the foundational myths of Afrikaner nationalism – in particular the idea of the Trek as the moment of emergence of the Afrikaner as the founding ethnic group of a new nation, "the white tribe," and the "divine right" of the Trekkers to the land. These myths are embodied through the structure of the monument itself – first through the seductive resolution provided by the narrative of encounter and conquest represented by the interior frieze, and second through the fact that the edifice houses what amounts to a cenotaph on its lower level, replete with "eternal flame," to the memory of Trekkers killed en route. This is strategically positioned: a shaft of sunlight was designed to strike the tomb each year on 16 December (the "day of the vow"). Third, of course, these foundational myths are reinforced through the prominent and confrontational positioning of the monument itself, directly opposite the Union Buildings – the site of British legislative authority' (28).

visit and the upheaval it causes in the village are narrated with distrust and humour in equal measures by a young boy. In this neglected backwater, where the state's presence is denoted by absence – absence of electricity, potable water, navigable roads – the very idea of a government-commissioned art project is absurd. This sense of absurdity is heightened by the physical differences between the white and black, urban and rural – 'At close quarters his flesh was overpowering. His temple was stuck with sea salt and grains of sand. His cheek was like a well-seasoned steak. The blisters on his ears had burst and the skin was peeling off in curls like pencil shavings' (Vladislavic 1996: 127). But nowhere is this difference more obvious than in the choice of model that the artist makes. Ignoring the host of eager and posturing villagers, the artist chooses the alcoholic, old and battered figure of Kumbuza: 'When Kumbuza was a young man he had gone to Johannesburg to work on the mines [...] [H]e left behind in Johannesburg the three longest fingers of his beautiful right hand [...] In his second season he slipped under the plough and mangled his left foot [...] He fell off a stile and knocked out his front teeth. On another occasion he tore off the lobe of his right ear with a carelessly cast fish hook' (131–32). What to the artist appear as idealisations of physical struggle and courageous labour are seen by the village community as banal drudgery – a symbol of their degradation, and as such, absurdly comical and rather insulting. When the artist appears with his callipers and measuring tools to record Kumbuza's dimensions, his actions echo those of the countless anthropologists and scientists whose measurements of the 'primitive' helped in the establishment of racist 'civilisational' scales that were amongst the prime ideological tools of colonialism and imperialism. Even Kumbuza reacts with horror at this approach. This cognitive gap between the liberal urban artist and his subjects persists when the young narrator finally makes it to Johannesburg and happens on the statue itself. It is not 'courage' he sees in the colossal figure of a gun-wielding soldier with Kumbuza's face, but bemusement. He is accosted by an urchin wielding a camera, one of the hordes of the 'casualised' mobile bodies that populate the city, and who offers to take a picture of him next to the living subject of the statue slumped on a nearby bench. It is Kumbuza, once again destitute and back in the city – except he is now mythologised in the sales pitch of the street photographer as 'the general', 'a true hero of the people'. The monumental function of statues in the 'new' South Africa is exactly comparable to that of 'old' South Africa – the homogenisation of historical tensions and contradictions into flat mystifications and platitudes that are seen as 'official' requirements of nation-building.

As we have seen in our brief look at urban theorists of contemporary South Africa, in addition to the issues of memorialisation, monuments can also raise disturbing questions about commodification, authenticity and fabrication. In 'Propaganda by Monuments' and 'The Whites Only Bench', Vladislavic makes these issues the fulcrum of his narrative. In the first story, a Russian translator working for the post-Soviet government receives a petition from Boniface Khumalo, a South African taxi driver, who wants to buy one of the statues of Lenin that are being destroyed in Russia, to decorate his new business venture, the 'V.I. Lenin Bar and Grill'.[7] The massive Soviet socialist monuments, whose presence gestured towards one version of heroic history, are now raw materials for banal everyday commodities such as door-knockers, railings, gravel, tombstones and, of course, 'monuments of the new heroes'. On hearing this news, Khumalo, a model citizen of the new South Africa, senses that he has an opportunity for making an entrepreneurial splash by importing one of the surplus Soviet statues. But this would be more than just a commercial gesture – Khumalo also wants to use his monument to make a statement against the planned space of the 'model' apartheid city:

> Then he looked out of the window at the drab veld of the valley dipping away from the road [...] On the far slope of the valley was a sub-economic housing complex, a Monopoly-board arrangement of small, plastered houses with corrugated-iron roofs, all of them built to exactly the same design. The planners of Van Riebeecksvlei had sought to introduce some variety into the suburb by rotating the plan of each successive house through ninety degrees, with the result that there were now four basic elevations which repeated themselves in an unvarying sequence down the long, straight streets. (Vladislavic 1996: 31–32)

But the seeming absurdity of a massive statue of the great Russian Communist leader in front of a bar amidst this gridlocked urban space reveals itself at a second glance to be perfectly reasonable. What is being memorialised here is a certain ethos – call it the GEAR ethos – in terms of which the 'developmentality' of enterprise is now enshrined as the legitimate desire of all new post-apartheid citizens. Khumalo muses on the cost of installing Lenin's statue – 'but surely it would cost a fortune just to build a pedestal of that size? What if he approached the SACP, or the Civic, or a consortium of local businessmen? [...] [M]y name can go on the plaque, I'll unveil the bloody thing myself!' (37). For him, the South African Communist Party, the new bureaucracy and a private consortium of businessmen are all interchangeable sources for funding, and the statue itself a chance of monumentalising his own name in the fabric of history.

The fabrication of history is also the subject of 'The Whites Only Bench', in which a group of artists and curators are preparing exhibits for the apartheid museum. Among these exhibits is one of the public benches reserved for 'Slegs Blankes/Whites Only' during the apartheid years – 'a beautiful object [...] The wooden slats were tomato-sauce red. The arms and legs were made of iron, but cleverly moulded to resemble branches' (1996: 55). The problem is that this bench is not 'authentic', but made by one of the museum's resident

---

7 Vladislavic writes about the conceptual origins of this story, and of the sources he used to write it, in Vladislavic 2006b.

artists, Charmaine, who has painstakingly researched and hand-made the object – 'But when you looked closer [...] you saw that all these signs of wear and tear were no more than skin-deep [...] Charmaine had even smeared the city's grimy shadows into the grain' (55). The revelation that the bench has been fabricated outrages the curator, who insists that museums, especially museums of apartheid, that are charged with preserving the memory of collective atrocities must be the preserve of the authentic, and orders the artists to find a 'real bench'.[8] At this point, Reddy, one of the researchers, gives the curator a demonstration of the necessarily fabricated nature of monuments and memory by showing her the iconic photograph of the 1976 Soweto rebellion – the one taken by Sam Nzima showing the wounded and dying body of the schoolboy Hector Peterson, shot by the apartheid police force. Reddy suggests that even, and especially, such iconic 'monuments' are sites of conflicting and contradictory memories. He reminds the curator that when – in an attempt to establish the absolute truth – the museum had asked witnesses to come forward, what they had gotten was a variety of stories and a whole box full of bullets, each claimed as the 'real one' that killed the boy – 'there were .38 Magnum slugs, 9mm and AK cartridges, shiny .22 bullets, a .357 hollow-point that had blossomed on impact into a perfect corolla' (63). Shaken but unbowed by this demonstration of the multivalence of 'truth', the curator relegates the 'fabricated' bench to the margins of the exhibition, and finds a 'real' bench to take centre stage. The museum continues to peddle the fiction about memorialising the 'real' nature of apartheid.

Vladislavic's short stories quite appropriately devote a lot of energy to the question of statues, monuments, memory, commodities and the everyday lives of things. But he is also interested in other registers of the uneven city. In 'The Journal of a Wall', the narrator is obsessed with a neighbour building a wall around his house. Walls, concretising the philosophy of apartheid and the desperate (and of course unavailing) reach for security in a severely unequal society, have attained a special aura in South Africa. In the narrator's

---

8 The device of a character narrowly and unswervingly committed to protocol, exactitude, formality and 'standards' is a staple of Vladislavic's fiction, enabling him to register both what changes and what does not change in the officially heralded 'transition' from the apartheid era to the time of the 'new' South Africa. One thinks of the narrator of 'The Book Lover' in *Propaganda by Monuments*, who introduces himself thus: 'I am not a snob, you see, but I am a stickler for standards' (1996: 87). Vladislavic has stated in interview that he was 'particularly pleased' with the narratorial voice in this story, 'which I would say is irritable, pedantic, obsessively detailed' (2007: 132). Contrast Aubrey Tearle, the blinkered, hilariously and almost heroically pedestrian narrator of the 2001 novel *The Restless Supermarket* – he is, tellingly, a retired proof-reader of telephone directories – who is also obsessively alert to every detail, and who sees everything but understands nothing of what is actually happening around him. The pun mobilised in *The Restless Supermarket* – 'end of an error' – brilliantly captures this general conceit. See also Charos 2008.

imagination, every brick of the wall seems invested with a kind of weight – 'It was reddish brown, with a cracked, cratered surface [...] It looked like it would plummet through the desk, the floor, sink down into the earth as if it were water' (1989: 32–33). Against this imagined weight and aura, the work of the narrator's neighbour is destined to appear thin and trivial – he seems not to be aware of what a wall *means* in South Africa. For him, the building is evidently just another everyday chore: this sacrilege maddens the narrator, who has wholly internalised the paranoid logic of apartheid:

> The sky above the wall was a blank, moronic space, as high as the stars. There was nothing in it that would provide comfort to a human heart [...] The world beyond the wall was empty [...] I was mad as hell [...] I should have gone right into their house and smashed up a few things. That would have been perfect, with the news in the background. I would have shown them unrest and rioting and burning, in three dimensions. I would have given them hell in the eye-level oven, and stoning with the bric-a-brac from the room divider. (41)

This narrative voice – unhinged, forever teetering on the brink of violence – reappears in 'When My Hands Burst into Flames': 'Wednesday afternoon, mid-winter, finds me at the counter in the United Building Society (Hillbrow), minding my business [...] when my hands burst into flames' (1989: 99). After initial hysterical panic, the narrator realises that these silent flames cause him no pain and do not seem to be burning him. Yet when he touches things external to him, they ignite. He comes slowly to an awareness not only that he possesses the new-found capacity to torch the entire city, but that this prospect rather thrills and excites him: 'I am starting to enjoy myself. I am highly flammable. Better, I am incendiary [...] Later, I think I will torch the park across the street. Meanwhile, I am content to play with fire' (103). The essential condition of the extreme city, its infectious, barely suppressed violent conflagration, is here expressed in the logic of an apparently unhinged consciousness.[9]

> 9 We draw here on the reading of this passage offered by one of the members of our writing collective, who, addressing himself to its historical denotation (rather than its spatial denotation or mapping, which is pre-eminently our concern here), writes of this short story that it 'simply cannot be understood outside of the specific ideological/experiential context of South Africa in the final years of apartheid, the "interregnum" as Nadine Gordimer called it – the South Africa in which "total strategies" were being devised paranoically by the state to defeat phantasmatic "total onslaughts", with the result that the mere presence, the mere physical existence, of most of the nation's people was projected as incipient criminality, latent terrorism. Vladislavic's protagonist initially responds to his "condition" with "horror and fear"; his hands unquenchably and inexplicably alight, he "wander[s] aimlessly for half an hour" (102). At some point, however, he begins to inhabit the identity capriciously imposed upon him – to find himself in it. "Finally I enter a shoe-shop with the express intention of setting something alight... I am starting to enjoy myself. I am highly inflammable. Better, I am

The narrators of these stories are also often caught between the compulsion to move and the urge to stay rooted. A part of the paranoia of the narrator of 'The Journal of a Wall' is precisely the fear of a loss of habitation, of a feeling of rootedness:

> Then it came again, the room trying to twist itself free from the rest of the house, rip up its tap-root and ascend into the sky [...] The whole place rattled and groaned, spun faster and faster, and then rose like an ancient flying machine, ripping roof-tiles like finger nails [...] The city was spread out below me like a map, but I couldn't get my bearings. There was my house, with its gaping wound. (1989: 25)

In 'Autopsy', the narrator follows an (imaginary?) figure – he takes him to be Elvis Presley – on a tour of the hyper-commercialised cityscape of the 'new' Johannesburg, whose every feature has been commodified. The imaginary Elvis is himself emblazoned with the fake logos of iconic global commodities like denims, sneakers and sports gear (1996: 41). The disappearance of this figure from his sightline causes the narrator (along with assorted passers-by) to chant praises to the Christ of our modern times – a thoroughly commodified Elvis – in an outburst of evangelical fervour. To follow this Christ is to be condemned to a restless traversing of a city that is more of a supermarket catering to globalised desires than a place of habitation.

Woven together by the statues, monuments, walls, violence, movement, paranoia, commodities, houses and townships of these early Vladislavic stories is the form of the restless city. As his writing has matured and gained in self-belief, Vladislavic's attention has turned increasingly and explicitly to Johannesburg, represented always as paradigmatic of the modern logic of combined unevenness. His first significant intervention in this respect took the form of an edited volume devoted to the subject of architecture in the apartheid and post-apartheid eras (Judin and Vladislavic 1998). With a diverse list of contributors from different disciplines, including architecture, sociology, literature, urban planning and visual arts, the volume immediately made two striking points. First, it took the unusual forms of a map with keys. The contents were not presented in a thematic or paginated sequence, but were clustered around geographical and conceptual positions. As the editors explained,

> An attempt was made to represent key architectural concepts in geographical terms [...] In this map, affinities were represented as proximities, tendencies by directions and intensities by accumulation. The map shows the major conceptual positions as landmarks [...] The map becomes a map of contents. Any essay discovered in the map of contents could now be located in the

---

incendiary" (102–3). By the story's end, he has started to "live the dream", even though it was not his dream to begin with, but the state's nightmare: "Later I think I will torch the park across the street. Meanwhile, I am content to play with fire"' (Lazarus 2011: 74–75).

body of the text according to these coordinates. (Judin and Vladislavic 1998: Introductory Note)

This form of the volume seemed to express an evolution in Vladislavic's thinking about representational strategies concerning the uneven city. To the formal tactics of mobility afforded by the short story is now added the idea of writing as a map with keys, where the content is directed by geographical and conceptual tendencies and intensities. Navigating the content via these routes, the reader is asked to proximate the experience of moving through the space-time of an extreme urban form.

The second thing that strikes the reader about *Blank* is that Vladislavic's own essay in the volume – 'Street Addresses: Johannesburg' – quite evidently bridges the concerns of his earlier short stories and his later, definitive work, *Portrait with Keys: The City of Johannesburg Unlocked*. The long-term focus on walls, fences and monuments is here intensified, and the development of new forms of racialised ghetto habitations is noted. By exploring with renewed energy the paranoid obsession with security, Vladislavic portrays a city of fragments on the point of an explosion:

> Long before he invented London, Dickens knew that cities exist primarily so that we can walk around them [...] We are entitled to envy Dickens. He lived in a city which offered the walkers 'miles upon miles of streets' in which to be lonely [...] A stranger, arriving one evening in the part of Johannesburg I call home, would think it had been struck by some calamity, that every last person had fled. There is no sign of life. Behind the walls, the houses are ticking like bombs. (Judin and Vladislavic 1998)

The narrator-figure is fascinated by such derelict, abandoned and superfluous spaces of this alarmed city as the Carlton Centre and the 'vanishing parkade'. He finds himself in dead ends, interstitial spaces that exceed or puncture the logic of urban planning. But paradoxically, he also realises that a 'rooted' sense of habitation emerges out of this very mobility and the circumnavigations to which it gives rise:

> It is also true that the complexity of cities, the flows of traffic across ever changing grids, coupled with the peculiarities of physical addresses, occupations, interests and needs, produces for each one of us a particular pattern of familiar or habitual movement over the skin of the earth which, if we could see from a vantage point in the sky, would appear as unique as a fingerprint. (Judin and Vladislavic 1998)

This narrator – mobile but also rooted, paranoid and alarmed but also attentive to new commonalities that are formed by the uneven city (the title of the essay, 'Street Addresses, Johannesburg', gestures towards the kindness and responsibility encapsulated in the act of giving directions to a stranger), disoriented but with an uncanny sense of direction, absurdist and alienated yet deeply attached to realism – emerges once again in *Portrait with Keys* (Vladislavic 2006a), in which he assumes the role of companion to the reader.

Following the formal experiments of *Blank*, *Portrait with Keys* provides its readers with narrative fragments that are grouped along various 'routes' of three varying lengths – long, medium and short. The contents of the fragments are given direction, as in the former volume, by conceptual 'tendencies' that accumulate in clusters. These 'tendencies' appear on the map as 'cycles', along which the reader might choose to move, or between which he or she might wish to take short cuts. This non-linear movement appears as the appropriate form for traversing what the narrator calls 'An Accidental Island', not only a place in which have occurred countless physical accidents, such as the narrator's trip and fall with which the book begins, but a place that is accidental in itself, 'made by geography and the town planners who laid out these city streets', far away from any source of water and yet recalling the flow and noise of the tide itself. An uncanny space, then, full of disoriented humans, such as the one whom the narrator calls the 'caged man', who paces all day, incessantly, next to a street cobbler:

> As it is, these turns in the opposite directions cancel out progress, create the impression that he is constantly retracing his steps, always forgetting why he is moving back and going back to the starting point [...] They are figures in a parable. The caged man is wearing out shoes as fast as the cobbler can mend them. But where does it start? Which panel of the diptych should we favour? Is the caged man making the cobbler work? Or is the cobbler making the caged man walk? (2006a: 38).

If fragments such as these are to be read as parables, it has to be said that they release a multitude of meanings and interpretations. This particular episode, for example, within a single moment, raises questions of movement and direction in the extreme city, of the possibility of 'progress' in the post-GEAR South Africa, of the productivity of the 'informal' economy, of the problem of waste (both wasted labour and wasted human beings) and, above all, of the possibility of reading as such. Should we take this as a *parable* on the say-so of a narrator whose uneasy, unmoored persona is gradually revealed over the course of the map?

The ground over which these urban creatures walk or labour often falls away suddenly, revealing as it does so the presence of the city's 'grounded' history of gold mining. The narrator is reminded that 'here we are still prospectors, with a digger's claim on the earth beneath our feet'. A brief peek into this underground city reveals beings who inhabit a parallel world – for example, the 'casualised' not-quite-labourers, members, evidently, of a vast reserve army – who use the spaces beneath manhole covers to store, in a disconcertingly orderly fashion, their meagre possessions, such as clothes, scraps of food, ragged bedding, bottles and pornographic magazines: 'There was a maze of mysterious spaces underfoot, known only to those who see it. And this special knowledge turned them into privileged ones, made them party to something in which, those who lived in houses with wardrobes and chests of drawers, and ate three square meals a day, could not participate'

(2006a: 50). Not only has a new principle of separation, of apartness, been reconfigured vertically across the city, but it obtains also along its horizontal axes. This brief underworld visit triggers a sense of disorientation in the narrator – 'I kneel on the pavement like a man gazing down into a well, with this small, impoverished, inexplicably orderly world before me' – and yet, this does not foreclose a defiant statement of belonging: 'This is our climate. We have grown up in the air, this light, and we grasp it on the skin, where it grasps us. We know this earth, this grass, this polished red stone with the soles of our feet. We will never be ourselves anywhere else. Happier, perhaps, healthier, less burdened, more secure. But we will never be closer to who we are than this' (76).

Nor are unplanned spaces revealed only in horizontal extremities and vertical depths; they are to be found also in the folds, cracks and recesses of the surface of the city. At the Johannesburg Public Library, walls have broken through and tunnels and walkways have suddenly appeared connecting basement parking garages and reception areas. In these folds, humans deemed as 'superfluous' by the GEAR regime might insinuate themselves. While visiting the toilet in an art gallery, the narrator sees 'a street child, as filthy as a chimney sweep' coming out of a cubicle and calmly washing his face at a basin, before disappearing once more into a crack in the wall: 'On my left, set into the curved wall that discreetly screens the toilets from the exhibition space, is a concrete ledge. There is an oddly shaped recess I would never have noticed. Two small boys are crammed into it. They smell of wood smoke and sweat' (33). Through the innumerable vanished gateways of the city – 'a garden path [that] leads to a fence rather than a gate, a doorstep [that] juts from the foot of a solid wall' (174) – the ghosts of these non-citizens come and go.

Human beings and things are *spectralised* alike by the extreme city: the things are those that have fallen outside the received circuits of commodification. Their eccentric existence renders them literally invisible to eyes accommodated to the logics of development and enterprise. Almost bumping into one such object on one of his expeditionary walks around Kensington, the Johannesburg suburb in which he lives – it is a metal pillar, something like a sawn-off lamp-post – the narrator exclaims,

> Impossible. I have walked along this pavement a thousand times, there isn't a detail I could have missed, never mind something so big. And such a peculiar, pointless thing too [...] On top is a turnip-shaped stopper, apparently welded to a shaft. Has it been lopped and plugged? Or was it made like this? [...] It's like something out of *2001: A Space Odyssey*. I can imagine that it was put here by an alien or left behind by an ancient civilization whose monuments I am incapable of recognizing. (162)

On the narrator's own construction, it is its very pointlessness that is the point of this object. It is literally *useless*: it cannot be bought, sold or built over; and yet, like the alien relic to which the narrator compares it, it simultaneously recalls a vanished history of social intercourse or exchange *and* serves as a kind of memorial to a future in which the commodity cycle that structures the present, and that seems so permanent, will have vanished as well. The very presence, the solidity, of this useless (or no longer useful) found thing – the narrator learns that there is a word for such things: *Tomasons* – defies any formulaic representation and demands the invention of a plastic language:

> It resists reduction [...] a Tomason is a thing that has become detached from its original purpose. Sometimes this detachment may be so complete that the object is turned into an enigmatic puzzle [...] Tomasons thrive in the man-made world, in spaces that are constantly being remade and redesigned for other purposes, where the function of a thing that was useful and necessary may be swept away in a tide of change or washed off like a label. They are creatures of the boundary, they gravitate to walls and fences, to entrances and exits. (162–63).

In other words, the very 'thingness' of Tomasons sums up the ceaseless flux of production, consumption, surplus and superfluity that is the motor of the long historical epoch we call modernity. The existence of such objects demands the kinds of reading and the forms of representational practice that Vladislavic's literary art yearns towards.

A good example of this elliptical, restless art is found in 'Engaging the Gorilla Cycle', a route through *Portrait with Keys* that traverses the forms of race and class consciousness that coagulate around the issue of security in post-apartheid Johannesburg. The 'gorilla' here has multiple referents: in Vladislavic's book the word refers simultaneously to the brand name of a car-locking device; to an actual gorilla named Max in Johannesburg Zoo, who, in a bizarre accident, is shot and seriously wounded by a burglar on the run from the police; to a black South African police sergeant who is racially abused by his (black) commissioner, who calls him a 'fucking gorilla'; and to the unknown assailants of a Johannesburg IT worker, one of whom is alleged, in the process of car-jacking the IT worker's car, to have bitten the hapless victim whilst proclaiming that he liked the taste of human flesh. Together, the surreal, absurd(ist) fragments that *Portrait with Keys* brings together in the 'Gorilla Cycle' trace the lineaments of a paranoid consciousness that inhabits the extreme city. It is partly a racialised consciousness: certainly, it is quite candid about its location on the privileged side of the class and colour boundaries that structure the city. But equally, it is a consciousness that demands our detached analyses of its own racialisation, insofar as the point of view that it narrativises serves to distance and defamiliarise readers from itself: readers of *Portrait with Keys* do not identify with the narrator, and are not invited to do so.

The narrator is fully aware of the fetish character of the gorilla car-locking system – 'Brute force is unthinking material force: there is no substitute for unbending steel. But it is also unfeeling animal force: there is no substitute for a powerful, dull-witted beast like a Gorilla' (57). And this fetishistic thinking leads unforgoably to the stereotypical representation of a savage urban jungle that, in its peculiar mix of anecdotalism, pseudo-science, historical amnesia and possessive individualism, is the default mindset informing the phenomenon of 'white flight'. Thus the narrator quotes his friend, Dave: 'In Joburg now [...] the hunter-gatherer is in the ascendancy. In fact, African cities everywhere are filled with roamers, intent on survival, plucking at what they can at the roadside' (39). Yet Vladislavic immediately allows us access to the historical-material nexus from which such racialised consciousness arises: 'In 1998, 107675 cars were stolen in South Africa (295 cars per day) [...] In 1998 [...] [e]xecutive salaries were sixty times higher than shop floor wages' (73). The empirical evidence of the extreme unevenness of the country, crystallised in Johannesburg, provides an explanatory gloss to the fetish and paranoia that the narratorial consciousness partially inhabits. The narrator's reflection on the everyday results of inhabiting such a consciousness is also made clear in an unsettling encounter with a black South African man in a car park, who appears to be trying to force himself into the car. The narrator registers immediate fear, and then the shame of feeling this fear 'He wants me to know who he is, to look at him. He wants me to recognize him when I see him again. His nose is almost inside the car [...] "I'm not a security," he says as the gap closes. "I'm not a security, I swear, but I wanna work with the people of the land"' (72). The desperate appeal to a commonality that this 'casualised' individual makes concretises the empirical data registering the actuality of unevenness and the realignment of segregation in the extreme city. It recalls another encounter at a car park, in which such commonalities must be appealed to because the commodification of social relationships has done violence even to the bond of language. The parking 'attendant' and the owner of the car cannot or do not speak to one another: the former merely hands the latter a card cut from discarded photocopier paper and bearing the text, 'I am not a beggar. My name is... I will watch your car while you are shopping' (114). When a bedraggled black youngster named Bongi is hired by the narrator, with considerable unease, to watch over the cars of guests arriving for a party as his house, the narrator speculates that the boy's appearance exemplifies the ruthless economic world of 'privatised' security: 'So far, he has only acquired the top half of a uniform, a navy-blue tunic that is too short in the sleeve [...] My theory is that he is earning the uniform item by item, as payment or incentive. After six months or so, he'll be fully qualified and fully clothed [...] This whole arrangement is immoral. Especially our part in it' (119–20).

Around these episodes that reveal the strata of the explosive city revolve the stories of Max the gorilla, the 'cannibal' car-jackers who attack the IT specialist, and Commissioner Selby, who racially abuses a junior officer but is cleared after an official enquiry because it emerges that he had used the word 'chimpanzee' rather than the word 'gorilla'. (It is successfully argued, on the basis of a contorted history of colonial semiotics, that to call somebody a 'chimpanzee' is not to be racially offensive.)

Yet restless movement and circulation may not be the only registers or keys to Vladislavic's city. We have seen that such restlessness and movement are often celebrated in avant-garde theory today as corresponding to the 'informalisation' of the economy and the 'creative destruction' of the social fabric. But Vladislavic's city is also very much concerned with habitation, inhabitation, fixity, rootedness – however contingent and imperilled these might be. We have already seen the narrator's declaration of belonging, a declaration achieved because of, not in spite of, the infectious restlessness of the city. When his house is turned inside out by repair work being carried out on his ceiling, the narrator becomes intensely aware of its status as a shelter: 'Suddenly I was aware not just of the icy air above the iron sheets, but of the musty air below the floorboards, and the damp soil below that. I was suspended, between the earth and sky, like an afterthought in brackets' (113). Precariousness notwithstanding, this consciousness of being sheltered, of being rooted between the sky and the earth, is further reinforced by the care and precision of the builder, whose routine work steadily returns solidity to the house and, in doing so, enables the narrator to measure the experiential and existential gap between a (mere) house and a *home*. In a city of Tomasons, of vanishing statues and gateways, the narrator also has time to notice that even the street hawker on Eleanor Street is concerned with intimacy and a sense of belonging:

> The hawker at No.12 Eleanor Street started with a couple of planks and tins, then added a trestle table, then a lean-to with a canvas roof. But her finest touch is a square of magic carpet laid down on the pavement [...] People think that the informal economy rests on hard-edged things like plastic milk-crates, cardboard boxes and supermarket trolleys, but it is floating on pillows of softly rounded air. (153–54)

In the city of edges, of fragments, of flight and of movement, the magic carpet – that mythical object of effortless transportation and transference – is also something that moors you to the ground.

Works Cited

Primary

Achebe, Chinua 1983. *Things Fall Apart* [1958] (London: Heinemann).
Antunes, António Lobo 1983. *South of Nowhere* [1979]. Trans. Elizabeth Lowe (New York: Random House).
Argueta, Manlio 1998. *Little Red Riding Hood in the Red Light District* [1977, rev. 1996]. Trans. Edward Waters Hood (Willimantic, CT: Curbstone Press).
Armah, Ayi Kwei 1974. *Why Are We So Blest?* [1972] (London: Heinemann).
Azuela, Mariano 2006. *The Underdogs* [1915]. Trans. Gustavo Pellón (Indianapolis: Hackett Publishing Company).
Ballard, J.G. 1995. *Crash* [1973] (London: Vintage).
Baroja, Pio 1922. *The Quest* [1903]. Trans. Isaac Goldberg (New York: Alfred A. Knopf).
Barreno, Maria Isabel, Maria Teresa Horta and Maria Velho Da Costa 1994. *New Portuguese Letters* [1972]. Trans. Helen R. Lane and Faith Gillespie (Columbia, LA, and London: Readers International).
Bolaño, Roberto 2009. *2666* [2004]. Trans. Natasha Wimmer (London: Picador).
Bombal, Maria Luisa 1995. *The Shrouded Woman* [1938]. *House of Mist and The Shrouded Woman: Two Novels*. Trans. Naomi Lindstrom (Austin: University of Texas Press).
Brown, George Mackay 2004. *Greenvoe* [1972] (Edinburgh: Polygon).
Bulgakov, Mikhail 1999. *The Heart of a Dog* [1925]. Trans. Michael Glenny (London: Harvill).
— 2007. *The Master and Margarita* [1966–67]. Trans. Richard Pevear and Larissa Volokhonsky (London: Penguin).
Burns, Charles 2005. *Black Hole* (London: Jonathan Cape).
Bykov, Dmitry 2010. *Living Souls* [2006]. Trans. Cathy Porter (London: Alma Books).
Carpentier, Alejo 1989. *The Kingdom of This World* [1949]. Trans. Harriet de Onís (New York: Noonday Press).
Chamoiseau, Patrick 1998. *Texaco* [1992]. Trans. Rose-Myriam Réjouis and Val Vinokurov (New York: Vintage).
Clowes, Daniel 2001. *Ghost World* (London: Fantagraphics).
Conrad, Joseph 2007. *Heart of Darkness* [1899] (London: Penguin).

Dickens, Charles 2001. *Bleak House* [1852–53] (London: Wordsworth Editions).
Djebar, Assia 1993. *Fantasia: An Algerian Cavalcade* [1985]. Trans. Dorothy S. Blair (Portsmouth, NH: Heinemann).
Dos Passos, John 2001. *U.S.A.* [1938] (London: Penguin).
Dostoyevsky, Fyodor 1972. *Crime and Punishment* [1866]. Trans. Constance Garnett (New York: Dell Publishing Co).
Dreiser, Theodore 2008. *The Financier* [1912] (New York: Penguin).
Eliot, George 2000. *Middlemarch* [1874] (London: Wordsworth Editions).
Faulkner, William 1973. *Requiem for a Nun* [1953] (Harmondsworth: Penguin).
Faulks, Sebastian 2010. *A Week in December* (London: Vintage).
Forster, E.M. 1972. *Where Angels Fear to Tread* [1905] (Harmondsworth: Penguin).
Franzen, Jonathan 1988. *The Twenty-Seventh City* (New York: Farrar, Straus and Giroux).
García Márquez, Gabriel 1970. *One Hundred Years of Solitude* [1967]. Trans. Gregory Rabassa (New York: Harper & Row).
Gibbon, Lewis Grassic 2006. *Sunset Song* [1932] (Edinburgh: Canongate).
Glukhovsky, Dmitry 2010. *Metro 2033* [2005]. Trans. Natasha Randall (London: Gollancz).
Gordimer, Nadine 1976. *A World of Strangers* [1958] (London: Cape).
Hamsun, Knut 2006. *Hunger* [1890]. Trans. Sverre Lyngstad (Edinburgh: Canongate).
Harris, Wilson 1985. *Palace of the Peacock* [1960]. *The Guyana Quartet* (London and Boston: Faber and Faber).
Haslett, Adam 2009. *Union Atlantic* (New York: Random House).
Hernandez, Felisberto 1993. *Piano Stories*. Trans. Luis Harss (New York: Marsilio Publishers).
Kelman, James 1998. *How Late It Was, How Late* [1994] (London: Vintage).
— 2007. *The Busconductor Hines* [1984] (Edinburgh: Polygon).
— 2008. *Kieron Smith, Boy* (London: Hamish Hamilton).
Kosztolányi, Dezsö 2010. *Skylark* [1925]. Trans. Richard Aczel (New York: New York Review Books).
Lampedusa, Tomasi di 2007. *The Leopard* [1958]. Trans. Archibald Colquhoun (London: Vintage).
Lanchester, John 2012. *Capital* (London: Faber and Faber).
Laxness, Halldór 2004. *The Atom Station* [1948]. Trans. Magnus Magnusson (London: Vintage).
— 2008. *Independent People* [1934]. Trans. J.A. Thompson (London: Vintage).
Lovelace, Earl 1996. *Salt* (London and Boston: Faber and Faber).
Lukyavenko, Sergei 2007. *Night Watch* [1998]. Trans. Andrew Bromfield (London: Arrow Books).
Machado de Assis, Joaquim Maria 1998. *The Posthumous Memoirs of Brás Cubas* [1880]. Trans. Gregory Rabassa (Oxford: Oxford University Press).
Mahjoub, Jamal 1989. *Navigation of a Rainmaker* (Oxford: Heinemann).
McEwan, Ian 1995. *The Comfort of Strangers* [1981] (London: Vintage).
— 2008. *On Chesil Beach* [2007] (Vintage: London).
Mudimbe, V.Y. 1993. *The Rift* [1979]. Trans. Marjolijn de Jager (Minneapolis: University of Minnesota Press).
Multatuli [Edouard Douwes Dekker] 1982. *Max Havelaar, Or the Coffee Auctions of the Dutch Trading Company* [1860]. Trans. Roy Edwards (Amherst: University of Massachusetts Press).
Murakami, Haruki 2011. *1Q84* [2009–10]. 2 vols. Trans. Jay Rubin (vol. 1) and Philip Gabriel (vol. 2) (London: Harvill Secker).

Neuman, Andrés 2012. *Traveller of the Century* [2009]. Trans. Nick Caistor and Lorenza García (New York: Farrar, Straus and Giroux; London: Pushkin Press).
Ngugi wa Thiong'o 2006. *Wizard of the Crow*. Trans. Ngugi wa Thiong'o (London: Harvill Secker).
Ouologuem, Yambo 1971. *Bound to Violence* [1968]. Trans. Ralph Manheim (London: Heinemann Educational Books).
Pelevin, Victor 1996a. *Oman Ra* [1992]. Trans. Andrew Bromfield (London: Faber and Faber).
— 1996b. *The Life of Insects* [1995]. Trans. Andrew Bromfield (London: Faber and Faber).
— 1998. *A Werewolf Problem in Central Russia and Other Stories* [1988]. Trans. Andrew Bromfield (New York: New Directions).
— 1999. *The Clay Machine-Gun* [1996]. Trans. Andrew Bromfield (London: Faber and Faber).
— 2001. *Babylon* [1999]. Trans. Andrew Bromfield (London: Faber and Faber).
— 2006a. *The Helmet of Horror* [2005]. Trans. Andrew Bromfield (Edinburgh: Canongate).
— 2006b. *Empire V* (Moscow: Eksmo).
— 2008. *The Sacred Book of the Werewolf* [2004]. Trans. Andrew Bromfield (London: Faber and Faber).
Pepetela 2002. *The Return of the Water Spirit* [1995]. Trans. Luís R. Mitras (London: Heinemann).
Pist'anek, Peter 2007. *Rivers of Babylon* [1991]. Trans. Peter Petro (London: Garnett Press).
Rivera, José Eustasio 2003. *The Vortex* [1924]. Trans. Earle K. James (Bogota, Colombia: Panamericana Editorial).
Robinson, Kim Stanley 2012. *2312* (London: Orbit).
Rulfo, Juan 1987. *Pedro Páramo* [1955]. Trans. Lysander Kemp (New York: Grove Weidenfeld).
Sahgal, Nayantara 1986. *Rich Like Us* [1985] (New York and London: W.W. Norton & Company).
Salih, Tayeb 2003. *Season of Migration to the North* [1967]. Trans. Denys Johnson-Davies (London: Heinemann).
Sinclair, Upton 2006. *The Moneychangers* [1908] (West Valley City, UT: Waking Lion Press).
Slavnikovna, Olga 2010. *2017* [2006]. Trans. Marian Schwartz (New York and London: Overlook/Duckworth).
Sorokin, Vladimir 2011. *Ice Trilogy* [2008]. Trans. Jamey Gambrell (New York: New York Review Books).
— 2012. *Day of the Oprichnik* [2006]. Trans. Jamey Gambrell (London: Farrar, Straus and Giroux).
Spark, Muriel 2006. *The Driver's Seat* [1974] (London: Penguin).
Stasiuk, Andrzej 2008. *9* [1999]. Trans. Bill Johnston (London: Vintage).
Sterne, Laurence 1983. *The Life and Opinions of Tristram Shandy, Gentleman* [1760] (Oxford: Clarendon Press).
Tanpinar, Ahmet Hamdi 2011. *A Mind at Peace* [1949]. Trans. Erdag Göknar (New York: Archipelago Books).
Tolstaya, Tatyana 2003. *The Slynx* [2000]. Trans. Jamey Gambrell (New York: New York Review Books).
Trollope, Anthony 1991. *The Way We Live Now* [1873, first published 1941] (Oxford: Oxford University Press).

Vladislavic, Ivan 1989. *Missing Persons* (Cape Town and Johannesburg: David Philip).
— 1996. *Propaganda by Monuments and Other Stories* (Cape Town and Johannesburg: David Philip).
— 2001. *The Restless Supermarket* (Cape Town: David Philip).
— 2006a. *Portrait with Keys: The City of Johannesburg Unlocked* (London: Portobello).
Vorpsi, Ornela 2009. *The Country Where No One Ever Dies* [2004]. Trans. Robert Elsie and Janice Mathie-Heck (Champaign, IL, and London: Dalkey Archive Press).
Welsh, Irvine 2013. *Trainspotting* [1993] (London: Vintage).
Yi Mun-Yol 2001. *The Poet* [1992]. Trans. Chong-wha Chung and Brother Anthony of Taizé (London: The Harvill Press).
Zola, Emile 2007. *Money* [1891]. Trans. Ernest Alfred Vizetelly (New York: Mondial).

Secondary

Abu-Haydar, Jareer 1985. 'A Novel Difficult to Categorise'. *Season of Migration to the North by Tayeb Salih: A Casebook*. Ed. Mona Takieddine Amyuni (Beirut: American University of Beirut): 45–53.
Adorno, Theodor W. 1985. *Minima Moralia: Reflections from Damaged Life* [1951]. Trans. E.F.N. Jephcott (London: Verso).
— 1991. 'Extorted Reconciliation: On Georg Lukács *Realism in Our Time*' [1961]. *Notes to Literature*. Vol. 1. Trans. Shierry Weber Nicholsen (New York: Columbia University Press): 216–40.
— 1992a. 'Commitment' [1962]. *Notes to Literature*. Vol. 2. Trans. Shierry Weber Nicholsen (New York: Columbia University Press): 76–94.
— 1992b. 'On Dickens' *The Old Curiosity Shop*: A Lecture' [1967, orig. publ. 1931]. *Notes to Literature*. Vol. 2. Trans. Shierry Weber Nicholsen (New York: Columbia University Press): 171–77.
— 2005. *In Search of Wagner* [1952]. Trans. Rodney Livingstone (London: Verso).
— et al. 1986. *Aesthetics and Politics* (London: Verso).
Ahmad, Aijaz 1987. 'Jameson's Rhetoric of Otherness and the "National Allegory"'. *Social Text* 17: 3–26.
Alberson, Hazel S. 1960. 'Non-Western Literature in the World Literature Program'. *The Teaching of World Literature* (Proceedings of the Conference at the University of Wisconsin, 1959). Ed. Haskell M. Block (Chapel Hill: University of North Carolina Press): 45–52.
Aldcroft, Derek Howard 2006. *Europe's Third World: The European Periphery in the Interwar Years* (Aldershot: Ashgate).
Allan, Michael 2007. 'Reading with One Eye, Speaking with One Tongue: On the Problem of Address in World Literature'. *Comparative Literature Studies* 44.1–2: 1–19.
Allinson, J.C., and Alexander Anievas 2009. 'The Uses and Misuses of Uneven and Combined Development: An Anatomy of a Concept'. *Cambridge Review of International Affairs* 22.1: 47–67.
Amireh, Amal, and Lisa Suhair Majaj 2000. *Going Global: The Transnational Reception of Third World Women Writers* (London and New York: Routledge).
Amyuni, Mona Takieddine, ed. 1985. *Season of Migration to the North by Tayeb Salih: A Casebook* (Beirut: American University of Beirut).
Anderson, Perry 1984. 'Modernity and Revolution'. *New Left Review* 144: 96–113.
— 1998. *The Origins of Postmodernity* (London and New York: Verso).

Annesley, James 2006. *Fictions of Globalization: Consumption, the Market and the Contemporary American Novel* (London: Continuum).
Appadurai, Arjun 1996. *Modernity at Large: Cultural Dimensions of Globalization* (Minneapolis: University of Minnesota Press).
Appiah, Kwame Anthony 1991. 'Is the Post- in Postmodernism the Post- in Postcolonial?' *Critical Inquiry* 17.2: 336–57.
Apter, Emily 1999. *Continental Drift: From National Characters to Virtual Subjects* (Chicago and London: University of Chicago Press).
— 2006. *The Translation Zone: A New Comparative Literature* (Princeton: Princeton University Press).
— 2013. *Against World Literature* (London and New York: Verso).
Arac, Jonathan, and Harriet Ritvo, eds. 1991. *Macropolitics of Nineteenth-Century Literature: Nationalism, Exoticism, Imperialism* (Philadelphia: University of Pennsylvania Press).
Arrighi, Giovanni 1994. *The Long Twentieth Century. Money, Power, and the Origins of Our Times* (London and New York: Verso).
Ashcroft, Bill, Gareth Griffiths and Helen Tiffin 1989. *The Empire Writes Back: Theory and Practice in Post-colonial Literatures* (London and New York: Routledge).
Ashman, S. 2009. 'Capitalism, Uneven and Combined Development and the Transhistoric'. *Cambridge Review of International Affairs* 22.1: 29–46.
Aziz, Barbar Nimri 1996. 'The Last Hakawati'. http://almashriq.hiof.no/syria/700/790/the_last_hakawati/. Accessed 28 September 2011. Originally published in *Aramco World Magazine* (January–February).
Bailey, Michael, and Des Freedman, eds. 2011. *The Assault on Universities: A Manifesto for Resistance* (London: Pluto).
Bakhtin, Mikhail 2003. *Problems of Dostoevsky's Poetics* [1963]. Ed. and trans. Caryl Emerson (Minneapolis: University of Minnesota Press).
Ballaster, Rosalind 2005. *Fabulous Orients: Fictions of the East in England 1662–1785* (Oxford: Oxford University Press).
Barchiesi, Franco 2011. *Precarious Liberation: Workers, the State, and Contested Social Citizenship in Postapartheid South Africa* (Albany: State University of New York Press).
Barker, Colin 2006. 'Beyond Trotsky: Extending Combined and Uneven Development'. *100 Years of Permanent Revolution: Results and Prospects*. Eds. Bill Dunn and Hugo Radice (London: Pluto): 78–87.
Barnard, Rita 2009. 'Fictions of the Global'. *Novel* 42.2: 207–15.
Bartlett, Robert 1994. *The Making of Europe: Conquest, Colonization and Cultural Change 950–1350* (London: Penguin).
Bartolovich, Crystal 2010. 'If Oil Could Speak: What Would It Say?' Unpublished paper prepared for the conference 'What Postcolonial Theory Doesn't Say'. University of York, 5 July 2010.
Bassnett, Susan 2006. 'Reflections on Comparative Literature in the Twenty-First Century'. *Comparative Critical Studies* 3.1–2: 3–11.
Bataille, Georges 1994. *The Absence of Myth: Writings on Surrealism*. Trans. Michael Richardson (London and New York: Verso).
Baucom, Ian 1999. *Out of Place: Englishness, Empire, and the Locations of Identity* (Princeton: Princeton University Press).
Bauman, Zygmunt 1987. *Legislators and Interpreters: On Modernity, Post-modernity and Intellectuals* (Oxford: Polity).
— 2004. *Europe: An Unfinished Adventure* (Cambridge: Polity).
Beaumont, Matthew 2011. 'Aleatory Realism: Reflections on the Parable of the

Pier-Glass'. *Experiments in/of Realism*. Eds. Anna Despotopoulou and Katerina Kitsi-Mitakou. Special issue of *Synthesis* 3: 11–21.

Beecroft, Alexander 2008. 'World Literature without a Hyphen'. *New Left Review* 54: 87–100.

Behdad, Ali 2005. 'On Globalization, Again!' *Postcolonial Studies and Beyond*. Eds. Ania Loomba, Suvir Kaul, Matti Bunzl, Antoinette Burton and Jed Esty (Durham and London: Duke University Press): 62–79.

Benjamin, Walter 2003. 'On Some Motifs in Baudelaire' [1939]. *Selected Writings Vol. 4: 1938–1940*. Eds. Howard Eiland and Michael W. Jennings. Trans. Edmund Jephcott and Harry Zohn (Cambridge: Harvard University Press): 313–55.

Berman, Marshall 1983. *All That Is Solid Melts into Air: The Experience of Modernity* (London: Verso).

Bessis, Sophie 2003. *Western Supremacy: The Triumph of an Idea?* [2001]. Trans. Patrick Camiller (London and New York: Zed Books).

Bhambra, Gurminder K. 2007. 'Multiple Modernities or Global Interconnections: Understanding the Global Post the Colonial'. *Varieties of World-Making: Beyond Globalisation*. Eds. Nathalie Karagiannis and Peter Wagner (Liverpool: Liverpool University Press): 59–73.

Bird, Emma Jane 2013. 'Reimagining Bombay: Postcolonial Poetry and Urban Space'. Unpublished PhD thesis, University of Exeter.

Bloch, Ernst 1977. 'Nonsynchronism and Dialectics'. *New German Critique* 11: 22–38.

— 1991. *Heritage of Our Times* [1935]. Trans. Neville and Stephen Plaice (Berkeley: University of California Press).

Bohrer, Karl Heinz 2012. '"Europe" as Utopia: Causes of Its Decline'. Trans. Ciarin Cronin. *New Literary History* 43: 587–605.

Boldrini, Lucia 2006. 'Comparative Literature in the Twenty-First Century: A View from Europe and the UK'. *Comparative Critical Studies* 3.1–2: 13–23.

Bond, Patrick 2000. *Elite Transition: From Apartheid to Neoliberalism in South Africa* (London: Pluto).

— 2004. *Against Global Apartheid: South Africa Meets the World Bank, IMF and International Finance* (London: Zed).

— 2006. *Talk Left, Walk Right: South Africa's Frustrated Global Reforms*. 2nd edn (Scottsville: University of KwaZulu-Natal Press).

Boschetti, Anna 2012. 'How Field Theory Can Contribute to Knowledge of World Literary Space'. *Paragraph* 35.1: 10–29.

Bourdieu, Pierre 1984. *Distinction: A Social Critique of the Judgement of Taste* [1979]. Trans. Richard Nice (Cambridge: Harvard University Press).

— 1993. *The Field of Cultural Production: Essays on Art and Literature*. Ed. Randal Johnson. Trans. Richard Nice (New York: Columbia University Press).

Brantlinger, Patrick 1988. *Rule of Darkness: British Literature and Imperialism, 1830–1914* (Ithaca: Cornell University Press).

Braudel, Fernand 1985. *Civilisation and Capitalism, 15th–18th Century* [1979]. Vol. 1: *The Structures of Everyday Life: The Limits of the Possible*. Trans. Miriam Kochan (London: Fontana). Vol. 2: *Wheels of Commerce*. Trans. Siân Reynolds (London: Fontana). Vol. 3: *The Perspective of the World*. Trans. Siân Reynolds (London: Fontana).

Breckenridge, Carol A., Sheldon Pollock, Homi K. Bhabha and Dipesh Chakrabarty, eds. 2002. *Cosmopolitanism* (Durham and London: Duke University Press).

Bremner, Lindsay Jill 2007. 'Memory, Nation-Building and the Post-apartheid City: The Apartheid Museum in Johannesburg'. *Desire Lines: Space, Memory and Identity in the*

Post-Apartheid City. Eds. Noëleen Murray, Nick Shepherd and Martin Hall (London and New York: Routledge): 85–104.

Brennan, Timothy 1997. *At Home in the World: Cosmopolitanism Now* (Cambridge and London: Harvard University Press).

— 2001. 'The Cuts of Language: The East/West of North/South'. *Public Culture* 13.1: 39–63.

— 2004. 'From Development to Globalization: Postcolonial Studies and Globalization Theory'. *The Cambridge Companion to Postcolonial Literary Studies*. Ed. Neil Lazarus (Cambridge: Cambridge University Press): 120–38.

— 2006. *Wars of Position: The Cultural Politics of Left and Right* (New York: Columbia University Press).

— 2013. 'Edward Said as a Lukácsian Critic: Modernism and Empire'. *College English* 40.4: 14–32.

Bretz, Mary Lee 2001. *Encounters across Borders: The Changing Visions of Spanish Modernism 1890–1930* (Lewisburg, PA: Bucknell University Press).

Brouillette, Sarah 2007. *Postcolonial Writers in the Global Literary Marketplace* (Basingstoke and New York: Palgrave Macmillan).

Brown, Nicholas 2005. *Utopian Generations: The Political Horizon of Twentieth-Century Literature* (Princeton and London: Princeton University Press).

Buchanan, Ian 2002. 'Reading Jameson Dogmatically'. *Historical Materialism* 10.3: 223–43.

— 2003. 'National Allegory Today: A Return to Jameson'. *New Formations* 51: 66–79.

Buck-Morss, Susan 2009. *Hegel, Haiti, and Universal History* (Pittsburgh: University of Pittsburgh Press).

— 2010. 'The Gift of the Past'. *Small Axe* 33: 173–85.

Buell, Frederick 1994. *National Culture and the New Global System* (Baltimore: Johns Hopkins University Press).

Buell, Lawrence 2007. 'Ecoglobalist Affects: The Emergence of U.S. Environmental Imagination on a Planetary Scale'. *Shades of the Planet: American Literature as World Literature*. Eds. Wai Chee Dimock and Lawrence Buell (Princeton and Oxford: Princeton University Press): 227–48.

Buzadhi, Sara 2011. 'Werewolves in Epaulettes and Other Bloodsuckers. *The Moscow News*. http://themoscownews.com/russian_tongue/20110704/188809471.html. Accessed 24 August 2012.

Calabrese, Andrew, and Colin Sparks, eds. 2004. *Toward a Political Economy of Culture: Capitalism and Communication in the Twenty-First Century* (Lanham, MD: Rowman and Littlefield).

Callinicos, Alex, and Justin Rosenberg 2008. 'Uneven and Combined Development: The Social-Relational Substratum of "the International"? An Exchange of Letters'. *Cambridge Review of International Affairs* 21.1: 77–112.

Calvet, Louis-Jean 2006. *Towards an Ecology of World Languages* [1999]. Trans. Andrew Brown (Cambridge: Polity).

Casanova, Pascale 2004. *The World Republic of Letters* (Cambridge: Harvard University Press).

Cervinkova, Hana 2012. 'Postcolonialism, Postsocialism and the Anthropology of East-Central Europe'. *Journal of Postcolonial Writing* 48.2: 155–63.

Charos, Caitlin 2008. '"The End of an Error": Transition and "Post-Apartheid Play" in Ivan Vladislavić's *The Restless Supermarket*'. *Safundi: The Journal of South African and American Studies* 9.1: 23–38.

Cheyfitz, Eric 1991. *The Poetics of Imperialism: Translation and Colonization from 'The Tempest' to 'Tarzan'* (New York and Oxford: Oxford University Press).
Chibber, Vivek 2013. *Postcolonial Theory and the Specter of Capital* (London and New York: Verso).
Chow, Rey 2004. 'The Old/New Question of Comparison in Literary Studies: A Post-European Perspective'. *ELH* 71: 289–311.
Cleary, Joe 2012. 'Realism after Modernism and the Literary World-System'. *Modern Language Quarterly* 73.3: 255–68.
Collini, Stefan 2010. 'Browne's Gamble'. *London Review of Books* 32.21 (4 November): 23–25.
— 2011. 'From Robbins to McKinsey'. *London Review of Books* 33.16 (25 August): 9–14.
— 2012. *What Are Universities For?* (London: Penguin).
— 2013. 'Sold Out'. *London Review of Books* 34.20 (24 October): 3–12.
Comaroff, Jean, and John L. Comaroff 1999. 'Occult Economies and the Violence of Abstraction: Notes from the South African Postcolony'. *American Ethnologist* 26:2: 279–303.
Connell, Liam, and Nicky Marsh, eds. 2011. *Literature and Globalization* (London: Routledge).
Coombes, Annie E. 2003. *History after Apartheid: Visual Culture and Public Memory in a Democratic South Africa* (Durham and London: Duke University Press).
Coombs, David Sweeney 2011. 'Entwining Tongues: Postcolonial Theory, Post-Soviet Literatures and Bilingualism in Chingiz Aitmatov's *I dol'she veka dlitsia den'*. *Journal of Modern Literature* 34.3: 47–63.
Cooppan, Vilashini 2001. 'World Literature and Global Theory: Comparative Literature for the New Millennium'. *Symploke* 9.1–2: 15–43.
— 2004. 'Ghosts in the Disciplinary Machine: The Uncanny Life of World Literature'. *Comparative Literature Studies* 41.1: 10–36.
— 2005. 'The Ruins of Empire: The National and Global Politics of America's Return to Rome'. *Postcolonial Studies and Beyond*. Eds. Ania Loomba, Suvir Kaul, Matti Bunzl, Antoinette Burton and Jed Esty (Durham and London: Duke University Press): 80–100.
Cornis-Pope, Marcel 2012. 'Local and Global Frames in Recent Eastern European Literatures: Postcommunism, Postmodernism, and Postcoloniality'. *Journal of Postcolonial Writing* 48.2: 143–54.
Culler, Jonathan 2006. 'Comparative Literature, at Last'. *Comparative Literature in an Age of Globalization*. Ed. Haun Saussy (Baltimore and London: Johns Hopkins University Press): 237–48.
Curtis, Adam 2011. 'How the "ecosystem" myth has been used for sinister means'. *The Observer* (Sunday 29 May). http://www.theguardian.com/environment/2011/may/29/adam-curtis-ecosystems-tansley-smuts. Accessed 11 October 2014.
Czeglédy, André P. 2003. 'Villas of the Highveld: A Cultural Perspective on Johannesburg and Its "Northern Suburbs"'. *Emerging Johannesburg: Perspectives on the Post-Apartheid City*. Eds. Richard Tomlinson, Robert A. Beauregard, Lindsay Bremner and Xolela Mangcu (London: Routledge): 21–42.
Damrosch, David 2003. *What Is World Literature?* (Princeton and Oxford: Princeton University Press).
— 2006. 'Rebirth of a Discipline: The Global Origins of Comparative Studies'. *Comparative Critical Studies* 3.12: 99–122.
— 2007. 'Global Regionalism'. *European Review* 15.1: 135–43.

— 2008. *How to Read World Literature* (Oxford: Wiley-Blackwell).
Davidson, Neil 2006a. 'Third World Revolution'. *Socialist Review* (December). www.socialistreview.org.uk/issue.php?issue=312. Accessed 17 January 2011.
— 2006b. 'From Uneven to Combined Development'. *100 Years of Permanent Revolution: Results and Prospects*. Eds. Bill Dunn and Hugo Radice (London: Pluto): 10–26.
Davis, Mike 2006. *Planet of Slums*. London and New York: Verso.
De Medeiros, Paulo 1996. 'Beyond the Looking Glass of Empire: The Colonization of Portuguese Literature'. *No Small World: Visions and Revisions of World Literature*. Ed. Michael Thomas Carroll (Urbana: National Council of Teachers of English): 43–57.
Denning, Michael 2004. *Culture in the Age of Three Worlds* (London and New York: Verso).
Derluguian, Georgi M. 2005. *Bourdieu's Secret Admirer in the Caucasus: A World-System Biography* (Chicago and London: University of Chicago Press).
Desai, Ashwin 2002. *We Are the Poors: Community Struggles in Post-apartheid South Africa* (New York: Monthly Review Press).
D'haen, Theo 2012. *The Routledge Concise History of World Literature* (London and New York: Routledge).
Dimock, Wai Chee 2006. *Through Other Continents: American Literature Across Deep Time* (Princeton and Oxford: Princeton University Press).
— and Lawrence Buell, eds. 2007. *Shades of the Planet: American Literature as World Literature* (Princeton: Princeton University Press).
Dirlik, Arif 2002. 'Rethinking Colonialism: Globalization, Postcolonialism and the Nation'. *Interventions* 4.3: 428–48.
Docherty, Thomas 2006. 'Without and Beyond Compare'. *Comparative Critical Studies* 3.1–2: 25–35.
— 2011. *For the University: Democracy and the Future of the Institution* (London: Bloomsbury Academic).
Donecker, Stefan 2009. 'Werewolves on the Baltic Seashore Monstrous Frontier of Early Modern Europe, 1550–1700'. *The Role of the Monster: Myths and Metaphors of Enduring Evil*. Ed. Niall Scott (Oxford: Inter-Disciplinary Press): 63–76.
Doyle, Laura 2010. 'Notes Toward a Dialectical Method: Modernities, Modernisms, and the Crossings of Empire'. *Literature Compass* 7.3: 195–213.
Drakulic, Slavenka 1999. *Café Europa: Life after Communism* [1996] (London: Penguin).
Durst, David C. 2004. *Weimar Modernism: Philosophy, Politics, and Culture in Germany, 1918–1933* (Lanham, MD: Lexington Books).
Eagleton, Terry 1990. *The Ideology of the Aesthetic* (Oxford: Blackwell).
— 1995. *Heathcliff and the Great Hunger: Studies in Irish Culture* (London and New York: Verso).
English, James F. 2005. *The Economy of Prestige: Prizes, Awards, and the Circulation of Cultural Value* (Cambridge: Harvard University Press).
— 2012. *The Global Future of English Studies* (Malden, MA, and Oxford: Wiley-Blackwell).
Esterházy, Péter 2005. 'How Big Is the European Dwarf?' [2003]. *Old Europe, New Europe, Core Europe: Transatlantic Relations after the Iraq War*. Eds. Daniel Levy, Max Pensky and John Torpey (New York and London: Verso): 74–79.
Etkind, Alexander 2011. *Internal Colonization: Russia's Imperial Experience* (Oxford: Polity).
—, Rory Finnin et al. 2012. *Remembering Katy'n: Memory Wars in Eastern Europe* (Oxford: Polity).
Fanon, Frantz 1968. *The Wretched of the Earth* [1961]. Trans. Constance Farrington (New York: Grove Press).

Farris, Sara R. 2010. 'An "Ideal Type" Called *Orientalism*: Selective Affinities Between Edward Said and Max Weber'. *Interventions: International Journal of Postcolonial Studies* 12.2: 265–84.

Feinstein, Andrew 2009. *After the Party: Corruption and the ANC* (London and New York: Verso).

Felski, Rita 2012. 'Introduction'. *New Literary History* 43: v–xv.

Fludernik, Monica, ed. 2003. *Diaspora and Multiculturalism: Common Traditions and New Developments* (Amsterdam and New York: Rodopi).

Friedman, Susan Stanford 2001. 'Definitional Excursions: The Meanings of Modern/Modernity/Modernism'. *Modernism/Modernity* 8.3: 493–513.

— 2006. 'Periodizing Modernism: Postcolonial Modernities and the Space/Time Borders of Modernist Studies'. *Modernism/Modernity* 13.3: 425–43.

— 2010. 'Planetarity: Musing Modernist Studies'. *Modernism/Modernity* 17.3: 471–99.

Fuentes, Carlos 2006. 'In Praise of the Novel'. *Critical Inquiry* 32.4: 610–17.

Furedi, Frank 2006. *Where Have All the Intellectuals Gone? Confronting 21st Century Philistinism*. 2nd edn (London: Continuum).

Ganguly, Debjani 2008. 'Literary Globalism in the New Millennium'. *Postcolonial Studies* 11.1: 119–33.

Gaonkar, Dilip Parameshwar 1999. 'On Alternative Modernities'. *Public Culture* 11.1: 1–18.

—, ed. 2001. *Alternative Modernities* (Durham: Duke University Press).

Geesey, Patricia 1997. 'Cultural Hybridity and Contamination in Tayeb Salih's *Mawsim al-hijra ila al-Shamal (Season of Migration to the North)*'. *Research in African Literatures* 28.3: 128–40.

Ghodsee, Kristen 2011. *Lost in Transition: Ethnographies of Everyday Life after Communism* (Durham: Duke University Press).

Gikandi, Simon 2001. 'Globalization and the Claims of Postcoloniality'. *South Atlantic Quarterly* 100: 627–58.

Givens, John 2010. 'The New Gothic, Mythic Prose, and the Post-Soviet Novel'. *Russian Studies in Literature* 46.1: 3–5.

Glissant, Edouard 1989. *Caribbean Discourse: Selected Essays*. Trans. J. Michael Dash (Charlottesville: University Press of Virginia).

GoGwilt, Christopher 2011. *The Passage of Literature: Genealogies of Modernism in Conrad, Rhys, and Pramoedya* (Oxford: Oxford University Press).

Goldman, Marshall 2008. *Oilopoly: Putin, Power and the Rise of the New Russia* (Oxford: Oneworld).

Gopal, Priyamvada 2012. 'How Universities Die'. *South Atlantic Quarterly* 111.2: 383–91.

Gosk, Hanna 2012. 'Counter-Discourse and the Postcolonial Perspective: *The Polish Complex* by Tadeusz Konwicki'. *Journal of Postcolonial Writing* 48.2: 200–08.

Gotz, Graeme, and AbdouMaliq Simone 2003. 'On Belonging and Becoming in African Cities'. *Emerging Johannesburg: Perspectives on the Post-apartheid City*. Eds. Richard Tomlinson, Robert A. Beauregard, Lindsay Bremner and Xolela Mangcu (London: Routledge): 123–47.

Gould, Rebecca 2013. 'Topographies of Anticolonialism: The Ecopoetical Sublime in the Caucasus from Tolstoy to Mamakaev'. *Comparative Literature Studies* 50.1: 87–107.

Graham, James 2008. 'Ivan Vladislavíc and the Possible City'. *Journal of Postcolonial Writing* 44.4: 333–44.

Gupta, Suman 2008. *Globalization and Literature* (Oxford: Polity).

Guy, Josephine M., and Ian Small 1993. *Politics and Value in English Studies: A Discipline in Crisis?* (Cambridge: Cambridge University Press).
Habermas, Jürgen (co-signed by Jacques Derrida) 2005. 'February 15, or, What Binds Europeans Together: Plea for a Common Foreign Policy, Beginning in Core Europe' [2003]. *Old Europe, New Europe, Core Europe: Transatlantic Relations after the Iraq War.* Eds. Daniel Levy, Max Pensky and John Torpey (New York and London: Verso): 3–13.
Hall, Catherine 2002. *Civilising Subjects: Metropole and Colony in the English Imagination 1830–1867* (Cambridge: Polity).
Hargreaves, Alec G., and Mark McKinney, eds. 1997. *Post-colonial Cultures in France* (London and New York: Routledge).
Harlow, Barbara 1985. 'Sentimental Orientalism: *Season of Migration to the North* and *Othello*'. *Season of Migration to the North by Tayeb Salih: A Casebook.* Ed. Mona Takieddine Amyuni (Beirut: American University of Beirut): 75–79.
Harootunian, Harry 2000a. *History's Disquiet: Modernity, Cultural Practice, and the Question of Everyday Life* (New York: Columbia University Press).
— 2000b. *Overcome by Modernity: History, Culture, and Community in Interwar Japan* (Princeton: Princeton University Press).
Harris, Wilson 1981. *Explorations: A Selection of Talks and Articles, 1966–1981* (Mundelstrup, Denmark: Dangaroo Press).
Hart, Gillian Hart 2002. *Disabling Globalization: Places of Power in Post-apartheid South Africa* (Pietermaritzburg: University of Natal Press).
Harvey, David 1985. *The Urbanization of Capital: Studies in the History and Theory of Capitalist Urbanization* (Baltimore: Johns Hopkins University Press).
— 1989. *The Condition of Postmodernity: An Enquiry into the Origins of Cultural Change* (Oxford: Basil Blackwell).
— 2001. *Spaces of Capital: Towards a Critical Geography* (New York: Routledge).
— 2005. *The New Imperialism* (Oxford: Oxford University Press).
— 2009. *Social Justice and the City.* Rev. edn [1973] (Athens and London: University of Georgia Press).
Hassan, Waïl S. 2003. *Tayeb Salih: Ideology and the Craft of Fiction* (Syracuse: Syracuse University Press).
Hayot, Eric 2012. *On Literary Worlds* (New York and Oxford: Oxford University Press).
Helgesson, Stefan 2004. 'Minor Disorders: Ivan Vladislavić and the Devolution of South African English'. *Journal of South African Studies* 30.4: 777–87.
Hickey, Kieran 2011. *Wolves in Ireland: A Natural and Cultural History* (Dublin: Four Courts Press).
Hirst, Paul, and Grahame Thompson 1996. *Globalization in Question: The International Economy and the Possibilities of Governance* (Oxford: Polity).
Hockx, Michel 2012. 'The Literary Field and the Field of Power: The Case of Modern China'. *Paragraph* 35.1: 49–65.
Hoesel-Ihlig, Stefan 2004. 'Changing Fields: The Directions of Goethe's *Weltliteratur*'. *Debating World Literature.* Ed. Christopher Prendergast (London and New York: Verso): 26–53.
Holmwood, John 2011. *A Manifesto for the Public University* (London: Bloomsbury Academic).
— and Gurminder K. Bhambra 2012. 'The Attack on Education as a Social Right'. *South Atlantic Quarterly* 111.2: 392–401.
Hotson, Howard 2011. 'Don't Look to the Ivy League'. *London Review of Books* 33.10 (19 May): 20–22.

Howes, David, ed. 1996. *Cross-Cultural Consumption: Global Markets, Local Realities* (London and New York: Routledge).
Huggan, Graham 2001. *The Post-colonial Exotic: Marketing the Margins* (London and New York: Routledge).
Hulme, Peter 1992. *Colonial Encounters: Europe and the Native Caribbean, 1492–1797* (London: Methuen).
Huyssen, Andreas 2005. 'Geographies of Modernism in a Globalizing World'. *Geographies of Modernism: Literature, Culture, Spaces*. Eds. Andrew Thacker and Peter Brooker (London: Routledge): 6–18.
Israel, Nico 2004. 'Globalization and Contemporary Literature'. *Literature Compass* 1.
Jameson, Fredric 1971. *Marxism and Form: Twentieth-Century Dialectical Theories of Literature* (Princeton: Princeton University Press).
— 1986a. 'Third-World Literature in the Era of Multinational Capitalism'. *Social Text* 15: 65–88.
— 1986b. 'On Magic Realism in Film'. *Critical Inquiry* 12: 301–25.
— 1986c. 'Reflections in Conclusion' [1977]. *Aesthetics and Politics* (London: New Left Books): 196–213.
— 1995. *Postmodernism, or, The Cultural Logic of Late Capitalism* [1991] (Durham: Duke University Press): 297–418.
— 1998. 'Notes on Globalization as a Philosophical Issue'. *The Cultures of Globalization*. Eds. Fredric Jameson and Masao Miyoshi (Durham and London: Duke University Press): 54–77.
— 1999. 'History Lessons'. *Architecture and Revolution: Contemporary Perspectives on Central and Eastern Europe*. Ed. Neil Leach (London: Routledge): 69–80.
— 2002. *A Singular Modernity: Essay on the Ontology of the Present* (London and New York: Verso).
— 2007. 'A Note on Literary Realism in Conclusion'. *Adventures in Realism*. Ed. Matthew Beaumont (Oxford: Blackwell): 261–71.
— 2008. 'How Not to Historicize Theory'. *Critical Inquiry* 34: 563–82.
— 2012. 'Antinomies of the Realism-Modernism Debate'. *Modern Language Quarterly* 73.3: 475–85.
— and Masao Miyoshi, eds. 1998. *The Cultures of Globalization* (Durham and London: Duke University Press).
Jarvis, Simon 2012. 'Phantasmal Disestablishment'. *South Atlantic Quarterly* 111.2: 402–11.
Jay, Paul 2001. 'Beyond Discipline? Globalization and the Future of English'. *PMLA* 116.1: 32–47.
— 2010. *Global Matters: The Transnational Turn in Literary Studies* (Ithaca and London: Cornell University Press).
Judin, Hilton, and Ivan Vladislavic, eds. 1998. *Blank: Architecture, Apartheid and After* (Rotterdam: Nai).
Jürgens, Ulrich, Martin Gnad and Jürgen Bähr 2003. 'New Forms of Class and Racial Segregation: Ghettos or Ethnic Enclaves'. *Emerging Johannesburg: Perspectives on the Post-apartheid City*. Eds. Richard Tomlinson, Robert A. Beauregard, Lindsay Bremner and Xolela Mangcu (London: Routledge): 56–70.
Kadir, Djelal 2004. 'To World, to Globalize: Comparative Literature's Crossroads'. *Comparative Literature Studies* 41.1: 1–9.
Kaiwar, Vasant 2014. *The Postcolonial Orient: The Politics of Difference and the Project of Provincialising Europe* (Amsterdam: Brill).

Kanneh, Kadiatu 1998. *African Identities: Race, Nation and Culture in Ethnography, Pan-Africanism and Black Literatures* (London and New York: Routledge).

Kaplan, Amy, and Donald E. Pease, eds. 1993. *Cultures of United States Imperialism* (Durham and London: Duke University Press).

Kapur, Geeta 1998. 'Globalization and Culture: Navigating the Void'. *The Cultures of Globalization*. Eds. Fredric Jameson and Masao Miyoshi (Durham and London: Duke University Press): 191–217.

Katz, Barry 1982. *Herbert Marcuse and the Art of Liberation: An Intellectual Biography* (New York: Schocken).

Keel, Aldo 2005. 'The View from Up Top: Core Europe from the Scandinavian Perspective' [2003]. *Old Europe, New Europe, Core Europe: Transatlantic Relations after the Iraq War*. Eds. Daniel Levy, Max Pensky and John Torpey (New York and London: Verso): 80–83

Kelertas, Violeta, ed. 2006. *Baltic Postcolonialism: On the Boundary of Two Worlds; Identity, Freedom and Moral Imagination in the Baltics* (Amsterdam and New York: Rodopi).

Kendall, Elizabeth 2002. 'Between Politics and Literature: Journals in Alexandria and Istanbul at the End of the Nineteenth Century'. *Modernity and Culture: From the Mediterranean to the Indian Ocean*. Eds. Leila Tarazi Fawaz and C.A. Bayly (New York: Columbia University Press): 330–43.

Kiberd, Declan 1997. 'Modern Ireland: Postcolonial or European'. *Not on Any Map: Essays on Postcoloniality and Cultural Nationalism*. Ed. Stuart Murray (Exeter: University of Exeter Press): 81–100.

King, Anthony D. 1997. *Culture, Globalization and the World-System: Contemporary Conditions for the Representation of Identity* (Minneapolis: University of Minnesota Press).

Klobucka, Anna 1997. 'Theorizing the European Periphery'. *Symploke* 5.1–2: 119–35.

Konuk, Kader 2010. *East West Mimesis: Auerbach in Turkey* (Stanford: Stanford University Press).

Kracauer, Siegfried 1995. 'The Mass Ornament'. *The Mass Ornament: Weimar Essays* [1963]. Trans. Thomas Y. Levin (Cambridge: Harvard University Press): 75–88.

Krzeminski, Adam 2005. 'First Kant, Now Habermas: A Polish Perspective on "Core Europe"'. *Old Europe, New Europe, Core Europe: Transatlantic Relations after the Iraq War*. Eds. Daniel Levy, Max Pensky and John Torpey (New York and London: Verso): 146–52.

Krishnan, Sanjay 2012. 'V.S. Naipaul and Historical Derangement'. *Modern Language Quarterly* 73.3: 433–51.

Krishnaswamy, Revathi, and John C. Hawley, eds. 2008. *The Postcolonial and the Global* (Minneapolis and London: University of Minnesota Press).

Kropywiansky, Leo 2002. 'Victor Pelevin'. *BOMB* 79. http://bombsite.com/issues/79/articles/2481. Accessed 24 August 2012.

Kruger, Loren 2006. 'Filming the Edge City: Cinematic Narrative and Urban Form in Post-apartheid Johannesburg'. *Research in African Literatures* 37.2: 141–63.

Lafargue, Paul 2002. 'Reminiscences of Marx' [1890]. *Marx and Engels Through the Eyes of Their Contemporaries* (Moscow: Progress Publishers, 1972). Online version: Lafargue Internet Archive (Marxists.org): http://www.marxists.org/archive/lafargue/1890/xx/marx.htm. Accessed 28 June 2014.

Laird, Sally 1999. *Voices of Russian Literature: Interviews with Ten Contemporary Writers* (Oxford: Oxford University Press).

Larsen, Neil 2001. *Determinations: Essays in Theory, Narrative and Nation in the Americas* (New York and London: Verso).
Larson, Susan, and Eva Woods 2005. 'Visualizing Spanish Modernity: Introduction'. *Visualizing Spanish Modernity*. Eds. Susan Larson and Eva Woods (New York: Berg): 1–23.
Lash, Scott, and Celia Lury 2006. *Global Culture Industry* (Oxford: Polity).
Lazarus, Neil 1999. *Nationalism and Cultural Practice in the Postcolonial World* (Cambridge: Cambridge University Press).
— 2002. 'The Fetish of "the West" in Postcolonial Theory'. *Marxism, Modernity and Postcolonial Studies*. Eds. Crystal Bartolovich and Neil Lazarus (Cambridge: Cambridge University Press): 43–64.
— 2004. 'Fredric Jameson on "Third-World Literature": A Qualified Defence'. *Fredric Jameson: A Critical Reader*. Eds. Douglas Kellner and Sean Homer (Basingstoke: Palgrave): 42–61.
— 2011. *The Postcolonial Unconscious* (Cambridge: Cambridge University Press).
— 2012. 'Spectres Haunting: Postcommunism and Postcolonialism'. *Journal of Postcolonial Writing* 48.2: 117–29.
— and Rashmi Varma 2008. 'Marxism and Postcolonial Studies'. *The Critical Companion to Contemporary Marxism*. Eds. Jacques Bidet and Stathis Kouvelakis (Leiden: Academic Publishers): 309–31.
Lebedushkina, Olga 2010. 'Our New Gothic: The Miracles and Horrors of Contemporary Prose'. *Russian Studies in Literature* 46.1: 81–100.
Lefebvre, Henri 1995. *Introduction to Modernity* [1962]. Trans. John Moore (London and New York: Verso).
Levy, Daniel, Max Pensky and John Torpey, eds. 2005. *Old Europe, New Europe, Core Europe: Transatlantic Relations after the Iraq War* (New York and London: Verso).
Lipovetsky, Mark, and Alexander Etkind 2010. 'The Salamander's Return: The Soviet Catastrophe and the Post-Soviet Novel'. *Russian Studies in Literature* 46.4: 6–48.
Liu Kang 1998. 'Is There an Alternative to (Capitalist) Globalization? The Debate about Modernity in China'. *The Cultures of Globalization*. Eds. Fredric Jameson and Masao Miyoshi (Durham and London: Duke University Press): 164–88.
— 2000. *Aesthetics and Marxism: Chinese Aesthetic Marxists and Their Western Contemporaries* (Durham and London: Duke University Press).
Lomnitz, Claudio 2012. 'Time and Dependency in Latin America Today'. *South Atlantic Quarterly* 111.2: 347–57.
Longhurst, Alex 1999. 'The Turn of the Novel in Spain: From Realism to Modernism in Spanish Fiction'. *Studies in Modern Spanish Literature from Galdós to Unamuno*. Ed. Anthony H. Clarke (Exeter: University of Exeter Press): 1–43.
Loomba, Ania 1989. *Gender, Race, Renaissance Drama* (Manchester: Manchester University Press).
—, Suvir Kaul, Matti Bunzl, Antoinette Burton and Jed Esty, eds. 2005. *Postcolonial Studies and Beyond* (Durham and London: Duke University Press).
Lowe, Lisa 1991. *Critical Terrains: French and British Orientalisms* (Ithaca and London: Cornell University Press).
Löwy, Michael 2007. 'The Current of Critical Irrealism: "A moonlit enchanted night"'. *Adventures in Realism*. Ed. Matthew Beaumont (Oxford: Blackwell): 193–206.
— 2010. *The Politics of Combined and Uneven Development* (Chicago: Haymarket).
— and Robert Sayre 2001. *Romanticism Against the Tide of Modernity*. Trans. Catherine Porter (Durham and London: Duke University Press).

Lukács, Georg 1962. 'Dostoevsky' [1949]. Trans. René Wellek. *Dostoevsky: A Collection of Critical Essays*. Ed. René Wellek (Englewood Cliffs, NJ: Prentice-Hall, Inc.): 146–58.
— 1979. *The Meaning of Contemporary Realism* [1958]. Trans. John and Necke Mander (London: Merlin Press).
Majid, Anouar 2000. *Unveiling Traditions: Postcolonial Islam in a Polycentric World* (Durham and London: Duke University Press).
Makdisi, Saree S. 1994. 'The Empire Renarrated: *Season of Migration to the North* and the Reinvention of the Present'. *Colonial Discourse and Post-colonial Theory: A Reader*. Eds. Patrick Williams and Laura Chrisman (Hemel Hempstead: Harvester Press): 535–50.
Mamdani, Mahmood 1996. *Citizen and Subject: Contemporary Africa and the Legacy of Late Colonialism* (Princeton: Princeton University Press).
— 2013. 'What Is a tribe?' *London Review of Books* 34.17 (13 September): 20–22.
Marais, Hein 1998. *South Africa: Limits to Change – The Political Economy of Transition* (London: Zed).
— 2011. *South Africa Pushed to the Limit: The Political Economy of Change* (London: Zed).
Marcuse, Herbert 1969. *Eros and Civilization: A Philosophical Inquiry into Freud* [1955] (London: Sphere Books).
— 1979. *The Aesthetic Dimension: Toward a Critique of Marxist Aesthetics* [1977]. Trans. Herbert Marcuse and Erica Sherover (London: Macmillan).
Marx, Karl 1965. *Capital*. Vol. 1 [1867] (Moscow: Progress Press).
— 1990. *Capital: A Critique of Political Economy*. Vol. 1 [1867]. Trans. Ben Fowkes (London: Penguin).
— 1991. *Capital: A Critique of Political Economy*. Vol. 3 [1894]. Trans. Ben Fowkes (London: Penguin).
— and Friedrich Engels 1998. *The Communist Manifesto* [1848] (London and New York: Verso).
Maskell, Duke, and Ian Robinson 2001. *The New Idea of a University* (London: Haven Books).
Mayekiso, Mzwanele 1994. 'The "Civics": Hope of the Townships'. *Times Literary Supplement* (1 April): 8.
McCallum, Pamela, and Wendy Faith, eds. 2005. *Linked Histories: Postcolonial Studies in a Globalized World* (Calgary: University of Calgary Press).
McClintock, Anne 1995. *Imperial Leather: Race, Gender and Sexuality in the Colonial Contest* (New York and London: Routledge).
McGonegal, Julie 2005. 'Postcolonial Metacritique: Jameson, Allegory and the Always-Already-Read Third World Text'. *Interventions* 7.2: 251–65.
McGurl, Mark 2012. 'The Posthuman Comedy'. *Critical Inquiry* 38: 533–53.
McLeod, John 2004. *Postcolonial London: Rewriting the Metropolis* (London: Routledge).
Meek, James 2008. 'Dead Not Deid'. *London Review of Books* 30.10 (22 May): 5–8.
Mejías-López, Alejandro 2009. *The Inverted Conquest: The Myth of Modernity and the Transatlantic Onset of Modernism* (Nashville: Vanderbilt University Press).
Meskell, Lynn 2007. 'Living in the Past: Historic Futures in Double Time'. *Desire Lines: Space, Memory and Identity in the Post-apartheid City*. Eds. Noëleen Murray, Nick Shepherd and Martin Hall (London and New York: Routledge): 165–80.
Mignolo, Walter D. 1998. 'Globalization, Civilization Processes, and the Relocation of Languages and Cultures'. *The Cultures of Globalization*. Eds. Fredric Jameson and Masao Miyoshi (Durham and London: Duke University Press): 32–53.
Miyoshi, Masao 1998. '"Globalization," Culture and the University'. *The Cultures of*

Globalization. Eds. Fredric Jameson and Masao Miyoshi (Durham and London: Duke University Press): 247–70.
— 2000. 'The University and the "Global" Economy: The Cases of the United States and Japan'. *South Atlantic Quarterly* 99: 669–96.
— 2005. 'The University, the Universe, the World, and "Globalization"'. *Gramma* 13: 49–68.
Molesworth, Mike, Richard Scullion and Elizabeth Nixon, eds. 2010. *The Marketing of Higher Education and the Student as Consumer* (London: Routledge).
Moore, Jason W. 2010. 'The End of the Road? Agricultural Revolutions in the Capitalist World-Ecology, 1450–2010'. *Journal of Agrarian Change* 10.3: 389–413.
— 2012. 'Cheap Food & Bad Money: Food, Frontiers, and Financialization in the Rise and Demise of Neoliberalism'. *Review: A Journal of the Fernand Braudel Center* 33.2–3: 225–61.
Moretti, Franco 1996. *Modern Epic: The World-System from Goethe to García Márquez* [1994]. Trans. Quintin Hoare (London and New York: Verso).
— 1999. *Atlas of the European Novel 1800–1900* [1997] (London and New York: Verso).
— 2003. 'More Conjectures'. *New Left Review* 20: 73–81.
— 2004. 'Conjectures on World Literature' [2000]. *Debating World Literature*. Ed. Christopher Prendergast (London and New York: Verso): 148–62.
— 2011. 'World-Systems Analysis, Evolutionary Theory, *Weltliteratur*'. *Immanuel Wallerstein and the Problem of the World: System, Scale, Culture*. Eds. David Palumbo-Liu, Bruce Robbins and Nirvana Tanoukhi (Durham: Duke University Press): 67–77.
— 2013. *The Bourgeois: Between History and Literature* (London and New York: Verso).
Moses, Michael Valdez 1995. *The Novel and the Globalization of Culture* (New York and Oxford: Oxford University Press).
Mudimbe-Boyi, Elisabeth, ed. 2002. *Beyond Dichotomies: Histories, Identities, Cultures, and the Challenge of Globalization* (Albany: SUNY Press).
Mufti, Aamir R. 2005. 'Global Comparativism'. *Critical Inquiry* 31: 472–89.
Murphy, Richard 1998. *Theorizing the Avant-Garde: Modernism, Expressionism, and the Problem of Postmodernity* (Cambridge: Cambridge University Press).
Murray, Martin J. 1994. *Revolution Deferred: The Painful Birth of Post-apartheid South Africa* (London and New York: Verso).
— 2008. 'The City in Fragments: Kaleidoscopic Johannesburg after Apartheid'. *The Spaces of the Modern City: Imaginaries, Politics, and Everyday Life*. Eds. Gyan Prakash and Kevin M. Kruse (Princeton and Oxford: Princeton University Press): 144–78.
Murray, Noëleen, Nick Shepherd and Martin Hall, eds. 2007. *Desire Lines: Space, Memory and Identity in the Post-apartheid City* (London and New York: Routledge).
Muschg, Adolf 2005. '"Core Europe": Thoughts about the European Identity' [2003]. *Old Europe, New Europe, Core Europe: Transatlantic Relations after the Iraq War*. Eds. Daniel Levy, Max Pensky and John Torpey (New York and London: Verso): 21–27.
Niblett, Michael 2012a. *The Caribbean Novel since 1945: Cultural Practice, Form, and the Nation-State* (Jackson: University Press of Mississippi).
— 2012b. 'World-Economy, World-Ecology, World Literature'. *Green Letters: Studies in Ecocriticism* 16: 15–30
— 2013. 'The "Impossible Quest for Wholeness": Sugar, Cassava, and the Ecological Aesthetic in *The Guyana Quartet*'. *Journal of Postcolonial Writing* 49.2 (2013): 148–60.
Nuttall, Sarah, and Achille Mbembe, eds. 2008. *Johannesburg: The Elusive Metropolis* (Durham and London: Duke University Press).
O'Brien, Kevin J. 2006. 'Science-Fiction Sales: The Post-Soviet Generation'. *New York*

Times. 29 October. http://www.nytimes.com/2006/10/29/technology/29iht-scifi. 3323704.html?pagewanted=all. Accessed 24 July 2012.

Ohmann, Richard 2003. *Politics of Knowledge: The Commercialization of the University, the Professions, and Print Culture* (Middletown: Wesleyan University Press).

Oushakine, Serguei Alex 2010. Book review. *The Sacred History Cultural Anthropology* 25.2: 380–85.

Outhwaite, William, and Larry Ray 2005. *Social Theory and Postcommunism* (Oxford: Blackwell).

Paik Nak-chung 1998. 'Nations and Literatures in the Age of Globalization'. *The Cultures of Globalization*. Eds. Fredric Jameson and Masao Miyoshi (Durham and London: Duke University Press): 218–29.

Palmary, Ingrid, Janine Rauch and Graeme Simpson 2003. 'Violent Crime in Johannesburg'. *Emerging Johannesburg: Perspectives on the Post-apartheid City*. Eds. Richard Tomlinson, Robert A. Beauregard, Lindsay Bremner and Xolela Mangcu (London: Routledge): 101–22.

Parry, Benita 1992. 'Overlapping Territories and Intertwined Histories: Edward Said's Postcolonial Cosmopolitanism'. *Edward Said: A Critical Reader*. Ed. Michael Sprinker (Oxford: Blackwell): 19–47.

— 2004. *Postcolonial Studies: A Materialist Critique* (London and New York: Routledge).

— 2005. 'Reflections on the Excess of Empire in Tayeb Salih's *Season of Migration to the North*'. *Paragraph*: special issue on 'The Idea of the Literary'. Ed. Nicholas Harrison (Edinburgh: Edinburgh University Press): 72–90.

— 2006. 'Countercurrents and Tensions in Edward Said's Critical Practice'. *Edward Said: Emancipation and Representation*. Eds. Adel Iskandar and Hakim Rustom (Berkeley: University of California Press, 2006): 499–512.

— 2009. 'Aspects of Peripheral Realism'. *Ariel* 40.1: 37–55.

— 2013. 'Edward Said and Third-World Marxism'. *College Literature* 40.4: 105–26.

Pavlyshyn, Marko 2012. 'Andrukhovych's *Secret*: The Return of Colonial Resignation'. *Journal of Postcolonial Writing* 48.2: 188–99.

Pelevin, Victor 2000. 'I Was Never a Hero'. *The Observer*. 30 April. http://www.guardian.co.uk/books/2000/apr/30/fiction. Accessed 24 August 2012.

Pizer, John 2000. 'Goethe's "World Literature" Paradigm and Contemporary Cultural Globalization'. *Comparative Literature* 52.3: 213–27.

Pollard, Sidney 1998. 'The Peripheral European Countries in the 19th Century'. *Uneven Development in Europe 1918–1939*. Eds. Jean Batou and Thomas David (Geneva: Librairie Droz): 59–84

Popescu, Monica 2012. 'Lewis Nkosi in Warsaw: Translating Eastern European Experiences for an African Audience'. *Journal of Postcolonial Writing* 48.2: 176–87.

Power, Nina 2012. 'Dangerous Subjects: UK Students and the Criminalization of Protest'. *South Atlantic Quarterly* 111.2: 412–20.

Pratt, Mary Louise 1992. *Imperial Eyes: Travel Writing and Transculturation* (New York and London: Routledge).

— 2002. 'Modernity and Periphery: Towards a Global and Relational Analysis'. *Beyond Dichotomies: Histories, Identities, Cultures and the Challenge of Globalization*. Ed. Elisabeth Mudimbe-Boyi (Albany: State University of New York Press): 21–48.

Prawer, S.S. (Siegbert Salomon) 1976. *Karl Marx and World Literature* (Oxford: Clarendon Press).

Ramazani, Jahan 2009. *A Transnational Poetics* (Chicago: University of Chicago Press).

Readings, Bill 1996. *The University in Ruins* (Cambridge: Harvard University Press).

Robinson, Paul A. 1969. *The Freudian Left: Wilhelm Reich, Geza Roheim, Herbert Marcuse* (New York: Harper and Row).
Rosenberg, Justin 1996. 'Isaac Deutscher and the Lost History of International Relations'. *New Left Review* 215: 3–15.
— 2005. 'Globalization Theory: A Post-mortem'. *International Politics* 42.1: 2–74.
— 2006. 'Why Is There No International Historical Sociology?' *European Journal of International Relations* 12.3: 307–40.
— 2007. 'International Relations: The "Higher Bullshit": A Reply to the Globalisation Theory Debate'. *International Politics* 44.4: 450–82.
Rowe, John Carlos 2000. *Literary Culture and US Imperialism: From the American Revolution to World War II* (Oxford: Oxford University Press).
Said, Edward W. 1979. *Orientalism* (New York: Vintage).
— 1993. *Culture and Imperialism* (London: Chatto & Windus).
Sampedro Vizcaya, Benita, and Simon Doubleday, eds. 2008. *Border Interrogations: Questioning Spanish Frontiers* (New York and Oxford: Berghahn Books).
Sandru, Cristina 2012. *Worlds Apart? A Postcolonial Reading of Post-1945 East-Central European Culture* (Newcastle upon Tyne: Cambridge Scholars Publishing).
San Juan, Jr., Epifanio 2006. 'Edward Said's Affiliations: Secular Humanism and Marxism'. *Atlantic Studies* 3.1: 43–61.
— 2008. 'Postcolonial Dialogics: Between Edward Said and Antonio Gramsci'. *Postcolonialism and Political Theory*. Ed. Nalini Persram (Lanham, MD, and Plymouth: Lexington Books): 99–120.
Santiáñez, Nil 2005. 'Great Masters of Spanish Modernism'. *The Cambridge History of Spanish Literature*. Ed. David T. Gies (Cambridge: Cambridge University Press, 2005): 479–98.
Sapiro, Gisèle 2012. 'Autonomy Revisited: The Question of Mediations and Its Methodological Implications'. *Paragraph* 35.1: 30–48.
Saul, John 2005. *The Next Liberation Struggle: Capitalism, Socialism and Democracy in Southern Africa* (New York: Monthly Review Press).
Saussy, Haun, ed. 2006. *Comparative Literature in an Age of Globalization* (Baltimore and London: Johns Hopkins University Press).
Schwarz, Roberto 1992. *Misplaced Ideas: Essays on Brazilian Culture*. Ed. John Gledson (London: Verso).
— 2001. *A Master on the Periphery of Capitalism* [1990]. Trans. John Gledson (Durham: Duke University Press).
Seikaly, Samir 1985. '*Season of Migration to the North*: History in the Novel'. *Season of Migration to the North by Tayeb Salih: A Casebook*. Ed. Mona Takieddine Amyuni (Beirut: American University of Beirut): 135–41.
Shapiro, Stephen 2008. 'Transvaal, Transylvania: Dracula's World-System and Gothic Periodicity'. *Gothic Studies* 10.1: 29–47.
Shepherd, Nick, and Christian Ernsten 2007. 'The World Below: Post-apartheid Imaginaries and the Bones of the Prestwich Street Dead'. *Desire Lines: Space, Memory and Identity in the Post-apartheid City*. Eds. Noëleen Murray, Nick Shepherd and Martin Hall (London and New York: Routledge): 215–32.
Shih, Shu-mei 2013. 'Global Literature and the Technologies of Recognition' [2004]. *World Literature: A Reader*. Eds. Theo D'haen, César Domínguez and Mads Rosenthal Thomsen (London and New York: Routledge): 259–74.
Shilliam, R. 2009. 'The Atlantic as a Vector of Uneven and Combined Development'. *Cambridge Review of International Affairs* 22.1: 69–88.

Shklovsky, Viktor 2006. 'Sterne's *Tristram Shandy*' [1921]. *The Novel: An Anthology of Criticism and Theory 1900–2000*. Ed. Dorothy J. Hale (Oxford: Blackwell): 31–53.
Shohat, Ella, and Robert Stam 1994. *Unthinking Eurocentrism: Multiculturalism and the Media* (London and New York: Routledge).
Simon, Rick 2009. 'Upper Volta with Gas? Russia as a Semi-peripheral State'. *Globalization and the 'New' Semi-peripheries*. Eds. Owen Worth and Phoebe Moore (Basingstoke: Palgrave): 120–37.
Simone, AbdouMaliq 2008. 'People as Infrastructure: Intersecting Fragments in Johannesburg'. *Johannesburg: The Elusive Metropolis*. Eds. Sarah Nuttall and Achille Mbembe (Durham and London: Duke University Press): 68–90.
Smith, Neil 1990. *Uneven Development: Nature, Capital and the Production of Space*. 2nd edn (Oxford: Basil Blackwell).
— 1996. *The New Urban Frontier: Gentrification and the Revanchist City* (London and New York: Routledge).
Spivak, Gayatri Chakravorty 2003. *Death of a Discipline* (New York: Columbia University Press).
Stasiuk, Andrzej 2005. 'Wild, Cunning, Exotic: The East Will Completely Shake Up Europe' [2003]. *Old Europe, New Europe, Core Europe: Transatlantic Relations after the Iraq War*. Eds. Daniel Levy, Max Pensky and John Torpey (New York and London: Verso): 103–06.
Strongman, Luke 2002. *The Booker Prize and the Legacy of Empire* (Amsterdam: Rodopi).
Subramani 1998. 'The End of Free States: On Transnationalization of Culture'. *The Cultures of Globalization*. Eds. Fredric Jameson and Masao Miyoshi (Durham and London: Duke University Press): 146–63.
Swanson, Philip 2005. *Latin American Fiction: A Short Introduction* (Oxford: Blackwell).
Szeman, Imre 2003. *Zones of Instability: Literature, Postcolonialism and the Nation* (Baltimore: Johns Hopkins University Press).
— 2007. 'System Failure: Oil, Futurity, and the Anticipation of Disaster'. *South Atlantic Quarterly* 106.4: 805–23.
Taussig, Michael T. 2010. *The Devil and Commodity Fetishism in South America* (Chapel Hill: University of North Carolina Press).
Teeuwen, Rudolphus, and Steffen Hantke, eds. 2007. *Gypsy Scholars, Migrant Teachers and the Global Academic Proletariat* (Amsterdam: Rodopi).
Tlostanova, Madina 2012. 'Postsocialist ≠ Postcolonial? On Post-Soviet Imaginary and Global Coloniality'. *Journal of Postcolonial Writing* 48.2: 130–42.
Todorov, Tzvetan 2005. *The New World Disorder: Reflections of a European* [2003]. Trans. Andrew Brown (Cambridge: Polity).
Tomlinson, John 1991. *Cultural Imperialism: A Critical Introduction* (London: Pinter).
Tomlinson, Richard, Robert A. Beauregard, Lindsay Bremner and Xolela Mangcu 2003. 'The Post-apartheid Struggle for an Integrated Johannesburg'. *Emerging Johannesburg: Perspectives on the Post-apartheid City*. Eds. Richard Tomlinson, Robert A. Beauregard, Lindsay Bremner and Xolela Mangcu (London: Routledge): 3–20.
— and Pauline Larsen 2003. 'The Race, Class, and Space of Shopping'. *Emerging Johannesburg: Perspectives on the Post-apartheid City*. Eds. Richard Tomlinson, Robert A. Beauregard, Lindsay Bremner and Xolela Mangcu (London: Routledge): 43–55.
Trotsky, Leon. 1967. *History of the Russian Revolution* [1932–33]. Vol. 1. Trans. Max Eastman (London: Sphere Books).
— 2005. *Literature and Revolution* [1925]. Ed. William Keach. Trans. Rose Strunsky (Chicago: Haymarket).

Turim, Maureen 1998. *The Films of Oshima Nagisa: Images of a Japanese Iconoclast* (Berkeley: University of California Press).
Urquhart, James 2008. 'A Supernatural Love Affair Where Nothing Is as It Seems'. *The Independent*. 5 March. http://www.independent.co.uk/arts-entertainment/books/reviews/the-sacred-book-of-werewolf-by-victor-pelevin-791241.html. Accessed 24 August 2012.
Velickovic, Vedrana 2012. 'Belated Alliances? Tracing the Intersections between Postcolonialism and Postcommunism'. *Journal of Postcolonial Writing* 48.2: 164–75.
Venuti, Lawrence 1998. *The Scandals of Translation: Towards an Ethics of Difference* (London and New York: Routledge).
Viswanathan, Gauri 1989. *The Masks of Conquest: Literary Study and British Rule in India* (New York: Columbia University Press).
Vladislavic, Ivan 2000. 'Interview with Ivan Vladislavíc' (Christopher Warnes). *Modern Fiction Studies* 46.1: 273–81.
— 2006b. 'X Marks the Spot'. *Scrutiny2* 11.2: 125–28.
— 2007. 'Delving into the Toolbox: Ivan Vladislavíc Interviewed by Andie Miller'. *Journal of Commonwealth Literature* 42.3: 131–43.
Walkowitz, Rebecca L., ed. 2007. *Immigrant Fictions: Contemporary Literature in an Age of Globalization* (Madison: University of Wisconsin Press).
Wallerstein, Immanuel 1974. *The Modern World-System: Capitalist Agriculture and the Origins of the European World-Economy in the Sixteenth Century* (New York and London: Academic Press).
— 1980. *The Modern World-System II: Mercantilism and the Consolidation of the European World-Economy, 1600–1750* (New York: Academic Press).
— 1989. *The Modern World-System III: The Second Era of Great Expansion of the Capitalist World-Economy, 1730–1840s* (San Diego, London, Boston, New York, Sydney, Tokyo and Toronto: Academic Press).
— 1996. *Historical Capitalism with Capitalist Civilization* [1983, 1995] (London and New York: Verso).
Warnes, Christopher 2009. *Magical Realism and the Postcolonial Novel: Between Faith and Irreverence* (Basingstoke: Palgrave Macmillan).
Watkins, Evan 1989. *Work Time: English Departments and the Circulation of Cultural Value* (Stanford: Stanford University Press).
Weinberger, Eliot 2001. 'Anonymous Sources: A Talk on Translators and Translation'. http://www.fascicle .com/issue01/Poets/weinberger1. Accessed 10 April 2010.
Widdowson, Peter 1982. 'Introduction: The Crisis of English Studies'. *Re-Reading English*. Ed. Peter Widdowson (London and New York: Methuen): 1–14.
Williams, Raymond 1976. *Keywords: A Vocabulary of Culture and Society* (New York: Oxford University Press).
— 1991a. 'Crisis in English Studies' [1981]. *Writing in Society* (London and New York: Verso): 192–211.
— 1991b. 'Notes on English Prose 1780–1950' [1969]. *Writing in Society* (London and New York: Verso): 67–118.
Wynter, Sylvia 1971. 'Novel and History, Plot and Plantation'. *Savacou* (June): 95–102.
Yaeger, Patricia 2011. 'Editor's Column: Literature in the Ages of Wood, Tallow, Coal, Whale Oil, Gasoline, Atomic Power and Other Energy Sources'. *PMLA* 126.2: 305–26.
Young, Paul 2012. 'Peripheralizing Modernity: Global Modernism and Uneven Development'. *Literature Compass* 9.9: 611–16.

Index

Abbasi, Muhammad, Sa'id el- 85
Abu Nuwas 84–5
Adorno, Theodor W. 19, 20, 83n4, 103
  'Extorted Reconciliation' (critique of Lukács) 57–60
  on realism and modernism 57–9, 66–7
Alberson, Hazel S. 23n38
Aldcroft, Derek Howard 128
Alencar, José Martiniano de 64, 78
All-India Progressive Writers' Movement 77
Allan, Roger 91n16
'alternative' modernities *see* modernity
American literary studies 3, 42–8
Amin, Samir 45
Anna Karenina (Leo Tolstoy) 50
Anderson, Perry 10, 127–8n9
Antunes, António Lobo
  South of Nowhere 16
Anzaldúa, Gloria 70–1n20
Appiah, Kwame Anthony 67–8
Apter, Emily 23–8
  Against World Literature 27n43
  The Translation Zone 5
Aral Sea 13
Arguedas, José María 80
Argueta, Manlio
  Little Red Riding Hood in the Red Light District 72n23
Armah, Ayi Kwei
  Why Are We So Blest? 91n18

Ashcroft, Bill 29
Asturias, Miguel Ángel 19, 80
Auerbach, Erich 5, 24, 30
Aziz, Barbar Nimri 84n5
Azorín (José Martínez Ruiz) 129–30
Azuela, Mariano
  The Underdogs 79

Bakhtin, Mikhail 16, 122n2
Ballard, J.G.
  Crash 93
Balzac, Honoré de 59, 78, 131
Baroja, Pio 122
  La dama errante 134–5
  The Quest 51, 127, 129–35
  The Struggle for Life (Trilogy) 129, 130
Bartlett, Robert 35
Bartolovich, Crystal 113–4
Bassnett, Susan 29, 39, 123
  'Reflections on Comparative Literature' 33–7
Bataille, Georges 93
Baudelaire, Charles 18, 122
Beaumont, Matthew 70
Beckett, Samuel 20, 65
Beijing 11
Benet, Juan 126
Benjamin, Walter 145–6
  'On Some Motifs in Baudelaire' 59n10
Berger, John 19
Berlin 123

Berman, Marshall 18, 120, 145–6
  'modernism of underdevelopment'
    61–2n13, 122–3
Bessis, Sophie 34n55
Bhagavad Gita 46
Bloch, Ernst 52–3
  'simultaneity of the nonsimultaneous'
    12
Blok, Alexander 106, 114
Blomkamp, Neill
  District 9 144–5
Bohrer, Karl Heinz 36n58
Bolaño, Roberto 19
  2666 68, 80n30, 97
Boldrini, Lucia 32, 124
Bombal, María Luisa
  The Shrouded Woman 79
Bombay 13, 14, 55
Boschetti, Anna 9
Botev, Hristo 18
Boudjedra, Rachid 126
Bourdieu, Pierre 50
  Distinction 9
Bradbury, Malcolm 127–8n9
Bratislava 116
  in *Rivers of Babylon* (Pist'anek) 115, 117
Braudel, Fernand 8
  Civilization and Capitalism 18
Brazil
  as peripheral formation in world-
    system (19th C) 62–5
Bremner, Lindsay 153
Breton, André 19
Bretz, Mary Lee 127, 129, 131–5
Brezhnev, Leonid 99
Brouillette, Sarah 9
  'global literary marketplace' 126n8
Brown, George Mackay 138
  Greenvoe 127
Brown, Nicholas 19–20
  Utopian Generations 15, 52
Brunner, John
  The Sheep Look Up 71n22
  Stand on Zanzibar 71–2
Brutus, Dennis 78n27
Buck-Morss, Susan 47
Buell, Frederick 5
Buell, Lawrence 42
Buenos Aires 55

Bugul, Ken
  The Abandoned Baobab 85n8
Bulgakov, Mikhail 100–1, 103
  The Heart of a Dog 104, 106
  The Master and Margarita 104, 106
Burns, Charles
  Black Hole 71n21
Buzadhi, Sara 100n3
Bykov, Dmitry
  Living Souls 98

Cairo
  in *Season of Migration to the North*
    (Salih) 85, 87
Calvet, Louis-Jean 26
Cape Town 145
capitalism
  and 'Afropolitan modernity' (Achille
    Mbembe and Sarah Nuttall) 149–51
  contemporary crisis 69–70
  'millennial' (Jean and
    John L. Comaroff) 143–4, 145
  misread in civilisational terms as 'the
    West' 28–41, 48
  resource exhaustion 108–9
capitalist world-system 8, 10–15, 41, 42,
    49, 52, 53n4, 54, 61, 68, 69, 128–9
  as world-ecological-system 96–7
Caribbean
  as peripheral formation in world-
    system 73–4
Carpentier, Alejo
  Kingdom of this World 72n23
  The Lost Steps 50
Casanova, Pascale 6, 42, 70–1n20
  The World Republic of Letters 8–9, 45,
    125–7
Cervantes, Miguel de 36
  Don Quixote 65–6n16
Césaire, Aimé 19
Chakrabarty, Dipesh 40
Chamoiseau, Patrick 74
  Texaco 72n23
China
  basis for Trotsky's theory of 'uneven
    and combined development' 10
  combined and uneven development
    in 11
  transition to capitalism 97

189

Chow, Rey 25n39, 26–7, 29, 33, 123
 'The Old/New Question of
  Comparison in Literary Studies'
  39–41
Chughtai, Ismat 19
Cleary, Joseph 68, 77
Clowes, Daniel
 Ghost World 71n21
Coetzee, J.M.
 Dusklands 16
Cold War 5–6, 13n24, 23n38, 47, 98, 119
Comaroff, Jean 143–4
Comaroff, John L. 143–4
Comparative Literature 3–6, 22–8, 33–7, 39–41
Conrad, Joseph
 Heart of Darkness 16, 35
 Lord Jim 16
Coombes, Annie 156n6
Cooppan, Vilashini 7n16
Copenhagen 123
Culler, Jonathan 22
cultural imperialism 9–10
Curtius, Robert 36n58

Damrosch, David 7n16, 50, 137–8
 How to Read World Literature 5
Dante Alighieri 36
 Divine Comedy 50
Daumier, Honoré 18
Denning, Michael 3n6, 80
 Culture in the Age of Three Worlds 132
Derluguian, Georgi 107
Derrida, Jacques 37n60
D'Haen, Theo 126–7
Dickens, Charles 18, 19, 59, 78, 131, 133
 Bleak House 70
 The Old Curiosity Shop 59n11
Dimock, Wai Chee
 Through Other Continents 42–8
Ding Ling 77
Djebar, Assia
 Fantasia: An Algerian Cavalcade 94n25
Docherty, Thomas 3
Döblin, Alfred 122
Donecker, Stefan 102–3
Dos Passos, John
 U.S.A. 71–2

Dostoevsky, Fyodor 19, 61–2, 66, 72, 101, 106, 133
 Crime and Punishment 120–2, 127
Drakulic, Slavenka 118–9
Dream of the Red Chamber (Cao Xueqin) 50
Dreiser, Theodore
 The Financier 69n18
Dublin 14
Durban 145

Eagleton, Terry 27, 65
Eliot, George 74
 Middlemarch 70
Elk City (Oklahoma) 12
Emerson, Ralph Waldo 47
Engels, Friedrich 5, 10
England
 as 'core' formation in world-system 52–4
English, James F. 3n7
English literary studies
 and Comparative Literature 24
 in crisis 2–4
Ernsten, Christian 154
Esterházy, Péter 38–9n60
Etkind, Alexander 104
Europe
 idea of 37–8, 118–20
 literary representation of
  post-communist transition 116–21
 'old' vs. 'new' 37–8
 and postcolonial studies 124–7
 post-communist transition 115–20
European literary periphery 120–4, 126–7, 132, 135, 138
Evan-Zohar, Itamar 56

Fanon, Frantz 77
Faulkner, William 55, 72, 126
 Requiem for a Nun 70–1n20
Faulks, Sebastian
 A Week in December 69
Feinstein, Andrew 147–8n4
'The Firebird' (Russian fairy tale) 105
Flaubert, Gustave 74
Fontane, Theodor 74
Forster, E.M.
 A Passage to India 90n13
 Where Angels Fear to Tread 55

Foucault, Michel 100
France 12, 38
  as 'core' formation in world-system 52–4
Frank, Andre Gunder 45
Franzen, Jonathan
  The Twenty-Seventh City 69
Freud, Sigmund 93n22, 93n23
Friedman, Susan Stanford 81–2, 91
Fuentes, Carlos 65–6n16, 80
Fuller, Margaret 47

Galdós, Pérez 18, 78
García Márquez, Gabriel 80, 126
  One Hundred Years of Solitude 50, 54–5, 110–1
Gaskell, Elizabeth 51
Geesey, Patricia 91n16
Germany 38
  as semi-peripheral formation in world-system (18–19th C) 52–4
Gibbon, Lewis Grassic
  Sunset Song 127
Gilgamesh 50
Givens, John 104–5
Glasgow 14
  in *The Busconductor Hines* 138, 140–2
Glissant, Edouard 72
globalisation 4
  and 'world literature' 4–6, 22
Glukhovsky, Dmitry
  Metro 2033 98
Goethe, Johann Wolfgang von 5, 30
  Faust 50, 53, 54
Gogol, Nikolai 101, 103
Gorbachev, Mikhail 99, 101
Gordimer, Nadine 19, 78n27, 143, 160n9
Gotz, Graeme 155
Graham, James 146
Grandville, J.J. [Jean Ignace Isidore Gérard] 18
Griffiths, Gareth 29
Guy, Josephine M. 3

Habermas, Jürgen 37–8
Hafez, Sabry 92n21
hakawati 52, 84
Halo (video game) 144
Hamsun, Knut 18, 122
  Hunger 127

Hardy, Thomas 55
Harootnunian, Harry 13–5
Harris, Wilson 74
  Palace of the Peacock 72–3
Harrison, Robert Pogue 44
Hart, Gillian 148–9
Harvey, David 69–70, 115, 138
Haslett, Adam
  Union Atlantic 69
Hassan, Waïl S. 91
Hawthorne, Nathaniel 18
Heine, Heinrich 19, 51
Helgesson, Stefan 145
Hernández, Felisberto 79
  Piano Stories 79n28
Hickey, Kieran 102
Hill, Geoffrey 19
Hirst, Paul 4n8
Hockx, Michel 9
Hölderlin, Friedrich 19
Hoffmann, E.T.A. [Ernst Theodor Amadeus] 18
Howells, William Dean 74
Huntington, Samuel 34–5n56
Huyssen, Andreas 82

Ibsen, Henrik 19
Iceland
  accelerated modernisation after World War II 135–6
The Iliad (Homer) 50
Ireland
  as semi-peripheral formation in world-system (18–19th C) 65
'irrealism' *see* realism (literary)
Istanbul 24, 25n40

James, C.L.R. [Cyril Lionel Robert] 74
James, Henry 47
Jameson, Fredric 1n2, 1–2n3, 8, 10, 16, 41, 49n1, 52, 62–3n14, 64n15, 70–1n20, 82, 110, 153n5
  'On Magic Realism in Film' 21–2
  on modernity 11–15, 21–2, 120
  'Postmodernism' 13
  on realism and modernism 60–1, 66–7, 72, 77–8, 80
  'Third-World Literature in the Era of Multinational Capitalism' 13, 21–2

Jay, Paul 3
Jelinek, Elfrieda 19
Johannesburg 143–4, 145–55,
   in *Portrait with Keys* (Vladislavic) 161–7
Joyce, James 59, 64
Judin, Hilton
   Blank (with Ivan Vladislavic) 161–2, 163

Kafka, Franz 19, 22, 59, 65, 101, 140
Kaiwar, Vasant 11n22
Kane, Cheikh Hamidou
   Ambiguous Adventure 85n8
Keel, Aldo 38–9n60
Kelman, James 122
   The Busconductor Hines 51, 127, 138–42
   How Late It Was, How Late 140n16
   Kieron Smith, Boy 138
Kempadoo, Oonya 74
Kendall, Elizabeth 25n40
Khartoum
   in *Season of Migration to the North* (Salih) 85, 86, 87
Kiberd, Declan 124n3
Kingston, Maxine Hong 70–1n20
Klobucka, Anna 125
Konuk, Kader 25n40
Koolhaas, Rem 150
Kosztolányi, Deszö
   Skylark 127
Kracauer, Siegfried
   'The Mass Ornament' 154
Kropywiansky, Leo 100
Kruger, Loren 151
Kutzwayo, Ellen 78n27

Lafargue, Paul 75
La Guma, Alex 78n27
Lagos 13, 150
Lahiri, Jhumpa 70–1n20
Laird, Sally 101
Lamming, George 74
Lampedusa, Giuseppe Tomasi di
   The Leopard 126n7, 127
Lanchester, John
   Capital 69
Lao She 19
   Rickshaw 50
Larsen, Neil 82

Larson, Susan 128–9
Lawall, Sarah 5, 28
Lawrence, D.H. [David Herbert] 55
Laxness, Halldor
   The Atom Station 51, 127, 135–8
   Independent People 137
Lazarus, Neil 119–20, 160–1n9
Lebedushkina, Olga 98–9, 103–4, 105
Lefebvre, Henri 17
   'What Is Modernity?' 12
Lenin [Vladimir Ilyich Ulyanov] 10
Lisbon
   'postcolonial' city 124
Liu Kang 11, 15n28
Löwy, Michael 59–60, 68, 83, 95, 101
Lomnitz, Claudio 13n24
London 12, 13
   imperial city in *Season of Migration to the North* (Salih) 85, 87
   'postcolonial' city 124
Longhurst, Alex 127–8n9
The Lost Steps see Carpentier
Lovelace, Earl 74
   Salt 17
Lowell, Robert 47
Lu Xun 18, 19, 77
Lukács, Georg 16, 83
   'Dostoevsky' 61–2, 66, 122
   on realism and modernism 57–62
Lukyavenko, Sergei
   Night Watch 98

MacDiarmid, Hugh 19
McEwan, Ian
   On Chesil Beach 21
   The Comfort of Strangers 93
McGurl, Mark 47n66
Machado de Assis 18, 51, 62–5, 66, 72
   The Posthumous Memoirs of Brás Cubas 63–5
Madrid
   in *The Quest* (Baroja) 130–1, 133–4
'magical realism' *see* realism (literary)
Mahasweta Devi 19
Mahjoub, Jamal
   Navigation of a Rainmaker 90n13
Majid, Anouar 85n8
Makdisi, Saree 91
Mali 12

Mamdani, Mahmood 11
Mandela, Nelson 147
Manto, Saadat Hasan 19
Mao Dun 77
Marcuse, Herbert 83–4, 93n22
   'affirmative culture' 117–8
Marinetti, Filippo Tommaso 20
Marx, Karl 5, 10, 76, 96
   Capital 69, 74–5, 102
   commodity fetishism 18
   (and Friedrich Engels) *The Communist Manifesto* 10n19
Mayekiso, Mzwanele 148
Mbembe, Achille 149–51, 154
Medeiros, Paulo de 41
Meek, James 139
Mendes, Alfred Hubert 74
Meskell, Lynn 153
Mickiewicz, Adam 19
Middlesbrough (UK) 12
Mistral, Gabriela 19
modernism 6, 17–22, 51–2, 116, 126–7
   'peripheral' 81–95, 120–4, 125, 135–8
   and realism 57–62, 66–8, 129–35, 139–42
   Spanish 127–35
modernity 11–15, 66–7
   'alternative modernities' 14–15
Moore, Jason W. 70, 96–7
Moretti, Franco 1, 6, 8, 10, 18n29, 26, 52–7
   Atlas of the European Novel 55
   The Bourgeois 54–5
   'Conjectures on World Literature' 7, 53, 55–7
   Modern Epic 52–4
   'World-Systems, Evolutionary Theory, *Weltliteratur*' 56–7
Morrison, Toni 70–1n20
Multatuli [Eduard Douwes Dekker] 51
   Max Havelaar 16, 50, 75–6
Munif, Abdelrahman 19
Murakami, Haruki 50
   1Q84 80n30
Mudimbe, V.Y.
   The Rift 91n18
Murray, Martin 146–7, 153, 154
Muschg, Adolf 37–8
Musil, Robert 59, 65

Nabokov, Vladimir
   Lolita 106, 112
Naipaul, V.S. [Vidiadhar Surajprasad] 74n26
Naylor, Gloria 19
Neuman, Andrés
   Traveller of the Century 27–8
New York 12
Ngugi wa Thiong'o 19
   Wizard of the Crow 72n23
Niblett, Michael 52, 72–4
Niedecker, Lorine 19
Nouadhibou (Mauritania) 13
novel
   as genre 16–17
   graphic 71
   and plantation system in the Caribbean 73–4
   'resource fiction' 97–8
   and (semi-) peripherality 51–7, 61–5, 78–80
   speculative 71–2, 97, 112–3
Nuttall, Sarah 149–51, 154
Nzima 159

O'Brien, Kevin 98n1
Ouologuem, Yambo
   Bound to Violence 67–8

Pardo Bazán, Emilia 78
Paris 125–6
   'postcolonial' city 124
Parry, Benita 31, 73
Pelevin, Victor 99–102, 105–14
   Babylon [*Generation П*] 100, 101–2
   The Clay Machine-Gun 99, 102
   Empire V 100, 102
   The Helmet of Horror 100
   The Life of Insects 100
   Oman Ra 99
   The Sacred Book of the Werewolf 51, 100, 102, 106–14
Pepetela
   The Return of the Water Spirit 72n23
Peterson, Hector 159
Petrarch (Francesco Petrarca) 50
Petro, Peter 115
Pist'anek, Peter
   Rivers of Babylon 51, 115–20, 127

Pizer, John 5
Poe, Edgar Allan 18
Pollard, Sidney 128
Prawer, S.S. [Siegbert Salomon] 74–5
Proust, Marcel 50, 59
Prus, Bolesław 74
Pushkin, Alexander 103, 106
Putin, Vladimir 101, 106, 108, 111

Quasimodo, Salvatore 126n7

Rayfield, Donald 115
Réage, Pauline 93
realism (literary) 66–80
 'irrealism' 51–2, 57, 67–80, 83–95, 101–2
 in Latin American fiction 54–5, 78–80
 'magical realism' 21–2, 54, 55, 57, 71, 79–80, 98, 104, 110–1, 134, 144
 and modernism 57–62, 66–8, 129–30
In the Realm of the Senses (film, dir. Nagisa Oshima) 93–4
Reed, Ishmael 70–1n20
Reykjavík
 in *The Atom Station* (Laxness) 136
Rio de Janeiro 13
Rivera, José Eustasio
 The Vortex 79
Rizal, José 18
 Noli Me Tangere 50
Robinson, Kim Stanley
 2312 71–2
Romania 119
Rosenberg, Justin 11n20
Rulfo, Juan 80
 Pedro Páramo 80n29
Rumsfeld, Donald (US Secretary of Defense) 38n61
Rushdie, Salman 80
Russia
 basis for Trotsky's theory of 'uneven and combined development' 10
 literary representation of post-communist transition 99–106, 110–1
 post-Soviet literary production 97–8
 as semi-peripheral formation in world-system 62–3, 109, 116–7, 121–2
 post-communist transition 97, 107–8

Saadawi, Nawal El 19
Sade, Marquis de 93
Sahgal, Nayantara
 Rich Like Us 33n54
Said, Edward W. 5, 89n11
 Culture and Imperialism 29–33
 Orientalism 32
Saint Petersburg 14, 62, 120–1
Salih, Tayeb 52, 72
 Season of Migration to the North 51, 81–95 *passim*, 97
Santiáñez, Nil 129–30
Sapiro, Gisèle 9
Saramago, Jose 19
Saussure, Ferdinand de 100
Sayigh, Tawfiq 92n20
Schreiner, Olive 51
Schwarz, Roberto 62–5, 66, 76, 78, 97
 A Master on the Periphery of Capitalism 63–5
Sciascia, Leonardo 126n7
Scotland
 effects of neoliberalism in 139–42
Selvon, Samuel 74
Serote, Mongane Wally 78n27
Shakespeare, William 36
 King Lear 50
Shanghai 11, 12
Shapiro, Stephen 96
Shelley, Mary 19
Shelley, Percy Bysshe 19
Shepherd, Nick 154
Sheppard, Richard 131
Shih, Shu-mei 54
Shklovsky, Viktor 65
Simon, Rick 117n1
Simone, AbdouMaliq 150, 155
Sinclair, Upton
 The Moneychangers 69n18
Slavnikovna, Olga
 2017 98
Slovakia 116–7
Small, Ian 3
Smith, Neil 124, 138
Snyder, Gary 45
Solzhenitsyn, Aleksandr 99
Sorokin, Vladimir
 Day of the Oprichnik 98
 Ice Trilogy 98

South Africa
  literary representation of neoliberal transition 99, 156–67
  post-apartheid transition to neoliberalism 146–55
Spain
  as semi-peripheral formation in world-system 127–35
Spark, Muriel
  The Driver's Seat 93
Spivak, Gayatri Chakravorty 33
  Death of a Discipline 3, 22–3
Spitzer, Leo 23–4
The Star (South African newspaper) 143
Stasiuk, Andrzej 127
Sterne, Laurence
  Tristram Shandy 65
Stoker, Bram 100n3
Sudan 86–7, 88, 89
Swanson, Philip 78–80
Szeman, Imre 98, 108

Tan, Amy 70–1n20
Tanpinar, Ahmet Hamdi
  A Mind at Peace 127
Taussig, Michael 96
Things Fall Apart (Chinua Achebe) 50, 76
Thompson, Grahame 4n8
Thoreau, Henry David 47
  Walden 46
Tiffin, Helen 29
Tlali, Miriam 78n27
Tolstaya, Tatyana
  The Slynx 98
transition to neoliberalism
  China 97
  Europe 115–20
  post-communist Europe 115–20
  Russia 97, 107–8
  South Africa 146–55
translation 25–8
Trollope, Anthony
  The Way We Live Now 69n18
Trotsky, Leon 10, 104–5, 110
  theory of 'uneven and combined development' 6, 10–11, 116
True Blood (TV series) 144n1
Twilight (Stephenie Meyer) 144n1

Upanishads 50
Urquhart, James 113

Valle-Inclán, Ramón María del 129–30
Vargas Llosa, Mario 126
Venuti, Lawrence 26
Verga, Giovanni Carmel0 126n7
Virgil 50
Vladislavic, Ivan 99, 145–6, 149, 151, 155–67
  Blank (with Hilton Judin) 161–2, 163
  Missing Persons 144, 155
  Portrait with Keys 51, 57, 162–7
  Propaganda by Monuments 155, 159n8
  The Restless Supermarket 159n8
Vorpsi, Ornela
  The Country Where No-One Ever Dies 127

Wallerstein, Immanuel 8, 15, 18–19, 43
  The Modern World-System 53
Walzer, Michael 44
Warnes, Christopher 80
The Waste Land (T.S. Eliot) 20
Weinberger, Eliot 28n44
Wellek, René (and Austin Warren) 39–40
  Theory of Literature 39
Welsh, Irvine
  Trainspotting 127
werewolf folklore
  Baltic 102–3
  Irish 102
  Russian 105–6
Whitman, Walt 51
Widdowson, Peter 2n4
Wieland (Charles Brockden Brown) 50
Williams, Raymond 2, 3–4, 30–1
  Keywords 8
  'Notes on English Prose 1780–1950' 59n10
Wolf, Martin 114
Woods, Eva 128–9
Woolf, Virginia 19
'world literature' 4–48 *passim*, 49–80 *passim*
  'combined unevenness' in 6–7, 10–22, 49, 51, 67, 72–4, 109–10, 116–24, 134–8, 144, 146, 155–67

and comparative literary studies 4–6,
    22–8, 124–7
and critique of Eurocentrism 5, 22,
    30–1, 33
and postcolonial studies 4–6, 67–8,
    124–7, 132
and (semi-) peripherality 51–7, 61–80,
    81–95, 127–42
and world-systems theory 7–10, 53–7,
    96–7, 125

'world-system' (concept) 8–10, 43, 51
Wynter, Sylvia 73–4, 76

Yaeger, Patricia 97–8
Yeltsin, Boris 101
Yi Mun-Yol
    The Poet 72n23

Zola, Emile 78, 122
    Money 69n18